ABRAHAM LINCOLN

AND THE FIFTH COLUMN

BOOKS BY GEORGE FORT MILTON

THE EVE OF CONFLICT—STEPHEN A. DOUGLAS AND
THE NEEDLESS WAR

CONFLICT—THE AMERICAN CIVIL WAR

THE AGE OF HATE—ANDREW JOHNSON AND THE RADICALS

ABRAHAM LINCOLN

This photograph was taken by A. Gardner, April 9, 1865, and is the last known photograph of Lincoln

Abraham Lincoln
and the Fifth Column

BY GEORGE FORT MILTON

1942

THE VANGUARD PRESS · NEW YORK

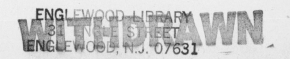

MANUFACTURED IN THE U.S.A. BY H. WOLFF, NEW YORK

TO ALICE FORT MILTON

DAUGHTER, COMPANION, AND FRIEND

I DEDICATE THIS BOOK

"Must I shoot a simple-minded soldier boy

who deserts, while I must not touch a hair

of a wily agitator who induces him to desert?"

ABRAHAM LINCOLN

CONTENTS

[ix]

ILLUSTRATIONS

Photographs numbered 3, 4, 5, 6, 7, 8, 9, 13, 15, 16, 17, 24, 25, are by Matthew B. Brady from files of the United States Signal Corps in the National Archives. Numbers 1, 2, 10, 12, 14, and 23 are from Brown Brothers. Numbers 11, 18, 19, and 22 are from the Bettmann Archive. Photograph number 21 is from the U.S. Signal Corps.

ACKNOWLEDGMENT

IN THE PREPARATION of this volume on Abraham Lincoln and the Fifth Column, the author has been fortunate in having had the thoughtful and generous aid of many people. Both in the investigation of source material, the quest for an understanding of the mass of data, and the critical analysis of the work from first rough draft to final book, this assistance has been invaluable.

The official documents of conspiracies, espionage and counter-espionage upon which, to a large extent, the book is based could not have been identified and examined except for the intelligent co-operation and assistance of the staff of the National Archives, at Washington. In addition, the burden of the actual writing of the manuscript was greatly lessened by the courtesy of that institution in making available a work-room in which the book could be written. The sagacious advice and friendly offices of Dr. Solon J. Buck, the Archivist of the United States, have put me greatly in his debt. Dr. Philip M. Hamer, Director of Reference, aided in many essential ways.

Among others at the National Archives who cooperated, let me testify my appreciation to Miss Elizabeth Drewry, of the Division of Reference, who was of especial aid in indicating the location of pertinent bodies of material. Dr. Ralph Lounsbury's suggestions were pertinent, and Mrs. Nadene Boyer

Acknowledgment

aided in many ways. Mr. Karl L. Trevor, the Librarian, was most co-operative, as was his assistant, Miss Irma Swank.

The quest of pertinent documents in the chaotic mass of War Department records could not have been nearly so fruitful had it not been for the aid of Mr. Dallas D. Irvine, Head of the War Department Division of the Archives, or that of Mr. Jerome Thomases, who suggested many interesting fields of inquiry; Mr. Robert Ballantine and Miss Marie Stark. The counsel of Mrs. Natalia Summers, of the State Department Division of the Archives was most helpful; Miss Julia M. Bland, of that unit, was prompt and competent in supplying documents desired.

Neither can I fail to mention the skill and understanding with which Miss Josephine Cobb aided in the selection of the Brady photographs which illustrate the volume; nor the artistry of Mr. Charles L. Perry, Jr., the photographer, in printing from the original Brady plates.

In the general formulation of the plan of the volume, the author is particularly indebted to Dr. James G. Randall, of the University of Illinois, one of the most sagacious of the historians of the Civil War period. Mr. Giles G. Hoffer, of Etna Green, Indiana, a graduate student under Dr. Randall, supplied some important original material and useful points of view. Mr. Alexander J. Wall, Secretary of the New York Historical Society, a long-recognized authority on the career of Horatio Seymour, was of aid; Mr. Lauriston F. Bullard, of Boston; Mr. Lloyd Lewis, of Chicago; Dr. William B. Hesseltine, of the University of Wisconsin, and Mr. Otto Eisenschiml, of Chicago, helped shape the pattern for the book.

Captain Cecil Holland, U.S.A., whose volume on General

Acknowledgment

John H. Morgan, is in the press; and Mr. Howard Swiggett, author of *The Rebel Raider,* helped clear up several gaps in the relation of Morgan and his aides with the fifth columnists. William H. Townsend, of Lexington, Kentucky, suggested several useful fields of inquiry, as did Dr. Thomas Clark, of the University of Kentucky, and Mr. Gilbert E. Govan, of the University of Chattanooga.

The author wishes to express his appreciation of the interest shown by Dr. Christopher B. Coleman, the Director of the Indiana State Historical Commission, at Indianapolis; and to Leland R. Smith, Indiana State Archivist, and Mrs. Hazel Hopper, of the Indiana State Historical Society. Mrs. Frank Hutchinson of Lawrenceburg, Indiana, kindly accorded permission to make use of the H. V. Johnson letter, the original of which is in her possession, and aided in research concerning it. Mr. Walter Locke, Editor of the *Dayton News,* undertook helpful inquiries as to the manuscript and other records of Clement L. Vallandigham in Dayton. Mr. Wellington Wright, of New York City, furnished interesting data on Fernando Wood.

Several thoughtful friends read the manuscript either in rough draft or final form, and were extremely helpful in forming the book's final shape and pattern. Mr. Edward Eyre Hunt's reflective philosophy was a useful guide to the evaluation of the factors in the fifth column struggle. The thoughtful, detailed criticism of style and arrangement by Miss Helen I. Slentz, of Washington, afforded a needed corrective to imprecise or repetitious writing. Miss Elinore Blaisdell, of New York City, gave many effective style ideas. The judgment of Dr. Pendleton Herring, of Harvard University, on proper perspectives proved most useful. Major Waldo Shumway, U.S.A.; Mr. Barnet Nover, the military expert of the *Washington Post*; Mrs. G. E. Forbush, talented detective writer of Washington, aided individual subject treatments. Judge Joseph C. Hutchinson, Jr., of the United States Circuit Court of Appeals, of Houston, Texas, and Dean M. T. Van Hecke, of the College of Law of the University of North Carolina, read the Vallandigham case chapters critically. Dr. J. A. Hall, of Washington, formerly of Paoli, Indiana, performed the same service for matters relating to Dr. Bowles and fifth column activities in Indiana.

But for the admirable and unflagging work of my secretary, Mrs. Pauline Rothfeld; and for the competent, attentive stenographic efforts of Miss Eleanor Wagner and Mrs. Janet Spiker, all of Washington, the production of the manuscript would have been greatly delayed. All three of them worked under extreme pressure to carry the narrative through from rough notes to finished manuscript. Mr. Joseph Greenbaum, of New York, prepared the index, with his accustomed meticulous care and skill.

Undoubtedly this volume contains many errors of commission, omission, and evaluation. For these, the full responsibility is mine. To the many who have generously aided the building of this book, let me express my heartfelt gratitude. Should some be interested in this picture of the way Abraham Lincoln defeated the Copperhead fifth column, this will be my most enduring reward.

GEORGE FORT MILTON

Washington, D. C.
July 4, 1942

ABRAHAM LINCOLN
AND THE FIFTH COLUMN

Chapter 1

LINCOLN FACES THE CRISIS

BEFORE dawn on Friday, April 13, 1861, a white-haired Prophet of Secession fired the first gun of the Civil War. The very morning that Beauregard's batteries bombarded Sumter, Abraham Lincoln, in Washington, received a committee from the Virginia Constitutional Convention to discuss with it the peaceful restoration of the Union.

Before they reached the White House that fateful day, the President had unofficial reports from South Carolina that Fort Sumter had been fired on. He informed the delegates of these dispatches, and declared that he would "repel force by force." Lincoln was well aware that the crisis had come, and that catastrophe might be close at hand.

For the next four years, this prairie politician commanded the ship of state during the nation's greatest crisis between Valley Forge and Pearl Harbor.

The eighty years since Sumter have been marked by great changes in the tools of war. Today death swoops from the sky, slinks on the surface of the seas, and charges in strange steel chariots over the land. These improvements in the tools of destruction and their tactical employment have put a new façade on the arts of war.

But there has been little change in the constants of human

nature. In the Civil War, as in our war today, we find the same common denominators. Nobility and heroism are hardy perennials—and so are baseness and cowardice. There are patriots and traitors, and disturbed, upset, uncertain men between. In each crisis, we find appeasers, agitators of revolution, and counter-revolutionaries too. Again and again the best families have their quota of the spiritually diseased.

Lincoln knew intuitively the many-sidedness of the task. The things he did, the means he used, the foes he overcame, afford fruitful analogies. This is true in his duties as Commander in Chief, in his handling of foreign affairs, and in his leadership in the fight against the fifth column in the Loyal States.

The literature of the conflict in arms is full of drama, death, and enduring fame. And equally important was the war of mind and mood, to persuade the people at home to keep up the sacrifices needed for victory. Here too Lincoln was a master of men. This book undertakes to tell of a Lincoln as shrewd in judging the strength of secret bands of traitors, and measuring their menace, as at length he became in finding enough men for the army and good generals to command them.

It would be well if each man who becomes the President of the United States possessed each of the great traits needed for meeting the varied problems of a democracy both in peace and in war. But in high crisis, it is most important that the Chief Executive shall be peculiarly equipped with a sympathetic understanding of the people's hearts and minds and souls. In such times he has done the best who has been poet and prophet and seer.

Such a man was Lincoln. He sensed almost intuitively the tangled moods of the people of the Loyal States, from the cabin on the prairie to the mansion on Fifth Avenue. In no one of the critical fronts did his genius show more quickly, and in none did it prove more indispensable, than in the fight upon the hidden front at home. Here we can measure the politician who grew to be a statesman, and record with satisfaction this great organic growth of character—a true test of a greatness which has resisted the acid bite of time.

Long before sunup the Sunday morning after the firing on Sumter, the President had arisen, and light was shining from a window of his study. Spring had begun to bud in the national capital, and in the early morning light the lawn stretching toward the Potomac seemed peaceful and inviting. But Lincoln paced the faded red carpet thinking how best to "preserve, protect, and defend the Constitution" and to win the war.

He knew the problem well. It had occupied his waking thought—or such part of it as greedy office-seekers would let him keep for problems of the nation's safety. And he knew, too, that the shells hurled at Sumter had been cast in the foundry of sectional division more than half a century before. All of it he had lived through, in much of it he had battled, and his election had been seized as the occasion, if not the cause, for the secession parade. He knew, too, that division had existed within each of the sections, and that in each the intrasectional debate had been carried on with bitterness and rancor.

He sensed also the great strength the North could exert once it was awakened and geared to the winning of the war. It was, indeed, a great and puissant region. It had broadened its sweep from the Eastern seaboard to the Missouri basin, adding both the prairie and the plains to the cold and stony shores of the North Atlantic coast.

The North was on the march as an industrial empire. It had domesticated the Iron Horse and made it a willing servant of

[*19*]

more nearly perfect union. It had Morse's telegraph as the whip with which to flick the steed. From the mere handmaiden of agriculture, commerce had become its equal, while industry gave promise of outgrowing either one. The North's record revealed the benefits of handicaps to overcome and goals to reach—of the dividends of harsh climate and stony soil; of the challenge of huge regions which must be harnessed to meet the needs of men; of a prolific people needing work to do and new frontiers to overcome.

But the matters that preyed on the President's mind that Sunday morning were of high emergency. Could the Border States be saved? Was Washington in danger? Where would troops be found, to enable him "faithfully to execute the laws"?

Later in the morning the Cabinet gathered at the White House to plan a program of action. Army and navy officers were consulted, old militia laws studied, and quotas of troops assigned to the different States considered. Definite word came from Charleston that Major Robert Anderson had surrendered Sumter. Then Lincoln drafted a proclamation which warned "treasonable combinations" to disperse, and summoned 75,000 men to three months' service, to repress rebellion. As the legal basis for this call to arms, he used a law of 1795.

Late in the afternoon the President told George Ashmun, Massachusetts Republican Congressman, of his "earnest desire for the support of the best men of the country." Then he asked Ashmun to ascertain whether Senator Douglas would come to see him at the White House.

This request of the President was of the greatest importance. At that time Stephen A. Douglas greatly overshadowed Lincoln in the public eye, and many deemed him the North's most important man. The Little Giant had been a Senator from Illinois for fourteen years.

His public record in the 50's had been conspicuous. He effected the Compromise of 1850, after Clay and Webster failed, and later engineered its repeal. He had been a popular candidate for the Democratic presidential nomination in 1852. As foremost champion of the doctrine of Popular Sovereignty, he had a large following. Opposed to Lincoln in the presidential election, at the Inauguration Douglas held the President's hat, a symbol that whatever happened, he would support the Union and the Constitution.

This background made it of extreme importance that this chosen leader of the North's Free Democracy should join hands with the President to preserve the capital and rebuild the Union of the States. Douglas and Lincoln together could rally the North. Lincoln alone could not withstand the storm.

Ashmun sped to the Senator's house on Minnesota Row, found him at home, and Adèle, Douglas's lovely wife, urged instant compliance with the President's request. The Senator drove immediately, with Ashmun, to the White House. Lincoln met Douglas "with outstretched hands and with a benignant smile," and handed him a copy of the proclamation which was to be published the next day.

Douglas did not think 75,000 men sufficient. He thought the call should be increased to 200,000 men. A map was brought, and he pointed out such places as Washington, Fortress Monroe, Harper's Ferry, and Cairo, Illinois, the efficient protection of which might require most of the men in the call. These two remarkable men continued in confidential conference for two hours.

When the Little Giant left, Ashmun said to him that it was

highly necessary that the country have a statement of the interview. The President's proclamation had already gone out over the wires, to be published in newspapers over the country on Monday. The fact that Senator Douglas, the North's leading Democrat, had endorsed the call must be printed at the same time, otherwise Lincoln's proclamation might be badly received. Referring again to the statement of the interview, to be published side by side with the proclamation, Ashmun said to Douglas: "I shall send it either in my own language or yours." Douglas went to his friend's room at Willard's, and wrote a dispatch for the Associated Press, which was published with the proclamation the next morning.

"Senator Douglas called upon the President," it began, "and had an interesting conversation on the present condition of the country. The substance of it was, on the part of Mr. Douglas, that while he was unalterably opposed to the Administration on all its political issues, he was prepared to fully sustain the President in the exercise of all his constitutional functions to preserve the Union, maintain the government, and defend the Federal capital.

"A firm policy and prompt action was [*sic*] necessary. The capital was in danger, and must be defended at all hazards, and at any expense of men and money. He spoke of the present and the future without any reference to the past."

Publication of these firm Union views brought many criticisms, but the Little Giant had put his hand to the plow. A Missourian wrote that his State did not indorse Lincoln's war policy, so how could Douglas do so? The latter answered that he deprecated war, "but if it must come, I am with my country and for my country under all circumstances and in every contingency." To another inquirer of the course Democrats should

[22]

follow, he wrote: "There can be but two parties—the party of patriots and the party of traitors. We belong to the first."

Nor did Douglas content himself with words, but applied his resilient, penetrating mind and constructive imagination to the organization of the national defense. The President consulted him again and again, while Winfield Scott, the brave old General of the Army, sought his advice on strategic problems. It was rumored that this Number One Democrat of the North was about to be made a brigadier general. When asked about it, Lincoln parried that he had no reason to think Douglas would accept such a post, but "I can imagine few men better qualified." In 1864 the President told Orville H. Browning that he had intended to make Douglas his General in Chief.

But fate soon frustrated any such intention. Before the close of the first week of the war, word from Illinois convinced Douglas that he could be of more help in the West than in the capital. Richard Yates, Illinois's Republican Governor, had called a special session of the legislature, but there were mutterings in "Egypt" (as the southern section of the State was called, because of Cairo, its chief city), and there was danger of an actual revolt there.

The Senator's trusted aides at Springfield telegraphed him there were grave reasons why he must be on hand when the legislature opened. He went to the White House and disclosed the situation to Lincoln. Both men knew the indispensable importance of the Northwest to the Union cause. (The Northwest of this era was of course the Old Northwest, the Northwest Territory—now Ohio, Illinois, Indiana, Michigan, and Wisconsin.) Both agreed that Douglas must go West at once. They shook hands in friendly farewell, and parted for the last time.

The fact of war had confronted Abraham Lincoln with two separate but somewhat overlapping problems of public opinion. The first in point of time, though not of importance, was whether or not the Border States could be kept within the Union. The other was whether he could command the support of the great body of the people of the North. Upon the issue of these questions depended the outcome of the conflict.

To the battle for the Border States, Lincoln brought a rare understanding. Fortunate was the circumstance that the man now oath-bound to preserve, protect, and defend the Constitution and the Union had been cradled in a Kentucky cabin, received his rudiments of schooling in Indiana, and then started law and politics in central Illinois. Heredity, background, and intuition helped him read the riddles of the Border.

He knew that there was little effective opposition to fire-eater control of Arkansas, so was not surprised by the heavy rhetoric of her Ordinance of Secession. He feared but expected disappointment in Tennessee, North Carolina, and Virginia. He knew that the outcome of the referendum in the Volunteer State in February, with its rejection of secession by 12,000 votes, would now be brushed aside. So he was not surprised at the telegram from Governor Harris that Tennessee would not "furnish a man for purposes of coercion." Soon Tennessee entered into a military league with the Confederacy, declared her independence, and based this action on the right of revolution. At a referendum, held in June, this action was sustained by a vote of more than 2 to 1.

North Carolina pursued a similar course. Her Governor declared that the Old North State would be no party to "this war upon the liberties of a free people." A Constitutional

Convention gathered, and on May 20 unanimously adopted an Ordinance of Secession.

Virginia had already acted. Governor John Letcher, on receipt of the proclamation, telegraphed the President: "You have chosen to inaugurate civil war"; the Virginia Convention brought up its own pending ordinance on April 17, and enacted it, by a vote of 88 to 55. An election held May 23 confirmed the action, by about 128,000 to 32,000.

Abraham Lincoln had expected these outcomes. But he was pinning his hopes to the more northerly of the Border States—Maryland, Missouri, and above all others, his native State of Kentucky. In the field political, these represented his most challenging problem, and his first great accomplishment in the struggle to keep the Union safe.

The physical location of the capital city of the country was such that troops for her protection must come through Maryland, and the secession of that State must be prevented at all hazards. Governor Thomas Hicks had resisted the demands of Southern sympathizers that he call the legislature into special session. Now the President's call for troops forced his hand; he summoned the legislature, but in his message urged that Maryland assume "a neutral position." The solons protested against the war, but took no steps to call a convention or to secede. That fall, Maryland's elections went heavily Union.

The Missouri outcome was more spectacular. In February, her voters had rejected secession by a majority of 80,000. But her Governor, Claiborne F. Jackson, was a thoroughgoing Southern sympathizer. He termed Lincoln's requisition of troops "inhuman and diabolical," and refused to supply them. He was promptly challenged by Frank P. Blair, Jr., son of Old Hickory's sturdy friend and brother of Montgomery Blair, now Lincoln's Postmaster General. The Missouri Blair offered four regiments of Home Guards, Washington accepted, and in the resulting political battle for public sentiment in the State, Blair trounced the Governor completely. In the summer, a Missouri Constitutional Convention deposed Jackson, and Missouri was fixed as a Loyal State.

It but remained to safeguard Kentucky for Lincoln's hopes to be complete. Beriah Magoffin, the Governor of this commonwealth already known in frontier legends as the "dark and bloody ground," was as ardent a Confederate sympathizer as Claiborne Jackson. But Magoffin, a man of less force, took no steps toward secession; the legislature met early in the Summer, and resolved that the State should stay neutral. The President used great care to prevent offense being given to her spirit. The congressional elections in June yielded a stalwart Union delegation. Two months later a new legislature was chosen, definitely Union in its feeling. Shortly thereafter the Confederates, commanded by Leonidas Polk, an Episcopal bishop become a general, invaded the State, and so outraged public opinion that any danger of her secession was ended.

One influence in keeping Kentucky secure was the gospel that Stephen A. Douglas carried West from Washington. He had left the national capital the end of the week after Sumter's fall. The journey was on the Baltimore & Ohio through western Virginia; the first stop was Bellaire, Ohio, just below Wheeling, in western, soon to be West, Virginia. News that the Little Giant was at the hotel spread like wildfire, thousands poured in on special trains from western Virginia, a throng gathered, and the Senator talked to them. His words were sober and thoughtful: "The very existence," he said, "of the people in this great valley depends upon maintaining inviolate and forever that great right secured by the Constitution, of freedom of trade, of transit, and of commerce, from the center of the continent to the ocean that surrounds it." The question was not only that of Union or Disunion, but "of order, of the stability of the Government; of the peace of communities. The whole social system is threatened with destruction."

"Unite as a band of brothers," Douglas urged them, "and rescue your government and its capital and your country from the enemies who have been the author of your calamity." He pointed dramatically to the Ohio River, and exclaimed: "This great valley must never be divided. The Almighty has so arranged the mountain and the plain, and the water-courses as to show that this valley in all time shall remain one and indissoluble. Let no man attempt to sunder what Divine Providence has rendered indivisible."

His speech, which brought frenzied cheers, had a powerful reaction throughout Virginia west of the mountains. Within a few weeks the loyalists there began a movement to create a new commonwealth. Before long West Virginia knocked at the doors of Congress for admission as a State.

The Little Giant reached Columbus, Ohio, late in the evening. A crowd gathered before his hotel, and he stepped out on the balcony and talked to them through the darkness. His appeal, deep and sonorous, evoked a great "Amen" from the crowd. The next day, in Indianapolis, he spoke again: "Our country is in danger"; the Northwest could never consent for secession to cut off its access to the ocean; it was the duty of all citizens, "Democrats and Republicans, to rise up and unsheathe the sword in defense of our constitutional rights and never sheathe it until they are secure."

He reached Springfield April 25, and went to work at once. Some Southern sympathizers from Egypt spoke bitterly to him,

[*27*]

among these John A. Logan, who had not yet switched to rabid Radicalism nor joined the army. "You have sold out the Democratic Party," Logan told him, "but, by God, you can't deliver it!" Yet this was exactly what the Senator undertook to do. That night he addressed the legislature in the Hall of Representatives, which was crowded as never before.

The circumstances were impressive, and the earnest passion of his plea gave it extraordinary force. It was "with a heart filled with sadness and grief" that he addressed them; for the first time since the adoption of the Constitution, there was a widespread conspiracy to destroy the Government. What should Illinois do?

The people of the great valley of the Mississippi (who in that era used New Orleans as the natural outlet for their products) had particular interests. They could never sanction being cut off from the oceans and made "dependent provinces upon the powers that thus choose to isolate us." Therefore, "it is a war of self defense on our part. . . . Hence, if a war does come, it is a war . . . in defense of those great rights of freedom of trade, commerce, transit and intercourse from the center to the circumference of our great continent."

The legislators had a clear duty; it was "to lay aside, for the time being, your party creeds and party platforms; to dispense with your party organizations and partisan appeal; to forget that you were ever divided, until you have rescued the Government and the country from their assailants."

As for himself, he said that he had "struggled almost against hope to avert the calamities of war and to effect a reunion and reconciliation." Providence alone could reveal the issue of the struggle, but the North must not yield to resentment or vengeance, "much less to the desire for conquest or ambition." He himself saw "no path of ambition open in a bloody struggle

for triumphs over my countrymen . . . but I believe in my
conscience that it is a duty we owe to ourselves, and to our
children, and to our God, to protect this Government and
that flag from every assailant, be he who he may."

From beginning to end, men of all parties in the Hall ap-
plauded this speech, the results of which were immediate and
enduring. The Little Giant had roused and rallied the loyal
strength of Illinois. In years to come, it was realized that but
for him there might have been "civil war in Illinois from Cairo
north to the doorsteps of Springfield." But instead of that,
Douglas "put 500,000 men in the Union Army, and 50,000
from Illinois alone."

He continued his canvass of the Prairie State, but when he
reached Chicago, a severe attack of rheumatism sent him to
bed. A little later high fever developed; by the end of May
Douglas was at death's door. But even in his delirium, his mind
was taken with the nation's ills rather than his own. On one
occasion he cried out: "Telegraph to the President and let
the column move on!"

Sunday afternoon, June 2, he rallied slightly, only to suffer
a bad relapse. About five o'clock the next morning his wife
asked if he had any message for his mother, his sister, and the
two boys. "Tell them," he said with an effort, "to obey the
laws and support the Constitution of the United States." With
these words the Little Giant died.

Chapter 2

BIRTH OF THE FIFTH COLUMN

THE firing on Sumter had occasioned a display of patriotic emotion through the North akin to a Holy Crusade. Thousands of men and women wore "badges of loyalty." In some cities a flag flew from every home. Pulpits were draped with the Stars and Stripes, and Sunday-school children wore bunting buttons.

Douglas had not been the only outstanding Democratic leader of the North to proclaim fealty to the Union. Many who the year before had supported John C. Breckinridge—then Vice-President and candidate for the White House, now a Confederate major general—came out boldly for the Federal cause. The list was a lengthy one. Daniel S. Dickinson of New York followed this course. John Cochrane, the Sachem of Tammany Hall, wanted "to crush the rebellion." On forty-four ballots in the Charleston Convention, Benjamin F. Butler of Massachusetts had voted for Jefferson Davis's nomination. Now he became a militia brigadier, was called to active service, and within a year won the appropriate nickname of "Beast." Secession-sympathizing John A. Logan had a sudden change of faith, got a brigadier's commission and the later sobriquet of "Black Jack." None exhibited more ardent zeal than such recent converts to the faith.

[*30*]

STEPHEN A. DOUGLAS

who put his country above his party

EDWARD M. STANTON
Secretary of War in President Lincoln's Cabinet

JOSEPH A. HOLT
Judge Advocate General of the United States Army

Andrew Johnson's case was quite different. This tailor, who won a seat in Congress, then was twice Governor, and now was Senator from Tennessee, had shown his Union loyalty, both in the closing scenes of the last Congress and in the defeat of Tennessee's first referendum on secession. After the fall of Sumter, he made his way from Washington through Virginia to East Tennessee, in peril all the way.

As soon as he reached his home, the plebeian politician took the stump, and his speaking tour carried him to nearly every county in that section of the State. Threats of violence were plentiful; in a church at Kingsport he put his pistol on the pulpit, covered it with a handkerchief, and spoke as usual. All over the region he pleaded for his country with a passionate earnestness that moved men's hearts. As a result, in the June election the East Tennesseans voted down disunion by a majority of over 19,000—almost as much as it had been in February. Angered by this, the secession cabal at Nashville determined to send troops and have Johnson summarily shot. Given warning, in the middle of June he left for the North. A militia general ordered his arrest as a traitor to the State, but not a man responded. He passed through Cumberland Gap into Kentucky, and was safe.

There were other figures in this general picture of Democratic support who at the beginning seemed surprisingly enthusiastic, but several of these carried no real promise that their enthusiasm would last. When the war broke out, there were four living former Presidents: John Tyler, Martin Van Buren, Franklin Pierce, and James Buchanan. Tyler, a Whig, lived in Richmond, Virginia. Each of the other three was a Democrat according to his own definition, and each declared in favor of the Union cause.

Buchanan did so April 19. "The North will sustain the Administration almost to a man," he wrote, "and it ought to be sustained at all hazards." But he did little to sustain it, and put in most of his time preparing a defense of his own years in the White House. Edwin M. Stanton was in Washington, his role almost that of "Old Obliquity's" contact man with the anti-Lincoln forces. In a few months Stanton saw the light and made up to the Radical Republicans. Until then Buchanan relished Stanton's sneers at Lincoln as a clumsy clown, and his likening Lincoln to Paul du Chaillu's ape.

Martin Van Buren's attitude was very different. Old Hickory's trusted lieutenant promptly made known his loyalty to the cause for which he had battled for so long. An old man, infirm and within about a year of his death, he was not feeble in spirit, and his faith was firm. Just a short while earlier he had proved it. Franklin Pierce had written him from Concord, urgently suggesting that the three living former Presidents in the North hold a conference to draft a proposal of policy for the new Chief Executive. What Pierce had in mind was a repudiation of the course Lincoln was pursuing. Van Buren had little but contempt for Buchanan, did not want to have any meeting with him, and he sent Pierce a firm though polite refusal.

Franklin Pierce made the weakest declaration of the three men. Ten years before, the pleasant bearing and Mexican War record of this New Hampshire local notability had led political intriguers to make him the dark-horse candidate to break a deadlocked Democratic National Convention. Once nominated, his publicity men dubbed him "Young Hickory," and ran him successfully against General Winfield Scott. The latter, who was known as "Old Fuss and Feathers" in mingled affection and derision, was as feeble as a candidate as he had been competent as commander of the march to the capital of Mexico. Pierce's victory was the nation's loss—it was well said that this "Young Hickory" was naught more than "a blighted burr from the mane of Andrew Jackson's warhorse."

When Lincoln's proclamation summoning troops to subdue the rebellion reached Concord, Pierce expressed himself as follows: "Should a war of aggression be waged against the National Capital and the North, there is no way for us as citizens of one of the old thirteen States, but to stand together and uphold the flag to the last." This was the high point of his Union preachment. In December, 1861, the former President was charged with having had a hand in the organization of the Knights of the Golden Circle in New England. The undiplomatic Seward wrote him of these charges and asked him for an explanation. Irritation over this lack of trust made Pierce an increasingly bitter opponent of the Administration. In a Fourth of July oration uttered the day after Gettysburg, he was to speak sadly of "a great mausoleum of hearts of men who had cherished liberty" in vain.

But whatever was to prove the future course of these Elder Statesmen, there was other lip service to loyalty to the Union by crafty fellows whose good faith was at once suspect. Fernando Wood, co-owner of the *New York Daily News* as well as mayor of that city, made a few statements of his veneration for the dear old flag, and then began to fill his paper with innuendo and subversive propaganda. Baltimore had an active secession group, as her April riots testified. The Ohio Valley States, largely peopled by settlers from Virginia, the Carolinas, Kentucky and Tennessee and their descendants, gave ample evidence of the dislike by many of "the coercion of the South."

In the main, these settlers were not hostile to the institution of slavery and many of them were distinctly sympathetic.

The Quakers from the Mecklenburg, North Carolina, region represented about the only offset to this attitude. Not only were these Southern members of the Society of Friends men of peace, but also they were believers in freedom for black as well as white. Quite a number settled in southern Indiana, cheek by jowl with their proslavery neighbors. In one southwestern Indiana county, Southern sympathizers dominated the French Lick Springs region, while only eighteen miles away the North Carolina Quaker element gave the core of strong Union support.

It should be said that, in 1860, the focus of Indiana population was in the central and southern portions of the State. Indianapolis had only recently passed New Albany, on the Ohio, as Indiana's largest city. Much of the Northern area was sparsely settled and undeveloped. Ohio's Western Reserve did not continue west across the neighbor State. This was one reason why Indiana was such a focus of pro-Southern fifth column activities.

The attitude was well illustrated by Dr. William Bowles, a wealthy physician of French Lick Springs, Indiana, in letters written to his family in April and May. The Doctor, who became increasingly conspicuous in the fifth-column record in the Northwest, started with Southern sympathies. He had been an officer in the Mexican War. His wife, who came from New Orleans, owned many slaves. Bowles tried to bring some of them to his Indiana home, but had to send them back.

After a visit to the Indiana town of Paoli, he wrote that the Republicans there "have taken new courage, and raised a pole which they call a Union Pole, and swear that fire and blood await the man or set of men who will attempt to cut it down or raise a Secession Pole." The war spirit was building up on all sides, and he feared that "the Douglas wing of the Democratic Party will go off with the Black Republicans—and if so, our fate is sealed." He expected Kentucky to secede, but too late to do any good.

Furthermore, he had reconciled himself to the coming of war: "We must pass from the present condition, for in it we cannot remain free and happy, and if the South can maintain its position, all will be well and the country generally may look forward to happy days. But if the North should happen to conquer, then this continent will be forever doomed to be a world of miserable mongrels, which will prove a pest and a curse to every social relation of mankind."

His disheartenment increased with the enlistment in Paoli of a Union company of 114 men, all armed and equipped for war. He felt that "if things don't change here very soon, we will have fighting here in our midst. Already many persons whom I supposed to be true to the South have been silenced and are now afraid to open their mouths in favor of Southern rights." Worse than this, some of them had already come out for the North, and were calling those who would not do so "Tories and traitors."

By the end of May, he became so anxious about Kentucky that he visited Louisville, found it "in a perfect tumult. . . . Everything is under great excitement and the Abolition Party is very strong." He termed Magoffin's effort to preserve a policy of armed neutrality "a perfect humbug." On his return to Indiana he thought his own life in daily peril. Nonetheless, he did not hesitate to send a friend to General Gideon J. Pillow, raising Confederate troops at Memphis, with a note, duly intercepted, that the man had "come south for the purpose of rendering himself useful in the cause of Southern Rights."

This was, doubtless, an extreme case of Northern Border sympathy for the secessionists. Yet throughout the southern portions of Ohio, Indiana, and Illinois, together with the whole State of Missouri, the organization of disaffection proceeded rapidly. With the early summer, a secret society spread over the whole region, with a full panoply of oaths, grips, recognition signs—and determination to aid the Confederate cause.

For the first few weeks after hostilities began, the authorities in Washington thought the capital in deadly peril of Confederate capture. Militarily, this probably was the case; but the leaders of the new revolutionary government still at Montgomery, getting ready to move to Richmond, thundered in the index only. Pierre G. T. Beauregard had several brigades at Charleston which could have been entrained for northern Virginia late in April or early in May. But the South moved slowly. After heartbreaking delays, alarums, and upsets, Union troops began to pour into Washington and the President had one less pressing fear.

Throughout May the environs of the city on the Potomac filled with new military encampments. Lincoln issued a second call, for 42,000 volunteers for a three-year term, to which the young men of the North responded eagerly. Troop totals mounted until, by the beginning of June, the Union forces in the eastern theater of war amounted to 60,000, almost double the Confederate strength.

With the shift, there came a corresponding alteration in the temper of Northern Republican leadership. During February and March Horace Greeley had urged in his *Tribune* that the Southern States be allowed to depart in peace. But by the end of May he had grown irascible over the failure of the Federal forces to march forthwith upon the secession capital on the James. "On to Richmond!" thundered his editorials, echoed every Sunday in sermons from a thousand pulpits. The patriots of platform and easy chair could not understand the delay. "Are not two more than one?" they would ask. "And have we not the two to our enemy's one? What dullards and laggards our generals must be to delay for a day or an hour!"

The President did not want to heed these demands. Stout old Scott, the General in Chief of the Army, in whom Lincoln had confidence both as a truly loyal officer and as a field commander who, through experience, knew the real problems of a military campaign, urgently advised against any dependence on an immediate movement. The "ninety-day wonders" must be turned into some semblance of soldiers before they were used as fighting men. Lincoln sensed this, but it did not solve his problem.

At the moment, he had the faults of his virtues. In March Douglas had epitomized them: Lincoln was "eminently a man of the atmosphere which surrounds him. He has not yet got out of Springfield. . . . He . . . does not see that the shadow he casts is any bigger now than it was last year. It will not take him long to find it out when he has got established in the White House. But he has not found it out yet." In the three months since the Little Giant had made this statement, the Man from Springfield had begun to discover a little about the power entrusted to his hands. He was on the path, but not very far along it.

In June, Chief Justice Taney added to the President's problems by a sharp challenge of the latter's suspension of the writ of habeas corpus. The Chief Justice was too old, too hardened in the arteries of his mind, to sympathize with the way Lincoln sought to meet the problems of a nation confronted by a fearful revolt, with fifth-column support in the Loyal States. While he was on circuit duty at Baltimore, an application for a writ

[*37*]

of habeas corpus came before him, for one Merriman, a young Maryland secessionist who had been drilling a company of Southern sympathizers, and had been arrested by the military. Taney granted the writ, but the Commanding General of the Military Department, on instruction from the Attorney General, refused to honor it.

In consequence, the Chief Justice filed with the Clerk of the Circuit Court a withering comment, concentrating responsibility on the President. The latter replied in his message to the Congress in special session, on July 4, in these words:

"Are all the laws but one to go unexecuted, and the Government itself to go to pieces lest that one be violated? Even in such a case, would not the official oath be broken if the Government should be overthrown; when it was believed that disregarding the single law would tend to preserve it?"

Lincoln was acutely sensitive to public sentiment—as had already been shown by his handling of sentiment in Maryland, Missouri, and Kentucky, this was one of his most conspicuously serviceable abilities. In the military instance it was to prove, at the immediate juncture, a harmful trait. For he had an over-acute perception of the hopes of the people that an immediate military victory would bring the war to an end. For this, and other reasons, the President temporarily let public opinion take the command of the army. Scott reluctantly ordered an advance through the northern part of the Old Dominion, and the tirades of the editorial columns led to the tragedy of First Bull Run.

About the time that he sent Scott these instructions, the President summoned the new Congress into special session. Until then he had not felt the need of the national legislature. The first steps for defense had been based on existing legislation, or on his own inherent powers as Commander in Chief.

The needs grew so great, however, that legislation became essential, either to cure earlier assumptions of authority, or to make new grants of power for the conduct of the war.

The Congress gathered early in July, gave heed promptly to the requests Lincoln made of it, and took a further step of great national consequence.

Most of the members of House and Senate agreed that the Congress was the one organ of the Government which, under the Constitution, formed and voiced the policy of the nation. They likewise felt that it had now become their duty to define, succinctly and forthrightly, the nation's policy in the war.

John J. Crittenden of Kentucky, Clay's successor as the Great Conciliator, took the lead in framing this statement. On July 22, he presented to the House a carefully drafted resolution. Its preamble emphasized that "the present civil war has been forced upon the country by the disunionists of the Southern States, now in arms against the constitutional Government, and in arms around the capital."

"In this emergency," it continued, "Congress, banishing all feelings of mere passion or resentment, will recollect only its duty to the whole country." Then came a clear declaration of the national purpose; it was the view of the House that:

"This war is not waged on their part in any spirit of oppression, or for any purpose of conquest or subjugation, or purpose of overthrowing or interfering with the rights or established institutions of those States."

Having thus pledged that neither punishment nor Abolition animated the Federal Government in the war, Crittenden's resolves then recited the affirmative purposes. The war was being waged "to defend and maintain the supremacy of the Constitution, and to preserve the dignity, equality, and rights of the several States unimpaired . . . As soon as these objects are accomplished the war ought to cease."

Four days later, Andrew Johnson, recently returned from Tennessee—and at the moment a Senator almost without a State—laid before the Senate a resolution in almost the identical words. This was promptly adopted, by a vote of 30 to 5. Soon the language of the resolutions was simplified into "the Union as it was and the Constitution as it is." This became the proclaimed purpose of the Government for the winning of the war.

The apparent unity was short-lived. Even as the rolls were being called, there was the best of evidence that the Radicals —the name then given the Republican extremists—were biding their time to destroy this structure. In the Senate, the Abolition-urging Charles Sumner refused to vote. On the House side, Thaddeus Stevens sat cynically silent, as did several other Radicals. There was this mute evidence that these men were as deeply committed to a secret revolution as they were to Federal success on the battlefield. Four months later, when the Congress met in its regular session, the Radicals began their open challenge of the course charted by the resolution.

The term opened December 2, 1861. Conservatives offered a resolution for the Congress to renew the pledge it had made in the Crittenden-Johnson document of five months before. By a vote of 71 to 65, the Radicals tabled it. This was a plain Radical declaration that they were against "the Constitution as it is" and would go the limit to make great changes in it.

They first moved to grasp the fact of power. They resented the way the President and his Cabinet had begun the war without Congress being on hand to instruct them. They felt bitter that they were not consulted about each general named, each plan of operation. Therefore they set out to take over the conduct of the war. William Pitt Fessenden of Maine told the Senate early in the session that he held it to be "our bounden duty, impressed upon us by our position here, to keep an anxious, watchful eye over all the executive agents who are carrying on the war at the direction of the people, whom we represent and whom we are bound to protect in relation to this matter." He refrained from suggesting how the Congress could do this without impeding, or thwarting, the Chief Executive in the latter's own oath-bound obligation to direct.

To this day it is an unsettled question how far the Congress should, or can, go in scrutinizing and seeking to control the employment by the President of powers which the Constitution vests directly in him—powers which are independent of any legislative statute, the most conspicuous of these being his designation as Commander in Chief of the Army and Navy of the United States of America.

Probably equally as large are the implicit residual powers which the President has by virtue of the express constitutional limits upon the powers that the Congress itself can exercise. The Constitution expressly declares that "all legislative powers *herein granted* shall be vested in a Congress." But it does not so limit the powers of the Chief Executive, declaring: "The executive power shall be vested in a President of the United States of America."

This language, designedly broad, is reported to have been framed in the Constitutional Convention of 1787 because General Washington himself deemed it wise to give this latitude. Washington is reputed to have thought that the new nation would surely be confronted with many foreign invasions and domestic tumults and insurrections, in which the power of the President to take complete and effective charge must be unquestionable. If this were the origin of the un-

trammeled power of the Commander in Chief, it constituted
another mark of the wisdom of the Father of His Country.

Lincoln believed this very definitely the case. He acted almost as though he held the implied powers of the office to be
as extensive as the need of any condition or situation that
called for action. Certainly throughout his White House years
he considered himself the repository of the residual Federal
power, and never hesitated to exercise it when he thought the
situation required it.

This doctrine and this line of conduct went directly counter
to the purposes of the Radical shapers of revolutionary change
in the national control. Their mode of checking the Executive,
in order to force him to kneel at their feet and obey their whim
and their will, was to set up a strange new structure of the
Congress, ostensibly to aid in winning the war.

The title of this was the Joint Committee on the Conduct
of the War. It was proposed in House and Senate before December ended. As a joint resolution of their own action and
self-direction of legislative duty, it called for no signature by
the President, hence could not be vetoed. The committee
started with some moderation, but within six weeks' time was
attempting to veto military appointments and plans made by
the Executive. In less than a month thereafter, it went beyond
the realm of veto, and arrogated the right to make affirmative
decisions.

The occasion for the committee was the refusal by Secretary
of War Cameron to furnish the Congress with certain records
about the disaster at Ball's Bluff, at which General Edward D.
Baker, a Radical Senator, had been killed. This led to the
passage of the joint resolution just mentioned. It was designed
to establish a committee with expansible powers to investigate

the conduct of the war. Senator Henry Wilson of Massachusetts did not seek to cloak the purpose, proclaiming that "we should teach men in civil and in military authority that the people"—that is, the Radicals—"expect that they will not make mistakes, and that we shall not be easy with their errors." By the end of the year this new experiment in government was at work.

Its central force was Benjamin F. Wade, its chairman. During the 50's this Ohio Senator had accepted the challenge to a duel of an irate fire-eater. Then, as the challenged party, he had chosen squirrel rifles at twenty paces. The fire-eater retreated in confusion, and the North shouted with glee over "Bluff Ben." This success led him to take the offensive against the Southerners, hurling a crude wit against their arguments and pretensions. His aggressive, caveman jaw gave him a savage look, not belied by his conduct. He kept his hold on the Ohio businessmen by being true to the protective tariff; he won and kept the masses through championing extreme causes: votes for women; a greenback currency; even the redistribution of wealth. But for all this addiction to eccentricities, he was a power on the stump. Wade, together with Zachariah Chandler of Michigan, determined the committee's policies.

Tall, grim, powerful, and relentless, Chandler had been in the Senate since the middle 50's. A shrewd and successful Detroit merchant, he built a machine to control the Republican party and the State. Lincoln turned over the Federal patronage for Michigan to him. This, together with straight cash, secured his control of his party at home. In Washington he clambered on the Radical juggernaut and already was close to the driver's seat.

Andrew Johnson was another member—the only Democratic

member whom the Radicals took to their bosom. He relished the assignment, which he hoped to put to service in getting a Federal army of liberation sent to his beloved East Tennessee. A certain jealousy of George B. McClellan's presidential expectations led Johnson to join the Radicals' attack on "Little Mac's" army record; the Senator suspected the General's political principles, and had 1864 ambitions himself.

The Tennessean stayed on the committee just two months. After Grant's capture of Fort Donelson, and the ensuing Confederate retreat almost to the line of the Cumberland Mountains, Lincoln began to think about the restoration of civil government. He asked Johnson to quit the Senate, go back to his State, and try to re-establish loyal civil government there, with the restoration of the Federal relation. On March 4, 1862, the President nominated and the Senate confirmed Johnson as Military Governor of Tennessee. Soon he left for Nashville, "the very furnace of treason."

House members of the new inquisition were Daniel W. Gooch, of Massachusetts, a Radical in conservative garb; George W. Julian, of Indiana, a Radical firebrand who thought McClellan a traitor; John Covode, of Pennsylvania, whose reputation had been built upon an investigation of the Buchanan Administration printing-contract scandals; and Moses F. Odell, a Brooklyn Democrat who denounced McClellan as a disloyal incompetent.

Gooch, a skillful cross-examiner, did much of the inquisitional work for the Joint Committee. Julian acted as the Abolitionist agent in the new program. Covode had an undeserved reputation as a sleuth and thief-catcher, because of his exposure of Cornelius Wendell, Buchanan's Public Printer and source of funds for needy henchmen. He did little of value for the Zach Chandler group. Odell grew so bitterly Radical

[44]

that the next year the Brooklyn Democracy read him out of the party.

These seven men made up the first Joint Committee on the Conduct of the War. From the beginning it was a mighty engine of control; in its later operations it stood revealed as a new, nonconstitutional organ of government, set up by the determined Radicals to run the military establishment for their own partisan ends. Ben Wade made no bones about this, but declared its function to be to secure for Congress and the Radicals the control of the policies and the conduct of the war.

Considered institutionally, it looked to the creation of a governmental organ never contemplated in the Constitution. The effect was to place a supreme executive of the legislature over the constitutional war executive—that is, the President as Commander in Chief. It represented a far-reaching experiment in the relation of the civil and military authorities in the nation at war.

The committee's operations supposedly were secret. Actually, while its hearings were not officially published at the time, committeemen never hesitated to make use, in speeches in the House or Senate, of any testimony before it. No witness hauled in to defend himself could ever know, officially at least, the nature of the slanders already uttered against him; nor could he be sure what of the things he said would be quoted privately or put in some report.

Lincoln did not, at first, seem to pierce through the pretended moral and ethical purposes of the new agency, and brought no pressure to head it off. But he never liked it, and by August, 1862, found it most harmful. At many critical junctures he was forced to discharge generals the committee hated, or to choose others politically attractive to the Radical cabal. Had he ignored its insistence on the choice of Hooker

[45]

to take over the Army of the Potomac early in 1863, and brought Sherman, Thomas, or Grant East for the job, the war might have been ended a year earlier.

The committee's record was not forgotten. When the United States entered the First World War in 1917, there was a move in Congress to establish a "Joint Committee on Expenditures in the Conduct of the War." Woodrow Wilson looked with horror on the prospect. Were this done, he declared, it would "render my task of conducting the war practically impossible." He warned that "the constant supervision of executive action which it contemplates would amount to nothing less than an assumption on the part of the legislative body of the executive work of the Administration."

Wilson went a step further; he called attention to "a very ominous precedent in our history, which shows how such a supervision would operate." This was the record of the Joint Committee on the Conduct of the War. President Wilson said that it "was the cause of constant and distressing harassment, and rendered Mr. Lincoln's task all but impossible."

The magnitude of this menace was not foreseen when the committee began its work. Nonetheless, many conservatives in Congress sensed the malice of its moving spirits, and feared its future course.

It likewise awakened the apprehensions of secession sympathizers and subversionists, both in the capital and in the country. While it was not the cause for the swift spread of the Copperheads, undoubtedly it did swell the ranks and increase the pace of the fifth column now forming in the Loyal States.

JAMES P. FRY
*Provost Marshal General of
the United States Army*

LAFAYETTE C. BAKER
*First Head of the United
States Secret Service*

THE OLD CAPITOL PRISON
where many Civil War Fifth Columnists were confined

Chapter 3

WARTIME WASHINGTON

EVEN before the outbreak of the war, Washington had seemed to offer a perfect place of concealment and field of operations for Confederate spies, domestic conspirators, and the disaffected and disgruntled of all sorts. This stemmed right out of its antebellum background.

Most of the long-time residents of the District of Columbia were Tory in the extreme, and had no sympathy with the personnel or the purposes of the Lincoln Administration. The neighborhood population, drawn from "Maryland Free State" and Virginia, had the divided loyalties of the Border region. Secession spies found it comparatively simple to get inside news of Federal activities and to send or take it through the lines.

The attitude of Washington's municipal government gave the Administration grave concern. At that time, and for thirty years thereafter, the capital city elected its own mayor and municipal legislature. Because of the political complexion of the city government at the outbreak of the war, its attitude was distinctly uncooperative. In June, the condition grew so bad that the Secretary of State ordered the arrest of James G. Berret, the mayor, and had him dispatched to Fort Lafayette. A little later Secretary Seward wrote the officer in command of that prison that Berret could be released, but only upon the condition that he would take the oath of allegiance to the Government of the United States, and at the same time would resign as Mayor of Washington. The prisoner accepted these conditions.

Lincoln himself was greatly concerned over the attitude of the courts of the District of Columbia, which were generally believed to sympathize with secession. During the first few months of the war, Sumner told the Senate that it "was notorious that we have about us many disloyal people, that there is here a very disloyal population," and cited the personnel of the District bench as example. His Massachusetts colleague, Henry Wilson, added the remark that the Chief Judge was disloyal; "I believe his heart is sweltering with treason." In the result, instead of invoking the slow process of impeachment, the Congress abolished the existing court structure, and thus ended the tenure of the suspected incumbents. At the same time it created a new local judicial establishment, and stalwart Republicans were put upon it.

The Government's first efforts to control the civil population were conducted by the Secretary of State, for reasons both personal and official. William H. Seward, the "Premier" of the Cabinet, had an unquenchable zeal for dabbling in everybody else's business. In addition, since the establishment of the Federal Government the office of the Secretary of State had been somewhat of a catchall for duties no other executive agency was designed to handle. With the war, and the new problem of subversion on the home front, Seward soon began to busy himself about arrests of political prisoners, their incarceration, and then the next step of setting up secret agents to ferret them out.

Lincoln likewise was acutely conscious of the need for detective work. In February, 1861, on his way to Washington, he heeded the warning of Allan Pinkerton, and permitted himself to be "smuggled" through Baltimore to the capital. The sneers which greeted this act of prudence did not lessen his belief in the Chicago detective, whom he later employed as a gatherer of military information for McClellan's army.

Seward made some use of Pinkerton in the summer of the first year of the war, but did not keep him long, perhaps because he felt that the detective was too close to the President, and Seward wanted his own man, whose loyalty would be direct to him. The first step he took was the quite proper one of establishing a listening post in Canada, not only to keep track of Confederate agents there but also to report the trend of sentiment in British North America. The day before Sumter was fired on, Seward appointed George Ashmun, the Massachusetts Congressman, special agent to Canada for three months. The salary was $10 a day and travel costs (which must be supported by vouchers); and Seward cannily advanced $500 cash on account.

This proved a false start, and for almost a year consular reports were burdened with appeals for confidential agents. Mr. Charles S. Ogden, at Quebec, insisted that "it requires ingenuity and judgment to watch the undercurrent"; consular fees were slim, but if the Government would be liberal in its allowance, he could frustrate the rebel plotters.

Reporting agencies were established at Halifax, St. John's, and other seaports, and reports flowed to Washington by mail and telegraph. Soon the Secretary was to learn that George N. Sanders had sailed for Liverpool, bearing dispatches from Davis. The Quebec Consul insisted Sanders left "disguised as a miner, carrying an old carpet-bag, wearing green goggles and a shaggy mustache"—a disguise which was in keeping with the excited imagination of this Kentucky stormy petrel.

The program in the United States itself started about the same time, but did not progress so quickly. As late as September, the head of the State Department wrote Flamen Ball, the United States Attorney at Cincinnati (a focus of Ohio Valley disaffection) that it is "our wish to make as few arrests as possible, compatible with the safety of the Government and never if they can be avoided for merely words spoken."

Seward expressed this attitude particularly in regard to the organization of a secret society of treason, which an informer in its ranks had written that he would be willing to betray—for a consideration. This was the Knights of the Golden Circle, then spreading like wildfire over Kentucky, Missouri, southern Ohio, Indiana, and Illinois. But Seward wrote Ball that "we have had disclosures from other similar persons, which have hitherto proved of little or no value"; the offer might be looked into, but with circumspection.

But the Secretary of State did not hesitate to advise Postmaster General Blair, about that same time, that the *Louisville Courier* was publishing some treasonable material, and he would "suggest the expediency of prohibiting the circulation of that paper by post." A little later, in reply to an inquiry from a dependable agent in New York, who desired to arrest an Irish firebrand although the latter had a British passport in good order, he wrote: "No passport is a protection for treason. If you have reliable evidence of facts, arrest Quinlan, passport or no passport. Hereafter no diplomatic or consular passport will be good unless countersigned by me."

Seward's "Secret Service Letter Book" for 1861 was full of inquiries dispatched to friends and trusted official associates throughout the country asking them to discover persons who could be put on important investigating tasks. He wanted "a discreet and active man" for the Northern frontier, to arrest spies seeking entrance from Canada, and offered to pay such a man $100 a month. A little later he appointed a special agent at Niagara Falls, to examine the persons coming over the Suspension Bridge, and seize and hold any who seemed suspicious. He sought, without immediate results, a good man for Chicago and another for Detroit. He authorized the United States Marshal at Boston to employ two detectives for two months' time, each at $150 a month. This was particularly urgent; therefore let the Marshal consult the governor of the State, "and take effective measures to break up the business of making and sending shoes for the Rebel Army."

But Seward's problem of getting an active man for the job of chief counterspy was not solved until he employed Lafayette C. Baker. This occurred in the late summer of 1861. It was the real beginning of the United States Secret Service.

In some ways this man Baker is a mysterious figure. The most direct evidence in print about him and his secret-service work is to be found in his book of reminiscences, which he entitled *The History of the United States Secret Service.* In this thick book of 693 pages, its author never hesitated to lay bare the confidential details, whether romantic or revolting, of the dangers he encountered. In it, he thoughtfully provided an introductory chapter describing his life, character, and accomplishments.

Born at Stafford, New York, in 1826, Lafayette went with his family to Lansing, Michigan. His boyhood in that Northwestern environment, he testified, gave him "circumspection and habitual self-control," together with a changeful and playful mood "in the unguarded enjoyment of social life."

In his middle twenties, Baker returned to New York. In

1853 he went via Panama to California, where he soon was a leading Vigilante. When he left for the East in January, 1861, a committee took note of his services and presented to him a cane of manzanita wood, with a head of polished gold quartz, embedded in which were nine stones, the whole being "richly mounted with solid gold and cost Two Hundred and Fifty Dollars."

This was but one of many presents this "bold, fearless and adventurous" character was to receive. And no matter whether it were a badge of gold marked "Death to Traitors," or "an elegant sabre with sash of china silk," or "the most elaborate finished saddles and trappings in the country," he made meticulous note that the value of the first was not less than $200, the second had cost about the same amount, while the third was worth $650.

Of average height, Baker weighed about a hundred and eighty pounds, and was lithe and sinewy. A profusion of brown hair surrounded his "forehead of intelligent outline"; he wore a beard; his gray eye, cold in repose, was sharply piercing when he interviewed "a victim of his vigilance." He was a fine horseman, and "probably the best shot in the country." Moreover, he had few vices; he did not curse, and had not tasted liquor for twenty years. "To those less fortunate than himself, and to his family, his fidelity and kindness of heart were well known."

Baker reached the East about the time the war began, and late in the summer Seward put him to work.

His first tasks were not overly important. He was ordered to arrest a Washington lady, find her treasonable correspondence, and turn it over to United States District Attorney Edward C. Carrington; he carried Parker H. French, a Confederate spy, to a cell in Fort Warren in Boston Harbor, and for the most part was assigned to matters of that sort.

After a brief investigation in Philadelphia, he telegraphed the Secretary of State: "It is highly important that certain correspondence should be examined here. Will you have a general order sent to the Postmaster here to that effect at once, allowing me to use my discretion in these investigations?" A little later he tried to stop smuggling across the Potomac, found the postmaster at Port Tobacco, Maryland, an active secession sympathizer, and would have arrested him but for the fact that the traitor "was confined to his bed with chills and fever, besides having a large family depending on him for support."

Baker was concerned, too, in the prison problem. When Seward had started seizing suspects, in June or earlier, he had sent them to forts in the Loyal States. But the commanders objected to having to treat these traitors with special consideration. Consequently, in July Seward issued instructions that the United States Marshals in the vicinity of these forts were to "supply decent lodging and subsistence for such prisoners unless they shall prefer to provide in those respects for themselves."

The Old Capitol, in which the Congress had sat before the new Capitol's completion, became the place of incarceration of political prisoners in Washington. At first, only suspected persons of the vicinity were confined there, but before many months people from points as far away as Dubuque, Iowa, were brought there by United States Marshals and thrust into dirty, overcrowded rooms. The Old Capitol Prison likewise became famous as the resting-place for Belle Boyd, Rose Greenhow, Madame Velasquez, and other Confederate suspects of the so-called weaker sex.

The War Department seemed to exert little influence in the

[*53*]

control of civil subversion so long as Simon Cameron continued as its head. But by the late fall of 1861 the procurement corruption of the Department began to be a public scandal. While not personally corrupt, Cameron seemed singularly insensitive to the swindling going on throughout the services of supplies. Contractors charged excessive prices for shoddy materials. In some military departments, such as John C. Frémont's at St. Louis, foreign thieves and native pirates vied in raids on the Treasury.

The President heard the stories and considered making a change. Cameron soon afforded him an added cause as well as excuse. The Pennsylvania boss, Radical in his political attachments, put in his annual report to Congress, without Lincoln's knowledge, a manifesto favoring immediate emancipation of the slaves. This blow to his Border State policy moved the President to send Cameron across the seas into honorific retirement as Minister to Russia.

One reason for the delay in cleaning up the War Department mess had been Lincoln's uncertainty over a successor. Intimate personal friends, like James Speed of Kentucky, pressed the name of Joseph Holt of that same State. At that time this magnetic platform orator was regarded as a coming man, perhaps Lincoln's successor in 1864. The President considered Holt for Secretary of War, then drafted him to set up the army's structure of counterespionage and control of civil conspiracies, and named him Judge Advocate General of the army. A little later, Lincoln established the Bureau of Military Justice and put Holt at its head, to give him more prestige.

This cleared the track for the choice of another aspirant to head the War Department. Edwin M. Stanton was urged by two groups which were at loggerheads with one another. Few Northern critics had sneered at Lincoln so much as this

Buchanan agent; but as soon as he saw the path to power he changed his course. Not only did he pay court to McClellan, who swallowed the bait, but he made pledges to the Radicals in Congress, and they took him to their bosom. Such was his greed for power that he shrank from no duplicity. On January 11, 1862, he became Secretary of War.

The stage was now set for the War Department to establish its own secret service. Within a few weeks the transfer was worked out. Seward gave up Lafayette C. Baker and the latter's agents, the control of the Old Capitol Prison, and the general handling of political and citizen subversion. Stanton took over the job, established a secret fund, and turned Baker over to General Holt. Lafayette C. Baker soon had the title of Chief of the United States Secret Service. Woe betide the sullen Copperhead!

The head of the new military establishment had many duties other than those connected with the fight against the fifth column. Notable among these was the attempt to control the morale (and so far as possible, the morals) of the soldiers stationed in or visiting the capital. This was one of his most time-consuming problems, because the presence of the men in uniform had confronted Washington with unsuspected social evils. Particularly after pay day, the Provost Guard was unable to restrain the soldiers. Soon after McClellan took command, he tried to introduce some slight military discipline in the capital, and forbade any officer or soldier to visit it except on public duty. The mayor moved up the closing hour for saloons from midnight to nine o'clock—but he did not change the hours for hotel bars and restaurants!

Congress tried to do its bit against John Barleycorn, and passed a vain act prohibiting the sale of liquor to any soldier.

Yet wherever soldiers were stationed, beer barrels and whisky demijohns abounded. Baker reported there were no fewer than 3,700 "fountains of ruin," and the "lowest places of intoxication" occupied two sides of the market square. In many places the whole stock in trade was a cask of beer and a gallon of unknown and villainous Bourbon whisky, dealt out in an old rusty tin cup at 10 cents a drink. Next as a source of corruption were the canterburies—concert halls where, nightly, men were drugged, robbed, and sometimes murdered.

Wartime Washington was filled with houses of ill fame, a few handsomely furnished and conducted in style. The girls, according to report, "were either young or in the prime of life, and frequently beautiful and accomplished." Not many were native Washingtonians; most came from New York, Boston, Philadelphia, and Chicago, stayed while the Congress was in session, and departed when the solons started home. The patrons were men "of moral respectability . . . the very best class of the city population," including Senators, Congressmen, governors, and a host of lawyers. They would come openly, exchange greetings, and "then go away and talk eloquently about morality and virtue."

There were gambling dens aplenty; in the summer of 1863, Stanton's chief spy reported that at least 163 of these were in full blast. Most of them were on or near Pennsylvania Avenue, some sumptuously furnished. Most had heavily curtained windows and an air of mystery and silence. The one in which Thad Stevens, Caliban of the Radicals in the House of Representatives, loved to spend his nights, had its floor thickly carpeted, its walls and ceilings frescoed, and was adorned with works of art. Chandeliers with many gas jets shining through cut-glass globes illumined the costly furniture. Liveried Negro attendants served the customers. Banquets were served, food and wine

[*56*]

being free, and the proprietor was "a gentleman of the bluest blood," as gamblers understood the term.

In such first-class establishments, "square" games alone were played, chiefly faro. The money was not on the table, ivory counters being used. Thousands of dollars changed hands in a night, and the country's great were often seen there. Nearly all of the stealings by paymasters and other handlers of public funds could be traced to these parlors of chance. But there were many others, low and vile, some with "female dealers to lure the unwary."

Confederate agents were habitual attendants at these palaces of chance, whether they dispensed wine, women, or song. There were reports that ardent female patriots of Dixie came to Washington to exchange their virtue for secret information from the patrons of their establishments. There were many authenticated instances of other agents who would supply funds to officials in distress because of gambling losses. The lolling tongues of the bars and the canterburies disclosed many important secrets. Baker and his men had to do the best they could to check these avenues of indiscretion or betrayal.

For all that, wartime Washington was a fascinating spot for the visitor. No longer was it a sleepy little Southern town. Even before Lincoln's inauguration it had begun to swell like one of McClellan's new gas balloons. By the time Baker got on the job, it had become the desperately overcrowded general headquarters of the nation at war.

The traveler coming to the capital from North, East, or West, had but a single way to reach the city—that is, unless he were willing to come on horseback with flapping saddlebags, or to jolt along in one of the few remaining stagecoaches over roads of almost unbottomed mud. By rail, he must come over the Washington branch of the Baltimore & Ohio. Incidentally, the trip from Baltimore to Washington was regarded as a high mark in modern transportation. Each day eight passenger trains went both ways; the most rapid needed only an hour and twenty minutes for the trip, and the fare was a modest $1.60. Each locomotive had a proper name of its own, the most famous being *Ten Wheel Perkins,* a voracious wood-burner, the fuel consumption of which forced occasional stops at convenient woodpiles. The passenger cars were quite varie-gated, some being little more than goods boxes on wheels. All had open platforms, with hand brakes. Inside were huge cast-iron stoves, in winter kept cherry-red by constant feeding of pine knots and "lightwood." The train crew wore light-blue double-breasted uniforms and military caps. There were news-butchers, who carried trays, took orders for gumdrops, and sold tobacco, apples, and cakes.

Before the war, the stations close to Washington had been desolate-looking hamlets, and the farmhouses of the region were dirty, dingy, and generally unpainted. The fields, full of stagnant pools, presented scenes of geese, pigs, and children swarming about, as one traveler said, "on a footing of perfect equality." With the war this doubly dilapidated atmosphere departed, and practically the whole distance from Baltimore to Washington became alive with soldiers, camps, warehouses, and artillery parks. After the train reached the Washington railroad yards, it made its way through a maze of tracks to a frame station, with tower and clock, at the corner of New Jersey Avenue and C Street. Some thought this a dirty, cheer-less hall, but the railroad magnates of the day called it a marvel of beauty and convenience.

Upon emerging on New Jersey Avenue, the visitor would be bewildered by a dense line of hacks and omnibuses, all the drivers and porters crowding around the exit and yelling at the top of their lungs:

"Willard's, whose a-goin' to Willard's? Every *gentleman* knows Willard's."—"Metropolitan 'otel, sir? Best 'ouse in the city, sir."—"The National, National! This way, sir. Only first-class 'ouse in Washington!"

On his first visit to the city, the traveler could not but be impressed by the great Capitol which loomed before him as he left the station. When finished in Monroe's Administration, it had seemed "a grand affair," but the country's growth, together with the Congress's growing sense of self-importance, led to a great extension, which was started in 1850. Twelve years later workmen were still putting on the finishing touches, and had not yet capped the dome with its headpiece, the great statue of Freedom. The Capitol had been modernized considerably; its "members' baths," finished in black walnut, with marble-tiled floors, had showers as well as tubs. The Capitol restaurant offered every delicacy of the season on its bill of fare.

The structure housed the Library of Congress, which had bought Jefferson's private library. Visitors here were under strict rules. Under no circumstances would anyone less than sixteen years of age be admitted, while visitors must remove their hats and talk in whispers.

From the base of Capitol Hill, a visitor's hack would swing into Pennsylvania Avenue, which at the time of the fall of Sumter was paved with cobblestones all the way to Georgetown. By 1862, it had been so hammered by army wagons and other unexpected traffic that its surface suggested that of corrugated-iron roofing; in many places deep mud covered the pavement, and teams of army mules often mired down. The brick sidewalks along the Avenue and elsewhere were in sorry shape.

The Avenue was full of life and motion. On its corners were

street vendors of an amazing variety. One sold "patent soaps warranted to remove grease spots most tenacious, in an amazingly short space of time." Near at hand, another sought to sell artificial insects attached to elastic strings. Candy men by the dozens stood by little stands chipping the hard sweets with little hammers. Then there were Italians roasting chestnuts, organ-grinders with dancing monkeys, telescope men proffering spyglasses at 10 cents a look. Bootblacks were everywhere, chiefly little inky fellows who would make a dive at your foot as you passed, and newsboys (exclusively white) were about as numerous. There were mounted guards at each street corner, swords drawn and waiting to seize the speeders of the day. Every two or three minutes horsecars clanked over the double track from Georgetown to the Navy Yard.

From early morn to latest night, wheeled traffic filled the avenue—hacks driven by Negroes being the most numerous, but with many private carriages with liveried coachmen, and government wagons and ambulances.

The Avenue was a museum without a Barnum. In one shop milady could buy a satin slipper, next door there was a load of hay for sale, and at the next, coffins up on end with a transparency suggesting that you be embalmed. The buildings on the north side were higher and more pretentious than the insignificant-looking shacks on the south side.

For all this surface tinsel, to world travelers Washington was a rather shabby and disappointing capital. In 1862 it had only one theater, no modern school buildings, and an indifferent spattering of monuments and statues. North of K and west of Fourteenth, there were few private houses until one came to Georgetown. East of the Capitol, dwellings were similarly well scattered. The only imposing official structures were the Capitol, the White House, the Treasury, and the Interior

Building. The State Department was housed in a tumble-down brick building at one end of the Treasury.

The War Department Building, to which Lincoln went so often and so anxiously, had originally been of two stories built of brick painted a drab color, having a wooden porch and heavy wooden columns. Already it looked battered and shattered. Not until the end of 1863 did the Post Office and the Patent Office near completion. The Center Market was a low row of sheds, open on both sides. The Washington Monument had climbed to only a third of its projected height, and ugly sheds and huge piles of rock and lumber clustered about its base.

The odorous B Street Canal and Tiber Creek ran through the center of the city—the last-named a little muddy stream which in summer was hardly liquid enough for geese; the two together made the city one vast stench. Other open pools, swamps, ditches, and sewers abounded, while horses, cows, goats, and pigs roamed at will.

Washington's noted hotels, the National, the Metropolitan, and Willard's, were all on Pennsylvania Avenue. The first-named, the city's largest, was at Pennsylvania Avenue and Sixth Street. Before the war it had been habited chiefly by Southerners, and during Buchanan's Administration a disease had been named for it—"the National Hotel disease"—the cause of which had been an oversimple kitchen sanitation. Across the street from it was Jesse Brown's establishment, first known as the Indian Queen, in the late 40's as Brown's Hotel, and in the Civil War bursting into the full effulgence of the title of the Metropolitan. On the Avenue at Twelfth was the Kirkwood House, unpretentious but bountiful.

Two blocks west, on the present site of the New Willard Hotel, was the inn of Caleb Willard, the most enterprising hotelkeeper the early capital had ever known. This was a rambling mass of rooms, six stories high. Obscure or unpretentious guests were assigned to the top-floor rooms farthest removed and had to climb five flights of steps; but the elite drew better quarters. Throughout the war Willard's was crammed to the eaves, and was said to house "more scheming, plotting, planning heads, more aching and joyful hearts, than any building of the same size ever held in the world."

Ladies visiting Willard's found a lavish drawing-room, with pianos, sofas, and easy chairs. For the men there was a barber-shop, where shaving was conducted "to a high degree of publicity." The menus were varied and bountiful. An English visitor noted carefully what one American ordered for his breakfast: Black tea and toast, scrambled eggs, fresh spring shad, wild pigeons, pigs' feet, two robins on toast, oysters, Thomas bread, and an ample supply of waffles! From Willard's the visitor could walk west past the Treasury at the next corner and come to the President's House.

The structure itself had been modeled pretty closely on the lines of the palace of the Duke of Leinster. Admiral Cockburn's raiders partially destroyed it in 1814, but it had been immediately restored. Its outer walls were freestone, painted white, from which fact, perhaps, it received its popular name of the White House. There were two lofty stories, and a roof with a balustrade around it. Ionic pilasters ornamented the outer walls; the north front had a handsome portico with four Ionic columns, and the main entrance led from this through a massive doorway into the main hall.

Within were thirty-one rooms of size. Those on the first floor—such as the East Room, with the Green, Blue, and Red rooms adjoining, and the large dining-rooms—were chiefly for ceremonial occasions. On the north front of the second floor

[*62*]

were six rooms which the President and his family used as bedrooms. On the south side were seven rooms: Antechamber, Audience Room, Cabinet Room, the President's Private Office, the Ladies' Parlor, and two other rooms not specifically assigned. There were eleven rooms in the basement, for such service purposes as kitchens, pantries, and butlers' rooms. To the left of the main entrance were the stairs to the upper story, and there a doorkeeper always was on guard, to keep improper characters from going up. The White House had an air of elegance as well as comfort, although it must be confessed that its furniture gave an impression of costliness rather than of taste.

Here it was that Lincoln lived during most of the war years. He was always accessible to visitors, but not before nine in the morning. Edward McManus, a shrewd little Irishman with pleasant smile and cheery word, was at the door. Butler for a succession of Presidents, from this experience he had gained a quick insight into character. It was said that he could "tell from a look the business and hopes of almost all callers." Most of the President's day was taken up with seeing office-seekers and officeholders, conducting hastily-called meetings of his Cabinet, and reading the Washington papers—and when he could get them those from Richmond, to which he always gave the greatest care. Such was wartime Washington in the battle-drenched years of 1861-65.

Chapter 4

THE KNIGHTS OF THE GOLDEN CIRCLE

THE month after the outbreak of the war, a resolution was introduced into the House of Representatives of the Kentucky Legislature that called for the appointment of a committee to investigate a new secret society which had begun to operate in that State—the Knights of the Golden Circle. Its operations were described as a menace to Kentucky's effort to be neutral, particularly because it was believed that this order was importing arms and ammunition. No investigation by the legislature followed. But for the next two years this band of Southern sympathizers disturbed the State and hampered the Administration's efforts to keep Kentucky in the fold.

From Lincoln's birth State—and that of Davis as well—the "castles" (the name given to the local lodges of the Knights of the Golden Circle) spread quickly over the immediate Border region. A little later they made their way into Iowa, Wisconsin, and Michigan, in the far Northwest; and into the coal-mining regions of Pennsylvania and the wards of New York City. There was even claim that units were established in the State of Maine.

What was the background of this secret society with such a romantic name? To what elements of the feelings of the people

[*64*]

did it make so immediate and commanding an appeal? Was it in fact a treasonable conspiracy? Or was it little more than a chance for impressionable youths to mumble rituals and swear oaths they neither intended nor understood?

The records do not disclose the answers to all these questions. After the war, there was naturally a flavor of disrepute to former membership in the K.G.C., as it came to be known in common conversation; and similarly to connection with any of its counterparts or successors, such as the Corps de Belgique, the Knights of the Golden Square, the Union Relief Society, the Order of American Knights, and the Order of the Sons of Liberty. This was so much the case that as late as 1918 historical inquirers who sought information from men known to have been in the ranks of one or another of these orders were met with evasion or stony silence. Most of the actual evidence available about the organizations was developed in the years of the war itself.

But no such mystery attached to the background of the Knights of the Golden Circle; on the contrary, the information about the order is voluminous, and traces deep into the past. While it was Southern in its direct organization, it was but one of the many manifestations of an addiction to oaths, grips, passwords, secret signs of recognition, and hidden meeting-places which marked all America for at least three decades before the Civil War.

One can find traces of the camp-meeting spirit, the Peter Cartwright revival so delightfully portrayed by Mrs. Trollope in her description of the *Domestic Manners of the Americans*. There were distinct resemblances to the open stealth of the Know-Nothings and other antiforeign movements of the 40's and the 50's. The magic of Masonry, with its "stations," variety of degrees, and solemnity of oaths, was conspicuous. In

the case of the Southern organizations, the general purposes
of extending the area of slavery, obtaining new opportunities
for expansion and excitement, and giving adventurous souls
new worlds to conquer, were ever present.

About 1850, for example, the Order of the Lone Star was
founded in New Orleans, with the secret purpose of seeking
to annex Cuba and other slave territory outside the United
States. A little later it was proposed to merge this body into
the K. G. C., as a larger society with parallel purpose; during
the negotiations, it was revealed that the oath of the other order required obedience to its Sachem, "without any reference
to and in spite of any oath they may have taken to support the
Constitution of the United States." Pierre Soule, then a Senator
from Louisiana, refused to take such an obligation and was required to leave the hall! But P. G. T. Beauregard and some
other army officers did not decline.

Another instance that came to light was the handiwork of
a Louisiana lawyer, one Phineas C. Wright, who in the late
50's had been employed in a famous litigation, the Gaines
case, the records of which went back to Revolutionary days.
In these records the attorney found papers about a secret
organization, together with its ritual and the obligations of
the oath. These led him to launch its counterpart, under the
title of the Order of American Knights. Within a short time,
however, Louisiana seceded and Attorney Wright moved to
St. Louis.

The real origin of the Knights of the Golden Circle was in
none of these, but in Ohio, whence it moved south. The
founder, Dr. George William Lamb Bickley, of an old Virginia family, moved to Cincinnati, Ohio, in the late 40's, and
in 1852 was appointed by the board of trustees of the "Eclectic
Medical Institute of Ohio" to the chair of materia medica,

therapeutics, and medical botany. He held onto this appointment until 1859 and occasionally performed its duties. But the greater part of his time was spent in the South in secret-order schemes.

These were the years in which the doctrine that it was the "Manifest Destiny" of the United States to seize and dominate the whole continent attracted a large part of the population. This led to such forays on the diplomatic front as the once-famous Ostend Manifesto. The prospect of extending the area of slavery into Mexico and Central America excited many Southern fire-eaters. The famous Nicaragua filibuster of General William Walker illustrated the lengths to which its disciples went.

These projected expansions southward fascinated Dr. Bickley, who organized the new secret order to provide a force to colonize and Americanize the northernmost provinces of Mexico. In 1854 he organized the first castle of the Knights of the Golden Circle in Cincinnati, Ohio—a city already noted for the earlier dubious honor of being the birthplace of the Know-Nothings and the scene of antiforeign riots. A few other castles were established in near-by towns. Its founder soon took the order to the Cotton South, where the idea was received with enthusiasm.

In 1863, when Bickley was a political prisoner in the Ohio State Prison at Columbus and was appealing frantically for release, he wrote Governor David Tod an elaborate justification of the presecession record of the order.

"The plan," according to his claim, "was to assist the Constitutional Party under President Benito Juárez to overthrow the Clergy Party under Miramón, by furnishing them men and officers, arms, munitions, and by shaping public opinion in the United States. For and in consideration of these services,

Don Manuel Doblado, Governor of Guanajuato, entered into stipulations with the Commissioners of the Knights of the Golden Circle organization in February 1860—all of which was reported, with duplicate of the articles of agreement, to the United States Government through Hon. Lewis Cass, then Secretary of State.

"Men were enlisted as colonists or emigrants, openly drilled in Baltimore, Washington, and in all the large cities of the South. It was a matter of newspaper notoriety both in this country and in Europe." While these men were not to be armed in the United States, "they availed themselves of a common right to emigrate to a foreign country, and when once there, to choose any mode of life compatible with their taste or interest."

This was magnificent understatement. The ritual of the Knights made the forthright statement that the purpose of the order was "the entire and speedy conquest of Mexico and the establishment of a separate and independent nation upon such a basis as to render it subservient to the march of American civilization."

In his letter to the Ohio Governor, Dr. Bickley continued that many emigrants from the United States had gone to Mexico, "and others were forming encampments on the Rio Grande when this terrible rebellion became imminent. By the order of the Texas authorities, the whole force was disbanded and the organization ceased its work."

This somewhat grandiose description of accomplishment was in part mirage; castles of the Knights were established throughout the South, there had been some drilling, and there was some emigration. But the actuality had been far short of the founder's claim.

It was Bickley's habit to report that plans on paper, and

The Knights of the Golden Circle

even dreams in his mind, were actual facts. Undoubtedly he was a facile orator, a good expounder, and a genius at devising rituals and oaths. But he seems to have been unable to make his good first impressions last. His leadership of the order was marked by many good starts, soon followed by the lieutenants' loss of confidence in Founder Bickley. Then the whole thing would have to be begun again.

In 1860, he encountered determined opposition within his own hierarchy of command, was ousted as the head of the society, and was taken back only on sufferance. Bickley later claimed to have dropped the secret-society work, to have supported the presidential candidacy of John C. Breckinridge in 1860, and then to have accepted Lincoln's election without objection.

Other letters of the founder told the story in several different forms, for Bickley was as untrustworthy as he was romantic. But it is a fact that the initial purpose of the organization was Mexican adventure. It is also true that it spread rapidly along the Texas border, and that its operations below the Rio Grande were brought to a sudden end.

During the secession parade, the fire-eaters who composed the junta of the new revolution undertook to energize every potential tool of effective resistance to the attacks they feared would be made upon the new Confederacy. Among these tools were the Knights of the Golden Circle.

They promptly shifted its focus from Mexican adventure to Confederate support. The change was made in due form. Bickley, who now preferred to be called General and not Doctor, made no objection to the espousal of resistance to the Union. The ritual was remodeled to declare that while the first field of operation remained Mexico, "we hold it to be

[69]

our duty to offer our services to any Southern State to repel a Northern Army." Another change prescribed that no candidate for the third degree, the level at which the hierarchy became military, would be considered unless either he came from a slave State, or if from a free State, was Southern-born, a Protestant, and a former slaveowner.

Bickley went to Montgomery, the first Confederate capital, where William H. Russell, famous correspondent of the *Times* of London, ran into evidences of his feverish activity. Official notification went to the members that after March 1, 1861, Montgomery would be general headquarters.

The spring of 1861 marked the end of the Knights of the Golden Circle in the Southern States themselves. Before attack on Sumter, its espousal of the secession cause had helped crystallize Dixie sentiment. But this value vanished when the Southerners took up arms. It was apparent that the secret order would be useful only in places where strong sympathy for States' Rights and slavery existed but expression of these sentiments was prevented by the Federal Government.

With the firing on Sumter and Lincoln's call for troops, it became apparent that there was no remaining merit to K.G.C. headquarters at the Confederate capital. Tennessee and Kentucky demanded attention, and after these, the South's friends farther north needed encouragement and organization. Bickley took the hint and hastened to Tennessee, and was active in Clarksville, in the heart of the dark-tobacco region. Then he went to Russellville, Kentucky, where he began the rapid organization of castles in an effort to stimulate volunteers for the Confederate Army. It was this frantic canvass which caused the introduction into the Kentucky Legislature of the investigation plea.

If the Unionists thought this threat of exposure likely to

daunt the Confederate agent, they were quickly disillusioned. Bickley had had a lifetime of controversy on the platform and in the press. In a few days he issued "An Open Letter to the Kentucky Legislature," which defied the threat. He boldly published the purported texts of the first and second degrees of the order. This was not a dangerous disclosure, because the treasonable pledges did not come until the higher and later degrees, and these were committed to memory and not to print. His "Open Letter" boasted of 8,000 members, with representation in every county of the State. It ended with the defiant declaration that he would keep up his efforts until the Stars and Bars flew over the Frankfort capitol.

The Union press reacted immediately and variously to this flaunt of treason. One paper predicted satirically that "many a man who puts his foot in a golden circle may get his neck in a hempen one." And George D. Prentice, editor of the *Louisville Journal,* compared Bickley to Catiline, and attacked his "hellish machinations." A little later he charged that the Knights of the Golden Circle were "the very heart, the brain, the breath, the soul, of the Secession Party in Kentucky." Bickley himself soon lost his fervor for organizing the subversive castles, and made his way to Virginia, purportedly to collect a fat legacy. But the Knights of the Golden Circle did not depart with him. They were in truth the developing danger to the Union cause in this Border State which Lincoln thought indispensable to victory.

Within a few weeks the order had spread outside Kentucky. By the middle of the summer, Dr. Bowles of French Lick Springs was actively installing lodges all over the southern part of Indiana. Similar activities developed in southern Illinois, in some counties of which the whole local administration was disloyal, and the officials from judge to sheriff to justices of the peace all belonged to the Knights. The Blairs might oust Governor Jackson in Missouri, but his friends countered with resort to the Knights, and a counterpart under the name Corps de Belgique, organized by a Southern sympathizer who held the office of Belgian consul at St. Louis. Seward finally canceled his exequatur, but not his zest for conspiracy.

The Federal authorities were not long in getting fairly complete information about this fifth-column work. For example, in June, 1861, one Jim Pumfrey deliberately joined the Knights in Kentucky, with the purpose of "ferreting out and giving to the military authorities such information of its plan of operation as would result in its overthrow." He was suspected, quit the order, and then "issued an exposition of its entire Ritual, which so frustrated the Knights that it resulted in an order being issued . . . to close all the castles."

About the same time, an anonymous pamphlet published in Indianapolis exposed the K.G.C. The next month a professional artist named John C. Brain was arrested at Michigan City, charged with membership in the society, and sent to Fort Warren. Governor Oliver P. Morton became alarmed over the expansion of the secret castles, and undertook the organization of an adequate spy service.

The Indiana Adjutant General, loyal Morton henchman in Radical politics as well as in State military control, set up a group for counterespionage. When he had his own group, under the State Adjutant General, in process of effective organization, the Governor appealed to Washington for Federal help. He did not ask for a group from Lafayette C. Baker's brigade of nondescript detectives. He sought the establishment of a com-

[*72*]

plete new military control over the State. Furthermore, he asked that Colonel Carrington of Ohio, in whom he had confidence, be put on the job.

Morton had, of course, a political motive in addition to a military one in asking that Carrington be sent to him. Henry W. Halleck, the General in Chief of the Army, railed against the part politics played in the army. "I have done everything in my power here," he wrote a department commander, "to separate military appointments and commissions from politics, but really the task is hopeless. The waste of men and demoralization of the army, by having incapable and corrupt politicians in nearly all military offices, high and low, are working out terrible results."

Be this as it may, the first six months of the war had shown both Federal and State authorities the need for new machinery to suppress subversive activities. Soon there came the creation of Military Departments in regions not in the theater of war. Each of these was divided into districts, generally one for each State. An elaborate apparatus of Provost Marshals was instituted, the better to discover plots and punish the conspirators.

Henry Beebee Carrington, who in the fall of 1861 became Morton's cunning left hand in the fight against the Copperheads, had an interesting background. He came of Connecticut stock, went through Yale University, and then read law. In 1848 he moved to Ohio and became a junior partner of William Dennison, an important force in the organization of the new Republican party in the State. This threw him in close contact with Salmon P. Chase, whose trusted friend Carrington became. During Chase's governorship of Ohio, immediately before secession, he drafted the lawyer to become Adjutant General, in order to reorganize the militia of the State.

[73]

In 1861, after Lincoln's proclamation, Carrington recruited nine regiments of Ohio militia for the Federal service. Dennison, who had succeeded Chase as governor, made Carrington a colonel and put him in command of a camp of regulars. He was also serving as Adjutant General of the State when Morton's call brought him to Indianapolis. There he quickly became Morton's trusted agent in the fight with the Copperheads—and his fight with the other Democrats, too.

Carrington's course was severe, sometimes brutal, almost always imaginative and excited. He knew no middle zone between patriots—which meant Radical Morton men—and traitors—which blanketed nearly every Democrat. With Morton's backing, but chiefly by virtue of his own boldness and ruthless force, he built a spy service which he soon believed the best in the land.

It was remarked at the time, and the reader today may be puzzled by the fact, that the really great exploits in the surveillance, detection, and crushing of the major conspiracies against the Federal cause were performed not by Lafayette C. Baker and the United States Secret Service which he commanded, but by special and often amateur staffs set up by General Carrington, Colonel Benjamin J. Sweet, and other District Commanders and State Provost Marshals. This was the result of two different but co-operating circumstances.

One was that the draft structure had an intimate and direct concern with fifth-column activities which forced the departments, districts, and boards to improvise every sort of counterespionage activity. The time urgencies were so great that the authorities had to make use of the human tools that were on hand, and learn how to do the task while actually doing it. But Baker's zone of action embraced not only the treasonable

activities of Copperheads, Butternuts, and more pretentious
traitors, but also the whole catalogue of soldier crime.

This meant that the United States Secret Service must attend to problems of smuggling; murder and robbery by soldiers both in the field and on detached duty or leave; efforts
to swindle the Government on war contracts; the defalcations
of paymasters, disbursing and finance officers, and others militarily accountable and responsible for Federal funds; the Confederate agents and spies who infested Washington, New York,
Niagara Falls, Detroit, Chicago, Cincinnati, and St. Louis;
and a variety of other detective duties. The operatives' reports
to General Baker were filled with information on such matters.
An important fraction of the time and attention of the Secret
Service was devoted to the struggle with the domestic fo-
menters of disaffection. But as the war went on, it seemed
more and more auxiliary in its role rather than the main director of the enterprise. Upon request, either direct or through
channel, Baker or his men would check up on some angle
Carrington or Sweet wanted looked into. But the principal
direction was by these men, who knew what they wanted and
how to get it. Quite a number of Baker's operatives were absorbed into the local secret-agent units. Carrington and others
sent their own men to Canada to unearth the true Confederate
plots.

Then there was another, and probably even more important,
factor. This was Baker himself. He started with Seward on an
odd-job schedule, and he seemed unable to focus his efforts
on the important tasks and delegate the small, routine jobs to
his rank and file. His energy spattered all about, without a sufficient concentration anywhere to achieve major results. The
Chief himself took pleasure in "shadowing" suspects, and in
interviewing spies who were trying to get inside his own or-

ganization to betray it to the Confederates—quite a number of them, of both sexes, did so, as the case of Madame Velasquez disclosed.

Had Baker been a strong man, like Holt or Carrington or Morton, he would have made his job as big as that of any one of them. The opportunity was there, but he never seemed quite able to see it or to grasp it. He became more and more of a pettifogger, and the really important tasks were seized and done by other hands.

At the same time, confidence in Baker's veracity and integrity grew less and less. There is no hint of this in his own *History of the United States Secret Service,* which proclaimed him the man but for whom the war could never have been won. But in 1867 there was evidence of the low esteem into which his work and his word had fallen.

This grew out of certain testimony that he had given before the Judiciary Committee of the House of Representatives, in connection with the proposed impeachment of President Andrew Johnson. The statement, without comment or rebuttal, made in a minority report from that committee to the House, said, in regard to Baker's testimony, and the examination by the committee: "It is doubtful whether he had, in any one thing, told the truth even by accident. In every important statement, he is contradicted by witnesses of unquestioned credibility. To his many previous outrages, entitling him to an unenviable immortality, he has added that of willful and deliberate perjury; and we are glad to know that not one member of the Committee deems any statement made by him as worthy of the slightest credit."

Be that as it may have been, Carrington's secret service was composed of spies, informers, betrayers, and outside secret agents. Inside officials who were jealous of more important leaders were worked on; the itch for money played a part; in quite a few instances, unsuspecting loyal men who had joined the castles were amazed at the lengths to which love of constitutional rights or Southern sympathies could carry the assertion of dissent. From many sources, and for almost as many motives, disclosures flowed in to Carrington's headquarters.

By May, 1862, the knowledge of the pattern of treason was plain enough for Carrington and Morton to take the next step—the public exposure and, if possible, the punishment of the leading Copperheads.

Carrington sought to do this in such a way that public opinion would be on his side. He was a keen student of the strange little quirks of the public mood. Ever since he had tackled the fifth column, he had studied the mind of the enemy. In this he was shrewd, for only by sinking one's own self into the mental and emotional processes of the antagonist can one gain sufficient grasp of the probable course of his path of judgment and decision to be able to sense in advance the next thing he will think, and the next step he will take.

It was this trait which made Napoleon the ogre of opposing commanders. On the battlefields in the Civil War, Sherman had it supremely on the Federal side; while among the Confederate leaders Stonewall Jackson and Nathan Bedford Forrest were masters of it. Indeed, Sherman once said of Forrest that "he is the only man on that side that I fear, because he knows what I am going to think before I think it myself." In the field of fighting treason, Carrington sought to exercise a similar self-identification with the enemy leadership, that he might learn how to checkmate it.

In time he came to the opinion that secret societies were "an inherent weakness with our people." His experience persuaded him that "their designs can be frustrated by the use of their own timid members, or by the patriotism of those who have been deceived into connection with them."

Some canvassers for members for the local lodges found it helpful to offer the prospect the chance to back out if he found this first degree not to his liking. One witness at a treason trial related that Stephen Horsey, who had solicited him to take the vestibule degree, had promised that once that were done, "he would show me the elephant, and if I did not like it after I was in, he would get me out."

This particular prospect had not been so anxious to be shown the elephant, but thousands were fascinated by the spectacular solemnity of the show. This played into the hands of the canny schemers. These used the form of a ritualistic secret society with ascending degrees to recruit a large rank and file of men and youths who liked the glamour of the secret meetings, but generally did not suspect the actual designs. By deliberate plan of the high command, the first or vestibule degree was so worded that almost anyone could take it without qualm of conscience or much fear. The revelations and instructions to the neophyte were treasonable by implication only. Most of the new members had no desire to take the succeeding steps.

The higher a member went, the thinner grew the mask of loyalty to the letter of the Constitution, until at the top there was hardly even a perfunctory effort to conceal the subversive purpose. But the ritual, at every level, provided poetry for the members' ears—and occasionally unconscious humor.

The *Guide to Enlistment* to an upper level of the military department of the Order of American Knights, a successor to K. G. C., was captioned "Headquarters of the Commander-in-Chief, and of the Illinois State Organization, Room No. 46,

McCormick's Building, Chicago, Illinois." It recited that it had been "Prepared by Authority" and described the "S.B." degree. The members of this degree constituted a "strong band" or brotherhood. A comrade in the society, declared the guide, "is also styled an 'S.B.' which has a strictly private meaning, explained only to members."

Morton, Carrington, and their lieutenants believed that the evidence on hand could be used to check, perhaps destroy, the Knights' organization in the State. The civil courts were still functioning—the extralegal devices of military courts had not yet been set up—so they determined to ask the Grand Jury of the United States Circuit Court to hold an investigation of the societies of treason. This was begun at once.

About the same time, the Indiana Republicans launched their canvass for the approaching elections. The Governor, who had a four-year term, had won with Lincoln in 1860; but the coming fall certain minor State officers, such as auditor, treasurer, and secretary of state, would be chosen—and so would be the whole Indiana delegation to the House of Representatives at Washington. The exposure of the Copperhead plots might well turn the political scales.

Under the subpoena of the Circuit Court, the United States Attorney summoned witnesses from every part of Indiana, to tell their stories to the Grand Jury. Leaves of absence were surreptitiously furnished new recruits for the Federal Army, and these men were sent back home, with instructions to join the castles of the K.G.C. and report what went on in the secret meetings. The accounts which resulted from this espionage told of active local lodges, which held regular meetings and drilled the members in military tactics.

The Grand Jury soon did its duty, and made a lengthy report. "A secret oath-bound organization exists," this declared, "numbering some fifteen thousand in Indiana, as estimated by the members of their Order commonly known as the Knights of the Golden Circle." Although their lodges had sprung up all over the State, "yet they have common signs, grips, and words" by which a member could enter a lodge anywhere in Indiana.

The Grand Jury went on that it had "abundant evidence of the membership binding themselves to resist the payment of the Federal tax and to prevent enlistment in the Army of the United States." Furthermore, wherever the Knights were strong "there has been a failure to furnish a fair proportion of volunteers." The meetings were held by stealth in unfrequented places, armed sentinels were generally posted to keep outsiders from intruding, and members often attended with arms in their hands.

Upon this evidence, the Grand Jury returned sixty indictments, for such crimes as treason, conspiracy to take and possess the property of the United States, and conspiracy to defeat the operations of the law. The report was made and the indictments returned on August 4, 1862.

The Democrats voiced anger over what they charged was nothing other than an effort to ensure Republican victory in the coming October elections. The party organ at the capital denied that there was any such order as had been reported. The Republican organ editorialized with great alarm that "nothing so seriously affecting the public safety of the Government has been developed since the outbreak of the rebellion." Governor Morton had already warned his fellow citizens against secret orders; now he repeated the charges and the threats. The Republican campaigners took to the hustings with every sort of story about what went on behind the guards at the castle meetings. Everywhere the charge was that treason and the Democratic party were identical.

But the election result demonstrated that the people were unimpressed by this Grand Jury conduct and the political use the Republicans had attempted to make of it. Of course this was not the only cause for the bad showing of the Administration candidates: McClellan's "change of base," Pope's disaster, the mixed victory of Antietam Creek, the draft law, the Emancipation Proclamation—all these contributed to the humiliatingly adverse outcome.

Another of the results, both of the official publication of the charges of treasonable conspiracy and of the loss of the State election and most of the congressional delegation, was the organization of the Union League by Administration followers. Its purpose was to have a countervailing secret society to support the vigorous conduct of the war. Similar clubs or lodges were being fostered throughout the Loyal States, and there are a few of them left today, with great plate-glass windows behind which distinguished citizens watch the passers-by.

Soon after New Year's Day, the Indiana Legislature met, and although the Democrats controlled it, a determined Republican member of the House tried to force a legislative investigation of the Knights of the Golden Circle. By a party vote, his resolution was laid on the table. On January 20, another Administrationist tried it again, and once more the House turned it down. There could be no doubt of the growing bitterness of the attitude of the peace forces in the State.

There is no question that a great deal of this description of disaffection was true. It was actively debated at the time, and has been a point of doubt since the ending of the war, whether the Confederate Government fomented and guided these treasonable efforts, or whether they probably resulted in the main from domestic feelings, without enemy stimulation. The answer to the questions remains difficult to discover. But there is some important new evidence that the Confederate leaders did have a hand in the fifth-column enterprises in the Ohio Valley.

In the years just before secession, Herschel V. Johnson was one of Georgia's ablest and most respected Democratic leaders. He was a Douglas man, and in 1860 was vice-presidential candidate on the Little Giant's ticket. He stood with Alexander H. Stephens in the Georgia Constitutional Convention at Milledgeville, opposing the Ordinance of Secession. Then, like Stephens, he "went with his State" and did his utmost for the Confederate cause.

In the early fall of 1862, Johnson smuggled himself through the battle lines, reached Cincinnati, and sought to stimulate the organization of Confederate sympathizers among the old Douglas Democrats of the States just north of the Ohio River. Many met him in Cincinnati. Some whom he had expected to appear failed him. Late in October, he wrote a Democratic politician of Lawrenceburg, Indiana, named Abiah Hays, this urgent solicitation:

"Cincinnati, Ohio, Oct. 29, 1862

"Mr. Abiah Hays

"Sir, I understand you are friendly to the Southern Cause, that you are a Democrat. We desire to know how many friends can be relied upon in your township or precinque [*sic*] and their names, in this way we can know exactly what to depend upon, and knowing act accordingly.

"In this way we wish to reinstate the old Democratic party, then such a compromise will be made as will be acceptable to the South, and if possible extend Slavery over all the States, and ultimately form an Empire, which is the best government in the world. Slavery is not congenial to a Republic.

"If we fail in this scheme, France is going to take Mexico, then form an Empire and place Prince Napoleon on the throne, then we will ask to be annexed, of course they will annex us, and when once annexed, the North will have to fight not only the Southern States but France, England and Mexico. You may easy judge what the result would be, with a Divided North as it now appears by the result of the late election, this will all take place in less than a year from this date. For this reason we wish to know our friends, so that we can provide them with fine positions under the new Government.

"Direct any communication you may think proper to make to W. W. White. I cannot stay long in a place, besides it would not do it might lead to detection, what you do, do quickly—after we have the knowledge desired we will organize in every state. Mr. Voorhees of your state assures me that we can get an army of 50,000 men in Indiana—write without fail.

"Yours sincerely,

"H. V. Johnson"

This presentation by a former Governor of Georgia and former member of the United States Senate was shrewdly devised to attract the conservative Democrats of the Ohio Valley, men who were not interested in the tinsel of secret-order ritual, but who were weary of the war. The Confederate agent mentioned Daniel W. Voorhees, who had just been re-elected to the Federal House of Representatives by the voters of his district. He could have mentioned many others in Indiana, Ohio, and Illinois who at the outset had been willing to co-operate to bring about the renewal of "the Union as it was and the Constitution as it is." But many of them, like the "Tall Sachem of the Sycamores," as admiring Hoosiers termed Voorhees then and thereafter, had resented the September preliminary Emancipation Proclamation, and began to work for peace at any price. Their names and positions were well known, and thousands followed the views of such men as Voorhees, Clement L. Vallandigham, Thomas A. Hendricks, George H. Pendleton, James W. Singleton, and others of their type.

About the same time, the rumor became persistent that the Confederates were determined to employ their daring cavalry raider, General John H. Morgan, to raise the flag of revolution in Indiana and Ohio. There were reports of the most careful preparation, that arms and ammunition would be brought in secretly through Kentucky; and also that the persons well affected to the Southern cause could place a star in a window of their homes, and that the gray-clad troopers would refrain from molesting them or burning their dwellings. There is inferential evidence that some such plan actually was proposed and considered, whether the Indiana leaders of the Knights agreed to it or not. The next summer, this note ran through the epilogue to Dr. Bickley's adventurous career as founder of the Knights.

It was June, 1863, when Dr. Bickley entered the picture again, and this time not as the head of the order in its new field of operation, but as a casualty of the general distrust and suspicion which seemed to attach to his personality and conduct.

We have taken note already of his work in Kentucky in the early summer of 1861, together with his dissatisfaction over the way the Confederate authorities treated him, which had resulted in his dropping the organizational work and departing for Virginia. His efforts there to raise troops in the south-western part of the State made no impression upon the authorities. In the early winter of 1863, he resumed his role of physician and became a surgeon in General Braxton Bragg's army. A little later, and for reasons which are not clear, Bickley procured a pass to cross the Union lines, ostensibly that he might proceed to his former home at Cincinnati.

General William S. Rosecrans allowed him to enter his lines, and questioned him at the army's headquarters at Tullahoma, Tennessee. The founder of the order was confronted with the direct charge that he was "the famous General Bickley" but denied it, claiming that he was the founder's nephew—a usual lie with him. At length the Federal General furnished him a pass and parole, and sent him on with definite instructions to report to General Ambrose E. Burnside at Cincinnati for identification. The plausible nature of the man was demonstrated by the way he persuaded officers at headquarters to advance him funds, for Brigadier General R. W. Johnson lent him $50.

Bickley did not obey the instructions. After going down the Cumberland River on a steamboat, he made several stops, and did a little injudicious and seditious solicitation. Rosecrans had suspected this would happen, and had sent a detective along to watch the loquacious Doctor. The latter was arrested at New Albany, Indiana, July 13, and after a short stay at Louisville, was sent to the Ohio State Penitentiary at Columbus for confinement as a dangerous political prisoner.

His baggage had been searched, and revealed ample evidence to sustain the charges. His wife had carried on her person the great seal of the order, which bore the emblem of a Maltese cross surmounted by a star. His trunk contained copies of the *Rules, Regulations and Principles of K.G.C.*, together with a

[85]

copy of Bickley's offer to the Confederate Secretary of War to raise a mounted brigade for its service; also there was a card on which a Confederate flag was engraved with the three letters of the order printed over it, and above and below the words "General George Bickley, Mexico and a United South."

The loyal press of the region exhibited satisfaction at the arrest, and termed Bickley "Morgan's spy." Furthermore, there had been a suspicious correspondence in the timing of his trip and Morgan's spectacular raid. There might have been some ground for the suspicion that he had gone to the Ohio Valley to raise a revolt by the Knights, which General Morgan could then lead.

Nonetheless, to the end of his confinement, first at Columbus, then at Fort Lafayette, and finally at Fort Warren, he protested complete innocence. The letter to Governor Tod, earlier referred to, insisted: "I have never forfeited my citizenship either to Ohio or to the United States. I have never taken up arms against her, and have in no way aided or abetted the rebellion. The K.G.C. organization was purely an American institution, and merited the support of every section of the common country. . . . It had nothing to do with politics, and as to the political organization, so called, in the West, it did not exist when I was here, and I know no more of it than a man in Russia or China."

For all these protestations, he remained in solitary confinement the rest of the war, and was not released until late in 1865. He sought to capitalize his notoriety by a lecture trip to England, but this was a failure. After his return to the United States, he lived in obscurity, and died in Baltimore in August, 1867. This man deserved the title of adventurer about as well as any of the Knights that failed in the Civil War.

Now we must return to the condition confronting Governor Morton and Carrington, who had just been promoted to be brigadier general because of the general satisfaction within the Administration over the effectiveness of his counter-espionage work. All through December the most alarming rumors reached Washington about the rapid development of conspiracies throughout the Ohio Valley, and particularly in Indiana, in which State the Copperhead orders had their greatest growth—and their most effective counterbattery.

In December, 1862, Secretary Stanton telegraphed Carrington for a report of the condition of the "Holy Brotherhood," or Knights of the Golden Circle. The Colonel responded promptly, and listed five purposes K.G.C. sought to achieve: to encourage soldiers to desert, and to bring their arms and animals home with them; to discourage volunteer enlistment; to resist and prevent the draft as a violation of constitutional rights; to stop the war as an "Abolition War"; and then finally, to thwart the Government in every way.

Within the next sixty days, the growing resistance to State drafts frightened the commander of this vital sector of the home front, and he almost fell into a panic. On January 31, 1863, a deserter from the army resisted arrest and troops were sent to seize him. But citizens of the neighborhood armed themselves. They fired on the party of twenty-five cavalrymen, and there was a sharp encounter. Carrington sent the Secretary of War a "confidential and urgent" telegram February 2, describing this disaster, and concluded with this comment: "The condition of things borders upon open resistance to Federal authority."

The *Indiana Sentinel,* charged with being a Copperhead sheet, had endeavored to telegraph what Carrington termed misleading dispatches to other anti-Administration papers in the country. He had stopped the telegraph companies from transmitting the stories. Now he appealed for summary powers to enable him to cope with the extraordinary danger. He closed with this startling statement:

"I express the firm conviction that a bloodless draft, in Indiana, would be, at present, impossible. . . . Volunteering is practically suspended. To convict before a jury is uncertain. . . . Is there no way of punishing these citizens and bringing to a head this plot?"

Two weeks later he wrote Stanton insistently: "Do you realize the extent and character of the secret order opposed to the Government?" He went on to relate an incident of a court trial that day. A member of the K.G.C. had been ordered to testify to the nature of his oath. He had declared in open court that he would "rot in jail before he would violate his oath to the lodge." There had been testimony that the membership in the State was 82,000. Carrington thought this a little exaggerated, but that there were perhaps 70,000, and that they were armed to a considerable extent.

The excitement increased all through the latter half of February and the early part of March, when the rumors that John Morgan was on his way were at their height.

Carrington wrote Stanton on March 19 that thousands believed this, and the photograph of the Confederate General was hung in many homes; "in some counties, his name is daily praised." The information was well authenticated that arms and equipment would be sent from Kentucky to the Indiana military branch of the Knights. He concluded that "the tension cannot last long—reaction or violence is certain."

In one sense, the General was quite right about it. The tension could not last long—and it broke two months later,

almost to the day. But opera bouffe, not tragedy, was the outcome, and the Knights of the Golden Circle were slain by
guffaws and jeers.

Late in April, the heads of Indiana's Democratic State organization called a mass meeting for Indianapolis, on May 20.
They expected such Indiana leaders as Daniel W. Voorhees and
Thomas A. Hendricks to make the welkin ring. In addition,
they invited former Congressman Clement L. Vallandigham of
Ohio and Governor Horatio Seymour of New York to attend,
and announced their expected presence. The purpose was to
stage a great party and public protest against the Lincoln Administration policies, particularly the draft, suspension of
habeas corpus, the indemnity act, and emancipation. Nor
would they spare Governor Morton, whose course they regarded as naked despotism.

The K.G.C. hierarchy determined to make use of the gathering for another purpose. They would assemble their "troops"
from the castles all over the State, stage a military demonstration, and perhaps attack Camp Morton, release the Confederate prisoners, and seize the arsenal. The Grand Commander
sent out orders for men to come armed and prepared for any
eventuality. Many castles responded to these instructions, and
their delegations arrived with arms and ammunition concealed on their persons, or under hay in the wagons that bore
them.

Vallandigham could not attend; as will be seen, he was in
a Federal military prison at Cincinnati, under order of banishment to the Confederate lines. Governor Seymour did not accept the invitation, although he sent a message which reprehended what he termed the unconstitutional conduct of the
Administration. Nevertheless, a crowd which has been esti-

mated as high as 12,000 gathered in the yards of the State capitol. Of these, perhaps a fourth were armed.

General Carrington, the commander of the Military District of Indiana, knew from his spies and informers the plans of the Copperheads. Governor Morton had his own secret-service tips. The two took measures to cope with any outbreaks. The Union troops in the city, together with the paroled Federal soldiers, were organized, and stationed over Indianapolis to guard the arsenal, military prisons, quartermaster depots, and so on. A heavy detachment at the Circle, just two blocks from the capitol, was ready with fixed bayonets, while a field gun was loaded and sighted at the State House.

Voorhees opened the meeting with a tribute to Vallandigham, who "has fallen a little sooner than the rest of us, perhaps, a victim to the base usurpation which has taken the place of public rights and of the Constitution." This gave the keynote for the day. The other speakers rang the changes on the loss of civil liberties, the outrages of the draft, and so forth. But none of them urged or intimated armed resistance to the constituted authorities.

While Hendricks was speaking, Federal troops took station around the capitol. Their orders were to check any "demonstration," but they took these as license to bait the crowd. Soon they began to cry "Copperhead," drew a cordon about the throng, and demanded three cheers for Abraham Lincoln.

About four o'clock, a squad with cocked rifles and fixed bayonets advanced through the crowd to the speaker's stand. No one knew what impended. Hendricks terminated his speech. Voorhees called for the report of the resolutions committee, put it to a vote, and adjourned the meeting.

The thousands of Democrats raged at this insolent troop interference with a public gathering. As they made their way from the scene, they expressed themselves loudly. The over-bearing soldiers seized many as "traitors," and rushed them to the guardhouse.

Visitors from out of town went to the railroad stations. As one train left the Indiana Central station, a shot was fired from a car. This touched off the temper of the troops. The resulting scene has been described by W. D. Foulke, Governor Morton's friend and adulatory biographer, in these words:

"The intention to create an armed disturbance now seemed clear, and the soldiers determined to give the remaining Butternuts a lesson. When the Indiana Central train left the station, a cannon was placed in front of it. The train stopped. A small body of soldiers was collected; and a policeman, accompanied by the soldiers, demanded the surrender of all firearms in possession of the passengers. Nearly two hundred weapons were given up.

"The train to Cincinnati was also stopped, revolvers were taken, and many others were thrown by their owners into Pogue's Run, at the side of the track. Weapons had been given to the women, in the belief that they would not be searched. Seven were found upon one woman. A knife nearly two feet long was discovered in the stove of one of the cars. In all, about five hundred revolvers were taken from those who had attended the meeting."

This humiliating epilogue to the State-wide Democratic protest meeting angered the members of the party, irrespective of whether they sympathized with the Knights' plans or not. The jubilant way the *Journal*, Morton's organ, hailed the incident, led the Democratic *Sentinel* to term Indiana as thoroughly ruled by troops as was France, Austria, or Russia.

Whether cause or mere coincidence, this incident, still known in Indiana folklore as the Battle of Pogue's Run, marked the end of the menace of the Knights of the Golden Circle in that State. The Knights had initiated more members in their Indiana castles than in any other Loyal State. Their lodges had sprung up in practically every county in central and southern Indiana, and especially in those close to the Ohio River. But the organization was loose, unsupervised, and ineffective. It brought odium on its members, and an unjust condemnation of the Democrats as a party of traitors. It had no record of accomplishments to offset these failures.

When John Morgan's men did cross the Ohio in July, as will be seen, they had neither aid nor comfort from the Indiana castles in that State. A few weeks later, the chiefs of the fifth column liquidated the Knights of the Golden Circle, and made a fresh start in the organization of treason.

Chapter 5

THE
STRUGGLE OVER EMANCIPATION

EMANCIPATION was the most conspicuous single issue of the year 1862. Before President Lincoln made up his mind to issue his preliminary proclamation in regard to it, he was harried on every side by friends and foes of the idea. Furthermore, he had considerable inner doubts of the need for it, and of its timeliness. The evidence indicates that at last he moved because of a feeling of war necessity. The preliminary Emancipation Proclamation in September, 1862, actually disclosed no more than that he intended at a future date, under certain conditions, to free the slaves in regions still in rebellion and not subdued and occupied by Federal forces.

The short-run consequences of the action were serious. Some months before its issuance, Chief Justice Samuel E. Perkins, of the Indiana Supreme Court, told Carrington that "if the President proclaimed emancipation, it would end the Government and each State would have the right to decide for itself." The Ohio Valley States felt very much this way about it. Certainly it intensified and quickened the transformation of such secret societies as the Knights of the Golden Circle from social groups entranced by the glamour of schoolboy ritual into active agencies of treason. A great many Union

[*93*]

soldiers, both in McClellan's Army of the Potomac, and in the Western armies under Buell, Rosecrans, Sherman, and Grant, felt let down, almost betrayed, by the new revolutionary purpose for which the war would be waged thereafter.

These conservatives, whether in the army or in the political campaigns at home, felt that the purpose of the war was the restoration of "Union as it was and the Constitution as it is." Such leaders among them as Horatio Seymour, New York Democratic leader who in November was to win the governorship of his State, hinted that if emancipation were the price the President had had to pay for continued support from the Radical Republicans, it had been used to buy men who were no longer loyal at heart to the Union cause. And there seemed some ground for this suspicion. The Abolitionists and the Radicals should have been happy because the Chief Executive had yielded to their pressure, but they rewarded him with the most grudging praise.

The election results were little short of calamitous. The Democrats carried New York, Pennsylvania, Ohio, Indiana—even the President's own State of Illinois. The opposition cut the Administration House majority to a mere 20, an unsafe margin for effective organization for war legislation.

None at the time assumed that these developments startled Lincoln. Many then refused to credit him with the possession of statesmanship, but all knew his wisdom in politics. When the casket that contained his remains was lowered into the grave at Springfield, an intimate friend whispered: "There lies the master politician of the age." The Emancipation consequences could not have been unexpected to a man so gifted with the ability to predict the probable public reactions to a step proposed.

For the first few months after the fall of Sumter, Lincoln

[*94*]

respected the point of view of the Border State conservatives, to a considerable extent agreed with it, and earnestly endeavored to conform, as far as he felt prudent, to the formula "the Union as it was and the Constitution as it is."

This point of view led him to persistent efforts, consuming a great deal of his time, to procure compensated emancipation for slaves in the slave States which did not secede—Delaware, Maryland, Kentucky, and Missouri.

In his report to the Congress in December, 1861, upon the state of the Union, he proposed three tests for such a program. Emancipation should be of the individual State's freewill action, without any duress from the Federal Government or army. In the second place, slaveowners in a State undertaking to free its Negroes should be paid for the slaves they lost. Again, the freedmen in such a State should be colonized.

On March 6 of the following year, Lincoln renewed his plea for legislation to set up a plan for freeing the slaves in the Border States. His message solicited a joint resolution of the Congress which would declare "that the United States ought to co-operate with any State which may adopt gradual abolishment of slavery, giving to such State pecuniary aid," and other help.

Lincoln urged that such a plan would be as economical as it was just. He showed that the war was costing so much money that if the bill for eighty-seven days of combat could be devoted to paying $400 to the owner of each slave manumitted, this would completely wipe out slavery in the loyal Border States, and in Washington as well.

It might have been a good plan for quiet consideration by thoughtful statesmen in a nation at peace. But the situation was emotional, not logical; prejudices and passions affected the participants. After considerable difficulty, the President assembled a group of leaders from the Border States, including local officials, important slaveowners, and members of the House and Senate. The President made practically no headway with them. Not even the proposed gift of government greenbacks to the manumitting slaveholder made any appeal; their fear of threatened social change could not be dispelled. Lincoln presented, on March 10, a modified plan involving not emancipation now, but rather "the decision at once to emancipate gradually." Of the thirty members of Congress who heard him, only a minority was impressed.

This was one of the greatest defeats Lincoln experienced in his effort to cushion the shock of change. He was not surprised at the antagonism of the Radicals, who approved Thad Stevens's description of his proposal as "the most diluted milk and water-gruel proposition ever made to the American nation." But he was sick at heart because the Border State leaders refused to go along.

In all probability this was a determining cause, as well as the occasion, of an important change of policy on the President's part. He began to admit to himself a coming change in the dominant Northern attitude. What had first been, on the part of certain controlling groups in the Loyal States, an unexpressed, and perhaps subconscious, desire was crystallized into the definite determination to conquer the South. This meant the adoption of methods of so drastic a nature that dictatorship in the North would be the inevitable result. If the conservatives of the Border States would not hearken to programs for gradual compensated emancipation, Lincoln would have to consider with real seriousness the alternative of emancipation as an act of war.

Since the beginning of the December term, the congressional Radicals had been setting the stage for this. Their earlier acts had been little more than whittling. The preceding August, a start had been made by the passage of legislation confiscating slaves employed for military ends against the Federal Government. This regularized Ben Butler's famous order defining fugitive slaves as "contraband of war," a flashing phrase which struck the country's sense of humor. This had been followed by the bill of Senator Wilson of Massachusetts for freeing slaves in the District of Columbia. The next step, on March 13, 1862, was the passage of an act to prohibit officers from returning to their masters any fugitive slaves who had come within the army lines, without regard to whether the master of the fugitive was or was not loyal. Three months later another act prohibited involuntary servitude "in the present Territories of the United States and in any that shall hereafter be acquired."

July brought the adoption of a bill sponsored by Senator Lyman Trumbull of Illinois. This ordered that all slaves escaping from disloyal masters and entering the lines of the army, "and all slaves captured from such persons or deserted by them and coming under the control of the Government . . . and all slaves found on or being within any place occupied by rebel forces and afterward occupied by forces of the United States, shall be deemed captives of war, and shall be forever free of their servitude." In addition, it gave the President the legal right "to employ as many persons of African descent as may seem necessary and proper for the suppression of this rebellion"—in other words, to use Negro troops.

In this way, the Congress had taken step after step toward emancipation. During its progress along the path, its power to go this far was subjected to vigorous attack. Conservative lawyers, statesmen, and other leaders pointed out that there was no such power inherent in the Congress, and that certainly none such had been expressly committed to it by the language of the

[*97*]

Constitution. As a matter of fact, Lincoln himself hesitated before signing the Trumbull measure, because of his own doubts upon this point. He knew that many of the things the national legislature had undertaken to do could constitutionally be done only by the President, and that they could be done by him only as an element of the almost unlimited powers conferred upon him as the Commander in Chief of the Army and Navy of the United States when the nation was at war.

Lincoln now realized that if any great step were to be taken toward freeing the slaves, he himself would have to take it, and abide the consequences. He saw with increasing clearness that it could be done only as an act of war, to aid the Government in suppressing the rebellion and bringing the Union together again. Furthermore, for several months his disappointment over the conduct of the war had been increasing; his estimate of the military situation was anything but optimistic, and he was searching desperately for some new weapon, psychological if need be, to strengthen the Federal cause.

From the day of his entry into the White House, Lincoln had sought to restrain the Abolitionist agitation for emancipation as a godlike act. This had taken great patience, for the campaign to force him to this fateful step had been intense—during his entire Presidency, probably no other pressure group beset him as continuously or as disrespectfully as the Abolitionists did. Thad Stevens expressed their viewpoint when he wrote that he wanted to treat the war "as a radical revolution, and remodel our institutions." He knew that this would "involve the desolation of the South as well as emancipation; and a repeopling of half the continent. This ought to be done but it startles most men."

Committees of ministers were frequent visitors to the second floor of the White House, making the most insolently insistent

[*98*]

pleas. Horace Greeley and other Radical editors backed them up with vitriolic objurgations. To one of these, Lincoln made public reply, in what ranks as a great state paper. The editor of the *Tribune* had printed what he called a "Prayer of Twenty Millions" for immediate freedom for the slaves. Lincoln replied to it, in order to disclose his basic policy as President and Commander in Chief.

"My paramount object in this struggle is to save the Union, and is not either to save or to destroy slavery," he wrote. "If I could save the Union without freeing any slave, I would do it; and if I could save it by freeing all the slaves, I would do it; and if I could save it by freeing some and leaving others alone, I would also do that.

"What I do about slavery and the colored race, I do because I believe it helps to save the Union; and what I forbear, I forbear because I do not believe it would help to save the Union. I shall do less whenever I shall believe what I am doing hurts the cause, and I shall do more whenever I shall believe doing more will help the cause. I shall try to correct errors when shown to be errors, and I shall adopt new views so fast as they shall appear to be true views.

"I have here stated my purpose according to my view of official duty; and I intend no modification of my oft-expressed personal wish that all men everywhere could be free."

The excited, often almost hysterical, petitions of the Abolitionists and their allies aroused the apprehensions of the conservatives. So did the tug of war over the command of the Army of the Potomac.

McClellan had organized his forces well, but he had treated the President unceremoniously, had refused to confide in him, and had encouraged a suspicion of his own fixity of purpose. Lincoln feared that the "Napoleon of the West" had developed grandiose political ambitions. Wade, Chandler, and other leaders of the Joint Committee on the Conduct of the War were leaving no stone unturned to harm the General, whose moderate views they feared more than they did the genius of General Joseph E. Johnston.

Conservative leaders like Horatio Seymour and his friend Dean Richmond, who had been the chairman of the Democratic National Committee which supported Douglas in 1860, James Guthrie of Kentucky, Senator Reverdy Johnson of Maryland, and several others wondered if there were not something they could do to uphold McClellan in this contest for the control of the army. By doing so, they believed that they could aid the President in his obvious desire to steer between extremes.

A number of them visited Washington in December, 1861, and again in January, February, and March of the next year. They found Stanton pretending to help the conservative Democratic General and at the same time giving every aid possible to the Radicals. They also found that McClellan himself had by no means as much caution in his conduct in things political as he showed in beginning the Richmond campaign. Lincoln had to force him to move at all, and the shift to the Peninsula did not cure his military "slows." But about that time the General received Fernando Wood, the New York City politician and newspaper proprietor whose loyalty was suspect.

Wood stayed several days at McClellan's headquarters, carried the General to the political mountaintop, and showed him the promised land of an 1864 Democratic presidential nomination. McClellan soon began to express ultraconservative political views, and eventually forced Lincoln to withdraw all confidence in him. This blunder of their key man brought to naught the plans of these particular conservatives.

The course of the war itself filled Lincoln with anguish. Try as he might, success would not attend the Union arms in the East. McClellan's failure to make the direct thrust through Centerville to Richmond was bad enough. The slow motion in the siege of Yorktown, and then the exasperatingly leisurely pursuit after the capture of the field of Williamsburg, made bad matters worse. The failure to develop and exploit the partial victory at Fair Oaks was disappointing. But the culminating blow was the Seven Days' Battle around Richmond, in which, at any one of a number of junctures, the Federal Commander might have defeated Lee—as, indeed, he did at Malvern Hill—only to continue his "change of base" and retreat to Harrison's Landing on the James.

Following this collapse of hopes for the capture of Richmond, Lincoln journeyed to McClellan's headquarters to study the situation on the spot. To his amazement, the General handed him an extraordinary letter concerned with politics.

McClellan did not undertake to disguise the critical situation of his army. Likewise he admitted that his views on public policy did not "strictly come within the scope of my official duties." At the same time the Government must adopt a policy "covering the whole ground of our national trouble"; unless the President did so, the cause was lost.

McClellan's letter stated that the rebellion had become a war, and must be conducted upon the highest principles known to Christian civilization. The Administration must not undertake to subjugate the people of any State; it must avoid confiscation, political execution, "Territorial organization of States, or forcible abolition of slavery." The Government ought to pay the owner of any escaped slave classed as "contraband" and used by the army. All private property and unarmed people ought to be protected, property taken for army use

[*101*]

should be paid for, and the only excuse for military law was to keep order and protect political rights.

Unless Lincoln would announce and the Government follow a "constitutional and conservative" policy of this type, McClellan warned, enlistments for the army would come to an end. Even worse, "a declaration of Radical views, especially upon slavery, will rapidly disintegrate our present armies."

Lincoln read this letter in silence, put it in his pocket, and took it back to Washington with him. His distaste for this ill-timed expression proved an important factor in the decision to which he soon came, to bring the General and his forces back to Washington, and to put his trust in General John Pope.

In the immediate issue, this was unfortunate, for Pope boasted that his headquarters were in the saddle, and General Lee commented, and the campaign proved, that Pope's "headquarters were where his hindquarters ought to be." The disaster of Second Bull Run filled the President's cup of woe to the very brim. He did not hesitate to put McClellan back in command of the Army of the Potomac, to reorganize the troops and force Lee's veterans out of Maryland. Lincoln made up his mind so swiftly on this that General McClellan had the army on the march before either Stanton or Halleck knew anything about it. The Wade-Chandler cabal could only protest after the event.

But at the same time Lincoln's mind had cleared of doubts about emancipation. On the steamer returning from Harrison's Landing, the President had written a first draft of the eventual Emancipation Proclamation. A few days later, he took Seward and Gideon Welles with him on a carriage ride. That evening, "Father Gideon" made careful note in his diary that the President had informed them that he had given earnest consideration to "emancipating the slaves by proclamation in case the Rebels did not cease to persist in their war on the Government and the Union, of which he saw no evidence." Lincoln now thought "that it was a military necessity, absolutely essential for the salvation of the Union, that we must free the slaves or be ourselves subdued. We have about played our last card, and must change our tactics or lose the game."

Seward thought this step a justified one, and perhaps expedient. Welles agreed with this. They heard no more of the matter until July 22, when Lincoln laid the draft of his proclamation before his Cabinet.

When he did so, he informed his constitutional advisers that his mind was already made up that such a step was desirable. But he did want their views on the language of the proclamation and the time that it should be made public. The reactions were unexpected; Chase seemed much disturbed, while Bates, of the Border State of Missouri, approved of the plan. Seward had changed his mind a little. Were such an announcement published after a defeat, it was likely to be regarded as "the last measure of an exhausted Government, a cry for help . . . a shriek on the retreat"; he would bring it out only after a victory. Lincoln thought this shrewd advice, and bided his time. McClellan resumed command of the Army of the Potomac, when Lincoln later revealed, "I made a vow that if McClellan drove Lee back across the Potomac, I would send the proclamation after him."

In the middle of September, the General did make contact with Lee's invading columns, and the Battle of Antietam Creek ensued. The first dispatches from the headquarters of the Army of the Potomac were indefinite, and it was not until September 22 that Lincoln felt himself authorized to issue the proclamation. Perhaps another and different pressure brought his final conclusion. The war governors of the North had called a con-

ference to meet at Altoona, Pennsylvania, September 23. Most
of the governors were Radicals, of the stripe of John A. Andrew
of Massachusetts; Oliver P. Morton of Indiana; Edwin D. Morgan of New York, and Andrew G. Curtin of Pennsylvania, who
had issued the call. They had been acting badly about honoring
Federal requisitions for troops, for they had become disgruntled because they were being deprived of officer patronage
and other elements of war policy control.

In any event, on September 22 the President summoned an
unscheduled session of his Cabinet, told them he had finally
made up his mind—the act and the consequences were his—
because he had vowed what he would do if Lee retreated, and
God had decided the question in favor of the slaves. But he
would like criticism of the language. The comments on this
were minor. But Montgomery Blair expressed fears that the
immediate effect might be to disturb the delicate balance of
political control in the Border States, so that the Copperheads
would sweep them at the next election. Welles commented that
the action on emancipation would be "momentous both in its
immediate and remote results, and an exercise of extraordinary
power which cannot be justified on mere humanitarian principles, and never would have been attempted but to preserve
the national existence."

The proclamation, which was published the next morning,
was preliminary, and essentially little more than a warning. It
declared that on the first day of the next year the President
himself would designate the States, or portions thereof, still in
rebellion against the Union, and that in those States, or portions thereof, in rebellion all slaves held would be free. It recited again the compensation and colonization views of the
President. Its style was clear and direct.

The Struggle over Emancipation

The reaction to this extraordinary employment of the power of the Commander in Chief—the greatest ever used by an American President in time of war—was immediate and profound. Now the worst fears of the conservatives had been realized. The Democrats of New York State, who had met in convention on September 10, must have had more than a premonition of what impended, for Dean Richmond had written resolutions denouncing all proposals for emancipation, and the delegates had unanimously and enthusiastically adopted them.

Two days after Lincoln had acted, the New York Republicans met to name a candidate for the governorship, to oppose Horatio Seymour, the Democratic nominee. The politicians had things arranged for the choice of General John A. Dix, a relatively middle-of-the-road political general. But this did not jibe with the views of Horace Greeley, who wanted the Radical James S. Wadsworth, then a brigadier general with the Army of the Potomac. The proclamation had so stirred the antislavery delegates that Wadsworth was put over on the first ballot. Later it was to be said that "Emancipation nominated Wadsworth—and defeated him."

Many of the old party war horses of Democracy thought that the Republic might as well suspend. Former President Franklin Pierce wanted the fall campaign pitched on the issue of Executive usurpation. He publicly proclaimed that in issuing the proclamation, Lincoln had been the tool of the Abolitionists, "their willing instrument for all the woe. . . . All the degradation, all the atrocity, all the desolation and ruin" of the country.

The voters did not go as far as Pierce had, but they went quite far enough to convince the politicians that politically the proclamation had been a mistake. The election outcome was definitely disastrous. So many States showed their disapproval that some of the President's weak-kneed brethren pleaded to him to withdraw and cancel the preliminary announcement. But Lincoln had learned to take the bitter with the sweet.

The issuance, on New Year's Day, 1863, of the definitive Emancipation Proclamation marked the failure of one of Abraham Lincoln's hopes. One fundamental purpose behind his announcement of intention on September 23 had been to send a combined warning and promise to the people of the seceded States. By inference, that proclamation had told them that if they would end the rebellion and re-enter the Union, their rights to hold slaves would not be interfered with by the Federal Government so long as their own States permitted it. But in the event that they did not cease their war and return to the Union, the North would fight through to victory, and when the South had been subdued, slavery there would be the first casualty of the defeat.

Between September 23, 1862, and January 1, 1863, there was opportunity for a negotiated peace between the Government of the United States and the people of the Confederacy. After that date, no real occasion was to present itself. Lincoln has been charged with having closed and bolted the door to the restoration of the Union as it was under the unamended Constitution. It was not a just charge. The real culprits in the matter were the leaders of the Confederate Government. Perhaps Jefferson Davis must bear chief responsibility for this. Determined resistance to any change of position, whatever might be the alteration of conditions and circumstances, was a habit to which he was peculiarly prone. The occupant of the Confederate White House had cast himself in the role of the George Washington of a Southern revolution for slavery and

States' Rights. From the beginning to the end of the war he would not countenance any suggestion of compromise that involved the surrender of the independence of the Government of the Confederate States of America. Nor did he now give any heed to the warning of the destruction of the South's "peculiar institution" in case the Federal Army won.

But there were many other men in strong positions in the Southern Government. A few gave some thought to the dangers, but in the main they did not believe that the North could defeat them on the battlefield. And there was another factor in which the Southerners had great confidence. They believed that the people of the North would not stand up to the war's continuing drain of men and material. They heard the most encouraging stories of disaffection, desertion, and conspiracies against the war. They placed faith in the fifth column, and began to hope that there would be a new secession—that the States of the Northwest of the 60's would join those of the Cotton South. Then there would be little but Abolition New England and commercial New York and Pennsylvania to sustain the Union cause.

Whatever the explanation, the Confederate Government made no move to explore the conditions for a negotiated peace. In particular, it ignored the favorable appearance of the Northern situation between the November elections and the beginning of the New Year. Davis and his generals let the chance go by. The Emancipation Proclamation came into force, and eventually it set powers to work which brought the rebellion to its end.

For some time after the September announcement, there had been an undercurrent of anxiety among the Abolitionists and the Radicals, who feared the President might change his mind about emancipation. They did not expect any outright cancellation of the preliminary proclamation. But they were suspicious of the attitude taken by Thurlow Weed and his paper, the *Albany Evening Journal,* for the Albany boss himself once said, and with much truth: "Seward is Weed, and Weed is Seward." Seymour had won the New York election on the thesis that there were two great objects to the war: to restore the Union; and to restore it as it was—not as it might be. He had predicted that a Democratic victory in that State would remind the Administration that the Civil War was being fought to crush a revolution, not to change the social system of the States. Weed urged him to stand by these views, "and our Government can be preserved."

This attitude of Seward's alter ego added to the fury with which the Radicals sought to force Seward out of the Cabinet. Lincoln foiled them by proposing to let Chase go at the same time. Radicals in the States commiserated the leaders of the cabal on their failure to force out the "envious, ambitious" Secretary of State, whom they called "the Unseen Hand" who was holding Lincoln back. Did his retention mean that the President would forego the formal issuance of the edict of freedom? Almost as bad, even if it were issued, might not Seward and the conservative generals keep it from being enforced?

Then there was a third fear—that the President's final act would be weak and timid in its expression. Sumner was urged to make sure that the proclamation yielded not only freedom "but all the fruits thereof, in the perfect right to use the Negro in every respect as a man, and consequently as a soldier, sailor, or laborer." Lincoln was heavily beset the last week of December, and the extremists warned that if he failed to issue the document, they would defeat all war appropriations. A Detroit paper quoted him as saying that if he had not issued the final proclamation, a dictator would have replaced him.

The document was issued on the scheduled day, but neither its language nor its immediate practical effect occasioned Abolitionist rejoicing. It proclaimed that all slaves in the rebellious States or parts of States were free, except those in all of Tennessee and certain parts of Louisiana and Virginia, which were held by the Federal forces. The disgusted Radicals complained that the President freed the slaves where his word meant nothing, but in the regions where he could have unlocked their shackles, he took care that they should remain in chains.

In addition, the critics regretted that the proclamation had not preached the Abolition gospel. Lincoln carefully refrained from declaring emancipation as a purpose of the war. He justified it as a military necessity, and in that way alone.

It was not strange, therefore, that many Radical papers attacked the feebleness of form and the exception of areas from the operation of the proclamation. Greeley demanded that the President furnish a further proof of his zeal for freedom. "The Proclamation of the President is not acceptable to the Radicals," the *New York Journal of Commerce* reported. "They argue that it is not universal and is therefore not up to the mark. They think it will not be effectual unless the President places men in the army who are in favor of it."

The conservative Republicans were cold, but for different reasons. Orville H. Browning, a trusted intimate of the President from his own section, recorded a dislike of it. Weed's paper in Albany attacked the proclamation because it had transformed a war for Union into an Abolition crusade, and all because of the Radicals "by whom the Administration is beleaguered, importuned, and persecuted." About the same time

[*109*]

the Weed paper, in comment on Seymour's inauguration as Governor, remarked that although almost half of the voters had cast their ballots against him, every one of them wished him well "in his avowed purpose to stand by the State and Nation in the pending conflict."

The Democrats and other conservatives exhibited various degrees of resentment. They claimed to be jubilant that at last the mask was off, and there was no need to give any further attention to the President's "glib talk" about a Union policy embracing all parties.

Governor Seymour sent his first message to the legislature on January 7. By inference, he challenged the doctrine of the proclamation. "We must accept the condition of affairs as they stand," the message stated. "Our armies in the field must be supported; all Constitutional demands of our General Government must be promptly responded to. But war alone will not save the Union."

Under no circumstances was the Governor willing to concede the division of the Union. He favored every exertion of power, but he called for the use of conciliation too: "We will hold out every inducement to the people of the South, to return to their allegiance, consistent with honor; we will guarantee them every right, every consideration demanded by the Constitution." This was a good statement of the pro-Union, antiemancipation attitude.

The epilogue to the Emancipation Proclamation was the move for a Constitutional Amendment, to universalize the freedom that it had undertaken to give. The Abolitionists were not slow in pointing out that the fundamental national charter must be changed if this new liberty were to endure. James M. Ashley of Ohio introduced a joint resolution proposing such an Amendment, soon after the new Congress met for its

December term in 1863. It was defeated in the House, but a companion measure passed the Senate.

The next year the issue came to life again in both houses, and the President announced on July 8, 1864, that he was strongly in favor of the Amendment then proposed to be submitted to the States for ratification. The following January, both houses having adopted it, the Secretary of State sent it to the State legislatures. Eleven months later the ratification of the Thirteenth Amendment was proclaimed.

But all this was far in the future. From the beginning of 1862 until the death of the Confederacy, emancipation continued to be a focal point for loyal debate, and an excuse for Copperhead conspiracy.

Chapter 6

SEYMOUR: LEADER OF THE
LOYAL OPPOSITION

DISPUTES over the suspension of the writ of habeas corpus, and the resort to the draft, soon widened the zone of controversy. The conflict of forces over these issues continued until the end of the war, with lingering echoes afterward. As the generally accepted leader of the loyal opposition, Horatio Seymour played an increasingly important part. We must take a good, steady look at him.

Today, Seymour is an almost unknown figure in the story of the Civil War—an undeserved semioblivion. In the critical years of the war, he at the same time chastened and sustained the Union cause. His protests subdued somewhat the excesses of the Lincoln Administration. But they enabled him likewise to exercise a moderating and restraining force upon the Copperheads.

In seeking appropriate historical analogy for the part he played, there come to mind those of several British statesmen who in the House of Commons bore the official title of "the Leader of his Majesty's Loyal Opposition."

Born in 1810 at Pompey Hill, Onondaga County (whence his nickname of "Big Pomp"), Seymour came of the patroons of the section. He was a promising cadet at the American

[*112*]

Literary, Scientific & Military Academy in Connecticut, and then read law. Admitted to the bar in 1832, he did not practice, because Governor William L. Marcy chose him as "military secretary." For six years Seymour was at Albany, learning government and politics, in both of which branches Marcy was a master hand.

In the 40's, Seymour's home county sent him three times to the Assembly. In the last of these terms he was chosen Speaker. It was in the legislature that his devotion for local self-government took shape. This theory, he said later, did not rest on any expectation that the people were necessarily virtuous and intelligent, but because "persons most interested in any matter manage it better than even wiser men who are not concerned therein." From this arose the need "to distribute each particular power to those who have the greatest interest in its wise and faithful exercise," whether township, county, State, or nation. He believed that the principle of "local and distributed jurisdiction" made for good government and good manhood.

The modernization of the Erie Canal seemed to Seymour essential to the economic future of the State, particularly in view of the developing productivity of the Middle West and its need for export outlets. For the Empire State to continue a dominating factor in trade with the West, he fought for new locks, connecting canals, wider channels. He was elected Governor of New York in 1852, and forced the program through.

He made a good governor, but the times hurled troubles at his head. The Maine prohibition law was sweeping over the country. The New York Legislature passed such a bill in 1854, but Governor Seymour vetoed it, to the anger of the godly. About the same time he had the hardihood to have Monsignor Bedini, a Papal nuncio, at dinner at his home, to the wrath of the Know-Nothings and other antiforeign groups. He sought

[*113*]

re-election, but the Democratic party split into factions, each with a separate ticket. After a bitter campaign, Seymour lost by some 300 votes out of a total poll of nearly 470,000.

The defeat he took philosophically, for his interests had wide range: politics; Erie Canal; land purchase and development in Wisconsin; dabbling in scientific botany; farming his wife's broad acres; hunting; and driving about in an old-fashioned buggy.

Seymour was tall, lean, alert, with hazel eyes, a wide mouth, a good smile, and a disarming grace of manner. As he grew older, he became stately, almost picturesque. His mobile face shifted expression like an actor's. His eye was clear, but his enemies said that the expression below it was one of indecision and introspection. He was given to soft answers, but these often did not turn wrath away. And he frequently made fun of himself, a very dangerous thing for a man in public life to do. He had a fine library and read voraciously, and in general made an art out of dignified ease, usually in a big desk chair which had come from Daniel Webster's library.

Like Webster, Seymour was never much of a fancier of freaks and fanatics. Bored with feuds, he was contemptuous of faction. He did not flaunt his love for humanity, and found public office such drudgery that it diminished his zeal for power.

In the 50's he was said to have "a golden voice," and took Edmund Burke for his model of speaking style. Even so, he believed short words were best, and that a man should speak and think at the same time. Perhaps he did not always practice what he preached in this, but it was remarked that whenever he made a set speech, he would have his right hand tucked into his tightly buttoned frock coat, and would get his words to his audience both forcefully and gracefully. Indeed, one of his biographers thought that "his grace, wisdom and charm probably caused his worst misfortunes."

This philosophical politician devoted the years between this defeat and the 1860 Democratic debacle chiefly to private business, the Wisconsin speculation, and reflective comfort. He became closely attached to two men who profoundly influenced his future career: Dean Richmond and Samuel J. Tilden.

Richmond, one of "Commodore" Cornelius Vanderbilt's ablest lieutenants, had a large part in putting together the various short railroad lines of western New York to make the New York Central system. This experience led him to apply a similar technique to Democratic politics. Richmond took the lead for Douglas; Seymour followed him, and respected his organizing skill and power drive. To Tilden he turned for the development of ideas and the formation of policies growing out of them.

Seymour was on a trip West when Sumter was fired on, and stopped off at Lansing, Michigan, to speak to the people. A few days later he was invited to address the Wisconsin Legislature. To both, he said that there was "but one course to follow"— unanimous support of the Lincoln Administration. While in Wisconsin he supplied funds for the equipment and expense of a company of volunteers.

That fall, New York had a State campaign for minor offices. Dean Richmond tried to save what he could out of the chaotic situation of the Democratic party. Seymour helped him, and one of his speeches gives a fair picture of his attitude. He reminded the crowd that a majority of the country's voters in 1860 had not preferred Lincoln for President. Still, the latter had been chosen constitutionally, and should have "just and generous support." But there was a limit to this; Lincoln deserved it only while he sustained the Constitution that had given him the office. This national charter was no mere "fair weather thing" but was intended to protect people in their civil and religious rights at the time that they needed protection.

Seymour pointed out that Alexander H. Stephens of Georgia, in 1861 the Confederate Vice-President, had disapproved of secession but nonetheless had followed Georgia out of the Union. Seymour had disapproved of Lincoln's choice, but had stayed in the Union with New York. The two sections hated one another because of bigotry and intrigue, feelings more noticeable at home than at the fighting front. But be all this as it may, the war was a fact, and it would be determined by force. The triumph would come "only by virtue of superior numbers, of greater resources, and a juster cause."

In closing this Utica speech, Seymour indulged in prophecy. "If this contest is to end in a revolution," he warned, "if a more arbitrary government is to grow out of its ruins, I do not believe that even then the wishes of ultra and violent men will be gratified. Let them remember the teachings of history. Despotic governments do not love the agitators that call them into existence. When Cromwell drove out from Parliament the Latter-Day Saints and Higher-Law men of his day, and 'bade them cease their vain babbling'; and when Napoleon scattered at the point of the bayonet the Council of Five Hundred, and crushed revolution beneath his iron heel, they taught a lesson which should be heeded this day by men who are animated by a vindictive piety or a malignant philanthropy."

Seymour's speech reflected the point of view of the loyal opposition. But this was only one of some four major groups which had conflicts of interest to be submitted to the electorate in the fall of 1862, and at many other elections to come. These four main segments of political opinion in the Northern States ranged from extreme right to extreme left, about in this wise:

1. *The disloyal opposition.* Here were the Butternuts and the Copperheads, the Knights of the Golden Circle, the Corps de Belgique, and the many thousands who felt as these did but were not joiners and did not "belong." In attitude, the disloyal opposition ranged from the active conspirators for Southern success, such as Dr. Bowles of French Lick Springs, who wanted a revolution in the Border States, to Clement L. Vallandigham, who believed in the syllabic inspiration of the Constitution, and preferred defeat to victory by ultraconstitutional means. At first this faction followed the letter of Constitutional Unionism, but it was not long until it made up the main troops of the Copperhead fifth column.

2. *The loyal opposition.* The leaders of this group objected to steps Lincoln took to win the war, particularly the suspension of the writ of habeas corpus, and his proclamation of prospective emancipation of slaves. Such men as Horatio Seymour disliked these extreme measures, which they believed breached the constitutional guarantees to the individual citizen. But at the same time they loyally supported the war, and never yielded their desire for the Union to be restored, at whatever cost in blood and taxes.

3. *The men in the middle of the road.* These made up the bulk of Lincoln's dependable support. They were represented in his Cabinet by such figures as Seward, Montgomery Blair, and Gideon Welles; in the party, by men like Thurlow Weed, the chief of the Albany wire-pullers, Henry J. Raymond, proprietor of the *New York Times,* Congressman, and influential in the party, and Judge David Davis, from Lincoln's State; in the army, such soldiers as Sherman, Thomas, Dix, and Banks gave it a fairly effective leadership.

The Republicans of this group were antislavery but not

Abolitionist. Its large number of Old Line Whigs had joined more because of its tariff and other economic policies than because of its social views. This element was led by such Elder Statesmen as Thomas Ewing of Ohio, whose shrewd advice had showed Lincoln how to escape from the dilemma of the seizure of Mason and Slidell. This part of the Northern population sustained the President from the beginning to the end of the war. It went with him when he moved forward. It held back with him when he resisted Radical demands. Probably it was the most important single segment of political opinion and action in the North.

4. *The Radical Republicans.* These were the extreme left of Civil War politics. Club-footed Thad Stevens captained this Jacobin band, the "godlike Sumner" was its high priest, and "Bluff Ben" Wade and Zach Chandler were in the hierarchy of command.

The congressional leaders had many powerful allies outside. Secretary Stanton connived with this crowd that hated Lincoln —and so did Chase, who wanted to use them to help him become President himself. "Beast" Butler had counterparts throughout the army—ambitious men who wanted the war won only by Radical commanders. Over the Loyal States there was a liberal sprinkling of these agitators and revolutionaries, who never hesitated to sacrifice the achievable good in an effort to attain the impossible best.

In the early winter of 1862, Dean Richmond flirted with the idea of strengthening Lincoln's hands in the beginning of the President's fight to retain executive control. Seymour went to Washington a time or two, in an effort to help make McClellan a conservative counterweight. But the General would not be helped. Then New York State politics warmed up in earnest.

It was the year for the choice of a new governor. Edwin D. Morgan, the Republican incumbent, announced that he would not seek re-election. The war had not been going any too well for the Republican cause, and Dean Richmond grew convinced that the Democrats could elect Horatio Seymour. The latter was reluctant—he never was an eager seeker of nominations, although after his party had put him forward, he would fight hard enough for the office. But Richmond set to work to draft him, which he did, with his accustomed skill.

By careful arrangement on Dean Richmond's part a group of Old Line Whigs was brought together at Troy September 9, in what they styled the Constitutional Union Convention. This body then proceeded to nominate Seymour its candidate for the governorship. This made him the choice of the old Fillmore men and other conservative New York Whigs. The Democrats, who held their state convention at Albany the following day, unanimously ratified the choice of the Whigs.

The nominee thus launched in the campaign he had not sought did not grumble, but got ready for "a sharp, bitter fight."

"I do not care about my election," he wrote his family. "That is not probable. But I want the opponents of the bad men who have brought our country into its present deplorable condition to be so much aroused as to make themselves felt and respected. If this is done, we shall have a strong, compact party that can defy violence and keep fanatics in check. We live in a fighting world, and in times like these, they are most safe who take strong grounds and call around them strong friends."

The campaign was waged not only in New York, but in every loyal State—and in some Border States which hardly shared the label. It was the year of the by-election midway in the presidential term. Each of the four contending political forces was

[*119*]

desperate to get as many of its own candidates chosen for the House as it could beg, buy, borrow, steal, or smuggle in.

Two weeks after Seymour's nomination, the President upset most of the earlier calculations of ballot-box probabilities by issuing the preliminary Emancipation Proclamation. We have already discussed the background, and the complex of reasons, for this extraordinary document. Within the same month, Lincoln took another step which added to the uneasiness of the conservatives. He suspended the writ of habeas corpus in the Loyal States, even though these were not the scene of military campaigns, and the civil courts in them were functioning undisturbed.

The conservative reaction against the Proclamation was terrific. This was evidenced both on the hustings and to an alarming degree in the army. Many officers of Indiana, Ohio, and Missouri volunteer regiments resigned their commissions. The instance of Lieutenant Colonel Horace Heffren, of an Indiana infantry regiment, is illustrative. He had been at the front from the beginning, fighting for "the Union as it was and the Constitution as it is." When the preliminary Emancipation Proclamation appeared, Heffren said that he had not joined up to free the slaves. He resigned, went home, joined the Knights of the Golden Circle, and became one of the most dangerous conspirators in Indiana. Thousands of enlisted men deserted, went on furlough and did not return, or malingered in the hospitals. Some regiments had to be disbanded and sent home.

The orders of conspiracy had a veritable field day. Almost at once the number of men anxious to take the K.G.C. vestibule degree doubled. Men on treason's political fringe denounced with new fury these unconstitutional activities of the Administration. The peace party grew apace through the States west of the Alleghenies.

The argument in New York was equally vigorous, equally against the Proclamation and the suspension of the writ, but it was pitched upon a definitely different, thoroughly Union plane. Seymour's opening statement, made to the convention the same day it had nominated him, urged that the country was on the verge of disaster. It was no time for intelligent opposition to be withheld. "Let the two great parties be honest and honorable enough to meet in fair and open discussion with well-defined principles and politics. Then each will serve our country as well out of power as in power. The vigilance kept alive by party contest guards against corruption or oppression."

The candidate insisted that the Democrats did not intend to embarrass the President, and protested against any abuse of him. After eighteen months of war, it had become clear that the country could not be saved by the Republicans, because these were in the grip of men who said the conflict had been "irrepressible." This meant that the Founding Fathers had formed a government which could not stand. This meant that the Republicans did not believe in the Constitution.

Seymour denounced this attitude. "We charge," he proclaimed as spokesman of the Democracy of New York State, "that this rebellion is most wicked because it is against the best government that ever existed. It is the excellence of our Government that makes resistance a crime. Rebellion is not necessarily wrong. It may be an act of the highest virtue—it may be one of the deepest depravity. The rebellion of our fathers is our proudest boast—the rebellion of our brothers is the humiliation of our nation—is our national disgrace. To resist a bad government is patriotism—to resist a good one is the greatest guilt. The first is patriotism, the last is treason."

The trouble with the Administration, he pointed out, was the strange variety of folk who claimed to support the Presi-

dent. Really it would strengthen Lincoln for the Democrats
to win the election. If the Radicals were to succeed in forcing
emancipation, it might bring armed intervention from abroad.
It was not the loyal Democrats who were the menace to victory
in the war—it was the Radical Republicans.

Then he pointed out the exact nature of Democratic policy
and position. "Opposed to the election of Mr. Lincoln," he
stated in careful words, "we have loyally sustained him. Dif-
fering from the Administration as to the course and the conduct of the war, we have cheerfully responded to every demand
made upon us. Today we are putting forth our utmost efforts
to re-enforce our armies in the field. Without conditions or
threats we are exerting our energies to strengthen the hands of
the Government, and to replace it in the commanding position
it held in the eyes of the world before recent disasters."

The Republican nominee, Brigadier General James S.
Wadsworth, was a thorough Radical, in favor of every elision
of constitutional guarantees that the President had made, and
likewise an ardent emancipationist. He remained at the battle
front throughout the campaign, an absence which was somewhat conspicuous. His lieutenants gave Seymour the hardest
blows they could, in which the charge of being a Copperhead
was relatively mild. Horace Greeley charged in the *Tribune*
that Seymour spoke "for the meridian of Japan." But this did
not bother the latter much, and he was able to put another face
upon the issue—the Union must win the war.

The Democratic candidate made a fine statement of this
fundamental. The past must be overlooked, and facts accepted
as they stand. The central point was the deadly conflict between
Union and rebellion. "The sword is now the arbiter. Not only
are the ranks of the armies arrayed in the defense of our flag
filled by our friends and relatives, but we know that upon the

results of battles hang the destinies of our country. Its greatness, its prosperity, its glory, are poised upon the turn of the
conflict."

A Democratic victory in the Empire State of the Union, he
declared, would remind the Administration at Washington
and the people of the country that the war was being waged
to crush a revolution, and not to change the social system. A
Democratic victory would be taken as a popular expression, at
a solemn referendum at the ballot box, that the people desired
the Government "to use all legitimate means to suppress rebellion, restore the Union as it was, and maintain the Constitution as it is."

The election outcome throughout the country confirmed
the worst forebodings of Lincoln and his Cabinet. About the
only place where the Radicals did well was the Border States.
Blair's fears that the Emancipation Proclamation would "disturb the delicate balance" between the parties there proved
unfounded. Or at least there were enough soldiers with bayonets watching the polls to more than offset it. The Republican
ticket won handsomely in both Kentucky and Maryland. In
Missouri, despite a bitter factional fight between two Republican factions, they did manage to elect a Radical legislature.

The September States, all in New England, voted before
Lincoln's proclamation had been made public. Vermont Radicals ran on a platform calling for "the confiscation of the slaves
and property of the rebels." But Republican majorities went
down, and Maine chose one Democratic Congressman.

The October results were much worse, the only solace coming from Minnesota, a featherweight in the scales. Ohio Democrats built their campaign about a platform plank of their
State convention that "we are, as we ever have been, the de-

voted friends of the Constitution and the Union, and we have no sympathy with the enemies of either." They took advantage of a trick of the 1861 Republican legislature. Greedy for a larger share of the congressional delegation, it had redistricted the State in such a way that Republican counties would be added to several congressional districts in order to shift them from a Democratic to a Republican majority. The gerrymander worked, but in reverse. The general swing was such that fourteen of the State's nineteen districts went against the Administration. In one hard-fought contest, Clement L. Vallandigham was defeated, but only because a heavily Republican county had been added to his old district. Each of the other counties gave him an increased majority over that of 1860. The Ohio Democrats determined to run him for the governorship the next fall.

The Pennsylvania result was about as bleak. In 1860 the Republicans had polled some 262,000 votes, against 230,000 for the Democratic State ticket. Two years later the Democrats ran a little ahead. Furthermore, they carried twelve of the twenty-four congressional districts of the Keystone State.

But Illinois hurt the worst. The President's own State elected eleven Democratic Congressmen, to three Republicans. One of the successful Democrats, who ran over the State at large, amassed a vote of over 136,000, which was 16,000 more than that for his opponent. A Democrat replaced a Republican as Mayor of Chicago, the anti-Lincoln party won the lower House of the Illinois Legislature by about two to one, and had a one-man majority in the State Senate. Sangamon County itself, in which Lincoln lived, sent Democrats to the Assembly.

The verdict in November was an even worse repudiation of the extreme war party. In States that went Republican, the 1860 majorities were badly cut.

The Indiana Democrats designed their campaign to show that Governor Morton did not reflect the people's sentiments. Its platform gave lip service to the war purpose, stating that the Constitution must be preserved and the rebellion suppressed. To that it added "that it is the duty of all good citizens to aid the General Government in all measures necessary and proper to that end." It was significantly silent about who should say what were the "necessary and proper" measures. The Democratic candidates for State office won by a good margin; seven Democrats were sent to Congress, to three Republicans; and a heavily Democratic legislature was elected.

New Jersey delivered a stinging rebuke to the secret-service efforts of the Administration. Some of Baker's men arbitrarily arrested James W. Wall, a popular conservative Democratic politician, rushed him out of New Jersey, and threw him into Old Capitol Prison at Washington. The indignant New Jerseyites picked a Democratic governor and chose Democrats for four of its five seats in Congress; both houses of the legislature were heavily Democratic. The legislature showed what they thought about his imprisonment by electing Mr. Wall to the United States Senate early the next year.

Most distressful of all was the result in New York State—at least, from an Administration standpoint. The voters had to choose a full ticket of State officers, most of the legislature, and the congressional delegation. The result was a blow to the Radicals.

Horatio Seymour won the governorship. The vote was close —305,000 to 295,000—but it was decisive. The Democrats split the congressional slate, winning seventeen Representatives to the same number for the Republicans; Roscoe Conkling, the upstate Radical, was one of those defeated. The Administration party kept the State Senate; because of the hold-over system only half were elected each two years. But the Democrats won a slight margin in the Assembly. They controlled the Empire State of the Union.

Even before the balloting, Seymour had suspected that he would be ahead of the Radical General. He realized that this was sure to be misinterpreted outside the State, the Radical Republicans taking it as the election of one little better than a traitor, while the Confederates from Davis down would exult that the North was about ready to give up the war. The Democratic candidate sought to undeceive the secessionists, and right after election addressed a powerful paragraph to Dixie:

"I wish that my voice could be heard throughout every Southern State. I would say, mistake not the conservative triumphs of the North. Listen not to the teachings of those who say we are not true to the Union, true to the Constitution. You know that we are those who battle for the Constitution, including your rights, when they were assailed and denounced. You know that at a time when you were safe within its folds, you deserted your country's flag, and you deserted us, too, who had been true to the principles of your Constitution. Read these triumphs aright, and they will tell you they bring into power men who love the Constitution as a tradition; men who inherit it from their fathers."

Would the South realize the real meaning of the choice of Seymour—that the people were for the Union of the Constitution, and would fight for it until victory had been won? Would Lincoln avail himself of what could become a new source of strength? Only time could give the answers to these questions.

Chapter 7

THE CONSEQUENCES OF THE
DRAFT

IT is believed by at least one half of the people of the Loyal
States"—so Governor Seymour wrote Lincoln, in August,
1863—"that the Conscription Act . . . is in itself a violation
of the supreme Constitutional law." In addition, he deemed it
a "violent, harsh policy," and an unnecessary one.

"The principle of the draft," the President wrote in an
appeal he never issued, "which simply is involuntary or enforced service, is not new. It has been practiced in all ages of
the world." At that juncture of the war effort, he continued,
the safety of the nation demanded it.

This difference of opinion epitomizes the outstanding issue
which beset the Lincoln Administration all through 1863. The
apparent purpose of the draft was the direct summons of the
citizen into the National Army—the title used in 1863 and re-
adopted in 1917. But Seymour thought the plan evasive and
dishonest, because its real purpose was to employ the threat of
conscription in order to revive voluntary enlistment sufficiently
to provide the needed troops. In addition, the plan was not any
too well framed, it was badly received, and much of the contemporary criticism of it would seem justified.

On April 13, 1861, the entire military establishment of the

Federal Union numbered only 17,000 men—and most of these on paper. Through a variety of devices, Abraham Lincoln at length had 1,000,000 soldiers in the field. Note has been taken, in the beginning of this volume, of the antique act to which the harassed Commander in Chief had to resort to raise his first and temporary contingent of 75,000 men. About a fortnight later he asked for 42,000 volunteers to serve a three-year term. The response was electric, and for about a year, the number of volunteers was ample. In the spring of 1862, about 640,000 men were on the rolls, a number considered much more than sufficient to capture Richmond, go down the Mississippi, and also master the Cumberland and the Tennessee.

Because of geography and terrain, aided somewhat by Lee and Jackson, this proved a miscalculation. In July, 1862, and again in August, the President called for 300,000 more. The stream of volunteers thinned out rapidly. The combination of disastrous defeats in the battlefield, Lincoln's own "change of base" in adding emancipation to the objects of the war, and the general sense of discouragement and disillusion threatened disaster to troop replacement and supply.

From the time of Antietam forward, the letter books of the Secretary of War were filled with reports of desertion, malingering, furloughed men who would not come back. At the same time that the mustering officers had trouble, the war governors showed increasing reluctance to raise new regiments, and there were numerous other evidences that the course of improvisation thus far followed would not work much longer.

This led to the most anxious consultation. The draft was an obvious alternative—but it was just the sort of substitute which Abraham Lincoln, essentially a man of the people and a believer in free choice, desired to avoid. Since the outbreak of the War of Independence, the new nation had never resorted to conscription. Indeed, fear and hatred of impressment was part of the American emotional heritage, and the occasion must be grave indeed before Lincoln could even think of employing it.

But the occasion was grave. Away down the Mississippi, Grant vainly fumbled at the gates of Vicksburg, and needed thousands of fresh troops to fill the ranks thinned by casualty and disease. Rosecrans at Nashville refused to move his army against Bragg until it was fully manned and appropriately equipped and supplied. "Fighting Joe" Hooker, who had taken over the battered Army of the Potomac, kept sending word from Falmouth on the Rappahannock that he needed new recruits by the thousands for "the best army on this planet." Such was the general burden of appeal. Lincoln reluctantly concluded that there was no escape from it—the call must be met, even at the price of a conscription bill.

At the request of the War Department, backed by the White House, a measure was introduced in the Senate in February, 1863, looking to the enrollment of soldiers direct into the Federal service. Hitherto the individual State had procured the soldier, and then had put him into company and regiment before it turned him over to the Union Army. Except for the Regular Army, an establishment which dated from President Washington's time, the Federal Government had always dealt with its component States—during major wars to the relish of the governors, who had the chance to pick the higher officers at the same time that the enlisted men elected the subalterns by viva-voce vote. The Regular Army was not expanded, except legislatively and chiefly on paper, until the Civil War was over. The new proposal established a completely new relationship between the Government of the nation and Abner Jones on his Cayuga farm.

This proposal brought instant attack from both Democratic

and conservative leaders, in and out of Congress. William A. Richardson, who had been one of Stephen A. Douglas's closest friends and now sat in his seat in the Senate, assailed the measure, as did the venerable Reverdy Johnson of Maryland and many others. The principal defenders were Henry Wilson, the Massachusetts Radical, and surly old Jacob Collamer of Vermont. Wilson pressed the need of men, Collamer defended its constitutionality, and the Senate passed it.

The House then staged an acrimonious debate. As usual, this went from the particular to the general. The opposition charged that the whole trouble with volunteering was that the people did not like the Lincoln policies, and had withdrawn their consent, not to the war, but to the way it was being conducted. The proponents of the draft made out the best case they could by charging that treasonable conspiracies, fostered by malignantly partisan Democrats, had prevented the people from responding to the call to the colors.

But all this was rhodomontade. All the members knew that these were set speeches for the record—and for the campaigns which would come in several States that fall. The net was a few minor House amendments, then a conference report, and on March 3, 1863, Abraham Lincoln signed the Conscription Act.

The provisions of this measure affected all able-bodied male citizens, and all men of foreign birth who had declared their intention to become citizens, between the ages of twenty and forty-five. These made up the new National Army, which embraced the entire enrollment from which troops could be called. The President was authorized to summon individuals to service through a draft. If it should prove necessary, he could call them all. While the initial call was for only a fifth of the entirety, this was expediency only—all could have been summoned at once. In each district the order of call of the individuals was to be determined by a lottery wheel.

The act directed the President to appoint an officer to be entitled Provost Marshal General and to head a bureau in the War Department. The States were to be divided into districts, with areas identical to that which elected the Representatives of the particular districts. Each Territory and the District of Columbia were constituted districts. For such districts a Provost Marshal was to be named, who would be assisted by a Commissioner and a surgeon, the three to constitute the board of administration and control. The district could be subdivided into as many parts as the area and population made it expedient to do. These districts were to begin immediately an enrollment of the potential soldiers therein.

For Provost Marshal General, Lincoln selected Colonel James B. Fry. This officer came of a Democratic family, had spent his life in the military service, and in 1862 had served as chief of staff for General Don Carlos Buell. It was said of the army career of this imaginative and erratic character, quite conservative in his political views, that his staff work was consistently good but his application of it somewhat inconstant. At any event, when Buell was removed from command of the Army of the Ohio, Fry was transferred to Washington as an Assistant Adjutant General of the Army. His service there was industrious, and later defenders of the operating record of the draft accorded to him traits of extraordinary tact and ability.

The Provost Marshals for the district were supposed to be selected from among those officers of the army who had proved their capacity to handle administrative detail. This was the hope, but all too often not the performance. As in the management of the military prisons and practically all other army-organized services of control and supply away from the fighting fronts, the commanders of the field armies were unwilling to detach, detail, or transfer their ablest subordinates, whether staff or line. But they were more than ready to dispatch the misfits, the maladjusted, and the incompetent. Many of these wound up as Provost Marshals, as did a large number of able officers who had been wounded or invalided home. Additionally, quite a few good administrators were commissioned direct from civil life and assigned to these new tasks.

Late in May, the machinery of the draft began to move. The first task was enrollment. In each district the experience was different, both because of the geographical location of the region and because of the characteristics of the members of the personnel of the district board. In some districts, the number of men affected was small, the enrolling officers were able to canvass the families within a few days or weeks, and there was no undue amount of excitement. But in other cases the experience was unpleasant, and in a few distinctly dangerous.

General Fry in his final report endeavored to put as good a face as he could upon the record. He declared that the opposition "could not be said to be serious; some of the officers were maltreated, and one or two assassinated, but prompt action on the part of the civil authorities, aided when necessary by military patrols, secured the arrest of guilty parties, and checked these outrages." There were conspicuous exceptions to this statement that the opposition was not serious. One was in the Border States, as will be seen in due course. A most disturbing situation developed in the anthracite region of Pennsylvania. The opposition in New York City exploded so violently that tired troops had to be rushed from the bloody field of Gettysburg to make sure that the riots would not be resumed.

As had been expected by the President and the Provost

Marshal General and his staff, the disturbances were vigorously promoted by the Knights of the Golden Circle and the new Order of American Knights, then in the process of replacing K.G.C. as the chief agency for organizing treason. But it was doubtful if this fifth-column activity was responsible for the majority of the resistance to the enrollment and summoning of the recruits. The provisions of the act itself helped shape the public attitude.

President Lincoln, Secretary Stanton, the Provost Marshal General, and his staff feared and at the same time expected that the men within draft ages would resent the new policy being undertaken. Some of them fell into the habit of blaming the secret societies and the antagonistic politicians for most of the trouble. But the fact was that one of the most important of the elements of the resentment was the way the draft was employed as a club to stimulate enlistment through other means.

After the war, Provost Marshal General Fry and his defenders boasted about the fact that "a comparatively small number of men was obtained strictly by the draft." During the four years from the time of the President's first call for troops until April 14, 1865, the aggregate number of men sent to service in the army, the navy, and the marine corps was about 2,690,000. Of these, not more than 170,000 were actually conscripted for the National Army under the terms of the Enrollment Act of March 3, 1863—and nearly 120,000 of these were substitutes. The actual net number drafted was 46,343!

The pressures for other types of enlistment were varied. The foundation for them was the quota system, theoretically a fair plan, but actually one which could be manipulated for purposes of reward or punishment—opponents of the draft, with or without reason, did not hesitate to charge, with intimate particulars, that such had been the case.

The theory of the quota system was that for each separate draft district in the country, a proportionate equality of sacrifice would be established. The formula for this quota involved a series of steps. The over-all number of men between the ages of twenty and forty-five, inclusive, was determined by the nation-wide soldier census. The number of troops that each district would be expected to supply, from the beginning to the end of the war, was determined by comparing the enrollment of that district with the total figure in the Loyal States.

But against this quota were certain offsets. Every man who had been furnished by that district through the State authorities; every man who had volunteered direct; the members of the Regular Army establishment from the particular district —all these were "credited" against the total. The remainder only was expected to be furnished by the district through direct compulsory conscription.

It soon became an important part of the promotion and propaganda of the office of the Provost Marshal General to stimulate the States to provide bounties, in cash or other tangible form, in order to lessen the odium of any actual draft there. States were expected to vie with one another in offering these additional compensations to volunteers. Cities, counties, and private organizations were similarly stimulated to offer bonuses. There seemed no bar to putting a cash price on patriotism.

Then there was an even more borderline device by which a drafted man could purchase his "commutation." The price was $300, an amount well beyond the pocketbook of the lowly and the humble, but meaning little to the well-to-do. Farmers, laborers, mechanics, and artisans felt, and with reason, that this helped make it the rich man's war but the poor man's fight. Cash instead of courage; the private circumstance of the citizen, together with his whim or mood or will—these determined whether or not he would offer the personal sacrifice for the cause of his nation. There was some criticism of the low ethics of this arrangement. And ever since there has been a growing wonder at this strange blind spot in a war which in part at least was fought to further high moral ideals.

Nor was this the worst of it. A citizen called to the colors was afforded still another path by which he could salve his conscience with a mask of patriotism at the same time that he stayed out of the army. For the law made it completely legal for a man called for active service to procure a substitute. The latter must be physically sound, of course, and within the required age limits. Whatever might be the reason for his willingness to take the place of the individual who had been drafted—whether it was family connection, personal friendship, sense of obligation, or straight-out employment—the Government accepted him in lieu of the one legally called. This led to many minor uncertainties and to ensuing controversies. Suppose the substitute became a deserter, would the liability to serve then revert to the original draftee? This was a practical question, for so many of these substitutes found it profitable to take the cash and let the credit go that they would desert continuously, hire themselves out over and over, under different names, much to the distress of the authorities. The "bounty jumper" was a well-known category in the North.

Another major objection was that the Administration consciously used the quota basis to harm anti-Administration governors and Congressmen. Seymour was deeply persuaded that this was the case, and all the expostulations of Fry, Stanton, and the President himself did not change the view of the

Democratic Governor of New York. His contention was that the 1860 census population basis was violated by the actual quota allocation to the districts. The Fry answer that the divisor was man power and not population was deemed a cover-up. Seymour and his lieutenants could not understand why the quotas for districts in New York City were so high while those for Republican areas in upstate New York were so much lower. Later apologists for the draft made elaborate calculations in the effort to prove that these discrepancies had resulted from the greater proportionate volunteering in rural New York, which was loyal, than in the city, where treason had many haunts.

There is little question that the President himself did not countenance discrimination of this sort; but the scrupulous sense of justice of the Stanton establishment was a little bit less certain. At any event, there was doubt of the good faith of the yardstick for the draft, along with irritation over the mode of its employment.

One of the chief purposes of the Copperhead fifth column, from its organization in the summer of 1861 until the final crash of the conspiracies in November, 1864, was to induce desertions from the Union soldiery. Every one of the chief secret societies—Knights of the Golden Circle; Corps de Belgique; Mutual Protection Association; Order of American Knights; Order of Sons of Liberty—made this a main effort.

Under the K.G.C. regime, as might have been expected from the incompetent leadership and co-ordination of that body, the results were disappointing to the Confederates. But Lincoln's preliminary proclamation of emancipation in September, 1862, stimulated desertion markedly, especially in the Ohio

Valley States. The Copperheads put particular emphasis on the soldier's bringing sidearms, equipment, and mount with him, and in some places paid a secret bounty to the deserter arriving home thus accoutered.

Great as had been the flow of deserters before the establishment of the Federal draft structure under the act of March 3, 1863, it was doubled thereafter. During the first two years of the conflict, whatever force used was that of the individual State, on the male citizens as members of the unorganized militia. Thenceforward it was the Government at Washington which, objectors claimed, invaded the domain of the State and interfered with the liberties of the individual citizen.

The over-all statistics on desertion reveal the virulence of the evil. In his carefully detailed work, *The Organization and Administration of the Union Army, 1861-65*, Fred A. Shannon concludes that throughout the Loyal States "the degree of reluctance to perform military service was indicated by the number of persons furnishing substitutes or commutation; and also by desertion."

Both exemption by the drafted man's "commutation"—paying $300 cash—and that through furnishing a substitute were sanctioned by an act of the Congress, and thus were covered with the cloak of virtue by the authorities. President Lincoln made a merit of necessity, and claimed pride in the fact that the money revenues of the Provost Marshal General's office, through the $300 fees, were so great that the administrative expenses of enrollment and draft required no appropriation by the Congress.

Horace Greeley indulged in an even more ambiguous type of justification. The *Tribune* of August 8, 1863, less than a month after the New York draft riots, made this appeal:

"If you are drafted, and can possibly leave your business,

Go. If you cannot, send your substitute—the best man whom money will obtain. If you cannot possibly get one, pay the commutation. But pay $500 for a substitute rather than $300 as commutation—if for no other reason than that, if you send a substitute, you cannot be drafted again while he continues to serve in your stead: Whereas, if you commute, that suffices only for this draft, and leaves you clearly liable to the next, if a next there shall be."

There were 86,724 men called in the draft who purchased exemption by commutation. The number of substitutes furnished, according to the *Official Records of the Union and Confederate Armies,* was 118,010, the two together making 204,736. This number of men used their purses to escape personal military service under the cloak of the absolution, perhaps tacit approval, of the law. The number was large enough, one authority says, "to include all men of wealth and their sons who were drafted, and most of the moderately well-to-do tradesmen and farmers as well. Since the method was so respectable, practically all who were able to do so availed themselves of it." This reference was to men of means who were drafted, not to the well-to-do in general. The Union forces had tens of thousands of such men and boys who had rushed to enlist, and fought splendidly through the war.

It is fitting to point out that procuring exemption from the draft became an organized business. On September 1, 1863, Thompkins and Co. No. 645 Broadway, New York City, advertised in the papers that "the New York Draft Assurance Association will this week, for $10, guarantee any undrafted party exemption from the draft. For $25 we will furnish any drafted party with an acceptable substitute. At these rates, we simply take the risks of an ordinary life insurance company." These schemes sound strange today, yet late in 1864 the War

[*138*]

Department officially validated and gave its approval to the insurance plan.

There were other devices which never received the official nod. A new class of grafters, tricksters, and dealers in sharp practice sprang up, called "exemption agents." These had runners to bring patrons to their offices, while scores set up shop in the lobbies of the New York City Hall, and offered affidavits at 50 cents apiece. Physical disabilities were at a premium; young men who were prematurely gray claimed to be over the age limit. Many eligibles made their ways to Memphis, New Orleans, and other places under the control of occupying troops, but beyond the zone of operation of the enforcement machinery of the Enrollment Act.

The number of deserters cannot be ascertained with precision, but it has been carefully estimated by army authorities. The figure, checked against the *Official Records,* comes to 421,625. This number is more than double the total of those who purchased commutation or furnished substitutes. It represents men who had no legal bar to punishment, but were called criminals for the action they took to evade military service.

The figures of desertion are divided between the men who had been enlisted and had done some troop service, put at 260,399, and the draftees who failed to report, numbering 161,-286. Provost Marshal General Fry estimated that about a quarter of the listed army desertions were "unintentional"; and that perhaps 30 per cent of failures of drafted men to report were similarly not culpable, or were repaired by their reporting later. Applying these corrections, the figures would be 195,255 deserters from the army, and 112,901 drafted men who did not report, or a total for the two categories of 308,156 actual deserters.

This is a formidable figure. It affords statistical proof of the general dislike of the draft. The Copperhead fifth column aided and abetted but it did not cause the "long, persistent, sullen, often virulent and sometimes violent resistance"—to quote Shannon—"which was encountered in practically every State of the Union whenever any draft was made at any period of the war."

Of the actual deserters, during 1863 and 1864 arrests were made of 76,526, or about a fourth of the entire number. It was not a task without hazard. Ninety-eight of the officers of the Bureau of the Provost Marshal General were killed or wounded by deserters resisting arrest, or by their friends. The number of soldiers or civilian peace officers killed or wounded while engaged in aiding the Provost Marshals is not separately reported, but is estimated at several times that figure. Casualties suffered by troops suppressing the riots in the Pennsylvania hard-coal region, and at New York, Troy, Boston, and elsewhere, further swell the figure.

In his last report, General Fry declared that, in seeking to arrest deserters or enforce enrollment, his men encountered physical opposition "in almost every house" they entered.

Resistance began so quickly that the War Department rushed out new General Orders providing for the punishment of any person who sought to obstruct the operations of district boards or their enrollment officers. These were soon supplemented by definitions of what constituted an impediment to the draft. Of course, anyone who attacked or obstructed the officers of registration and selection should at once be put under military arrest. But in addition it was made a crime for a citizen to stand silent when he was questioned as to the whereabouts of a man wanted by the draft authorities.

Doubtless the necessities of the situation demanded such interference with the accustomed habits of the people. But quite occasionally, however, these new powers were misused by the military bureaucrats of Stanton's office. They illustrated what Lord Acton, the eminent English historian, was later to say, in another but not dissimilar connection: "All power corrupts, and absolute power corrupts absolutely."

Furthermore, absolute power is always resisted, and sometimes with a ferocity and an evil passion even more terrible than the uncontrolled power which is its inciting cause. In three major instances, the opposition was heinous and despicable.

Probably the most extraordinary situation with which the enrolling officers had to contend was that in the hard-coal region of Pennsylvania. From the fall of 1861, there had been persistent reports of subversive organization in the Keystone State, and one of Lafayette C. Baker's first arrests had been that of an organizer of the Knights of the Golden Square, the ritual and printed purpose of which were almost word for word those of the order of General Bickley. A little later, word came that castles of the Knights of the Golden Circle itself were being organized in the neighborhood of Reading.

The passage of the Conscription Act by Congress transformed the incipient disaffection into flaming rebellion. By the summer of 1863, large organized bands numbering several thousands had established so complete a control of the anthracite region that the Union authorities, both State and Federal, were appalled. For almost a year thereafter, their efforts to cope with these bands continued ineffective. The Secretary of War, nervously excited as usual, tried to get at the bottom of the trouble. In the official correspondence that ensued was contained what today might be termed a first-class sociological report.

On January 29, 1864, Major General Darius N. Couch, commanding the Department of the Susquehanna, wrote from Chambersburg to Stanton that "you are aware, Mr. Secretary, that civil law is wholly inoperative in a large portion of the anthracite district unless backed by United States soldiers. The people there do not look to the State authorities for protection. I have been urged by the most prominent citizens to declare martial law." With this letter he enclosed the reports of the subordinate commanders on the spot.

Captain H. L. Johnson, Deputy Provost Marshal for the Eleventh District of Pennsylvania, had reported from Mauch Chunk to General Franz Sigel, a district commander subordinate to General Couch. The Captain thought it would help to give "a brief statement as to the state of the society in Banks Township, Carbon County, and in the adjoining districts during the last eight or ten months." He continued:

"Under the influence of bad political leaders, who counseled opposition to the draft, and to all other efforts to sustain the Government, frequent meetings were held in said coal region, and combinations formed to oppose the draft. The men so organized were mostly Irish of the Donegal Clan. By degrees they became more and more insolent and defiant. The lives of our best citizens were threatened, and Welshmen, Germans, English, and Americans were notified to leave or suffer death.

"A number of well-disposed workmen were driven away, some mysteriously disappeared and others were murdered. Proprietors of mines were notified by 'committees' that the draft must be suspended, the war stopped, or the production of coal should cease, and thus the United States Navy should be deprived of this indispensable article. The local authorities were unable to collect the taxes, all law was suspended except only the law of the Irishmen."

Parenthetically, it should be said that the Provost Marshal's blanket indictment of the Irish was not well advised, in view of the fine battle service for the Union of New York's famous "Fighting Sixty-ninth," and other stalwart Irish regiments. The employer-labor relation had been bad, the Donegal immigrants resented it. Also they were almost exclusively Democrats—a fact which made Radical officers attack them on slight provocation.

One incident Captain Johnson described was that of the jail delivery of a conspirator who had assaulted a judge. "Our District Attorney" (who was a Democrat), continued the recital, "refused to take any steps to arrest anyone." Nor could the State authorities of the region, Democratic in affiliation, be energized into any effective co-operation.

It developed that the War Department had sent to the military district in question only an indifferent type of troops, chiefly companies of "invalids"—men recovering from wounds or illness. When these sought to open the agencies for registration and enrollment, they were quickly brushed aside and run out of the mining towns. After a particularly outrageous murder, in which a mob of the insurgent coal-miners broke into the home of an operator who was working with the Federal officers and killed him in the presence of his wife and children, the Tenth New Jersey Infantry was rushed in to take control.

This precipitated house-burnings galore, further riots, and murders, until soldiers did not dare go through the country in less strength than at least a platoon. The Department Commander began to make arrests right and left. Immediately the political allies of the Clan of Donegal applied for writs of habeas corpus, and began to flood Washington with protests against the illegality and unconstitutionality of the repressive acts, and against the scandalous conduct of the New Jersey infantry. Some of the Democratic Congressmen of eastern Pennsylvania, actively anti-Administration and somewhat tarred with the brush of the Copperheads, laid siege to Stanton. But General Sigel stood by his men: "I do not know whether the remedy applied by the coal operators and Captain Rauch will have a permanent good effect and whether or not other more salutary measures will be necessary to prevent the congregation of a low and degraded people at certain places in the coal region.

"There seems no doubt but that the Provost Marshal has acted under the advice and pressure of the loyal class of the people, and the coal operators, who saw in the congregation of many families of a low character, united and assisted by outlaws and rioters . . . a danger for the rest of the community." Therefore there had been many arrests of these Mauch Chunk rioters. Sigel had "no doubt of their guilt," and was determined that they be kept in custody, and the only problem that remained was to prove the charges "in some form" before the Military Commission.

In the sequel, a little better surface was put on the registration in this region, but enlistment there was practically nil until the end of the war. This was the very same region in which, a few years later, the "Molly Maguires" took command and established a reputation as desperadoes which lingers to this day. These highhanded bands made mass murder a fine art, and counted the day a sorry one when at least one detective of the Reading Railroad was not "removed."

The machinery for the draft had been particularly tardy in the City of New York. The boards there, like those for the other districts over the Loyal States, had finished their enrollment, the quota had been assigned to each district, and the stage was set for this great "lottery of life." Right at this juncture, Lee marched down the Gunbarrel Road into Pennsylvania, there was the most urgent call for able-bodied soldiers, and New York City was denuded of all but a handful of Federal troops. During this pre-Gettysburg climax, Governor Seymour extended himself to the limit to co-operate with Stanton at Washington.

At the same time that he had hastened the dispatch of the troops to the dangerously close theater of war, the Governor had asked Washington to postpone drawing the names of draftees in the lottery until fresh troops could be got back to Manhattan, and also until certain complaints that had been made against district quotas had been determined, either administratively or by adjudication before the courts. He seems to have been wise in these expostulations, for surely this was a most injudicious moment at which to publish the names of the drafted men. But Provost Marshal General Fry declined to interfere with the schedule which the district boards had announced. The order for drafting in New York was issued July 1. Under the administrative setup, each district had the right to fix its own time for its own lottery. Several of those in New York City were late. Furthermore, the *New York Daily News* had seized the occasion of the city draft to attack the whole procedure as "an outrage on all decency and fairness," the object of which was to "kill off Democrats and stuff the ballot boxes with bogus soldier votes." This incendiary organ, which had the largest mass circulation in New York City, made use of a Seymour statement in his draft correspondence with Washington to sustain its propaganda. From some quarter, printed bulletins and handbills were passed around the labor section in the northern part of the city.

The draft began on July 11, at the corner of Forty-third

Street and Third Avenue. It passed without any especial disturbance. But on Sunday, excited meetings began to be held. Monday morning, trouble was at hand.

No sooner had the Commissioner for the Ninth District begun to turn the lottery wheel than the excited crowd in front of the office of the board took action. A huge block of Belgian marble came hurtling through the window, knocking over some spectators, and was followed by a volley of stones. With this, the crowd became a mob, burst through, smashed the office, and fired it. When the fire companies arrived, rioters prevented their using the fire hydrants, and the office could not be saved.

The mind of the mob followed the usual course; from burning the enrolling office of the Ninth District, they attacked those for the Eighth. Adjoining stores were looted, and the mob rushed from place to place in the city with arson and murder in its heart.

Late that afternoon they attacked the Colored Orphan Asylum at the corner of Fifth Avenue and Forty-fourth Street. Several hundred Negro children were inmates, and the mob desired to take revenge on them for the role the slaves had played in occasioning the war. A handful of police held the crowd back long enough for the orphans to escape, but then the rioters broke in and looted and fired the orphanage.

For three days the riots continued unabated. At no time were they city-wide. The members of the mob would go from place to place, as the whim happened to seize them. The mind of the mob fell, as almost always has been the case, to the level of the lowest member of it. Arson, looting, murder, even a case or two of rape, were included in the catalogue of its sins. Sometimes it would gather outside the City Hall, then would turn to an attack upon the office of Greeley's *Tribune*, which last was saved from destruction only by the chance arrival of a troop of police.

Governor Seymour, who was at Long Branch in New Jersey, heard of the trouble late Monday evening. He left immediately for New York City, but did not reach there until Tuesday morning. Then he went immediately to the City Hall, to counsel Mayor George Opdyke and help end the disturbance. A reasonably orderly crowd gathered in front of the City Hall, there were calls for the Governor, and about noon on July 14 he addressed the gathering. His exact words were not recorded. The *New York Times* of the next morning described another speech, made in Wall Street, which it said was the same in substance as that delivered from the City Hall steps. Its account recited: "He said he had sent to Washington to ask that the draft in this State might be suspended until the Courts could decide upon its legality. To the decision, when it came, all owed obedience. If they decided it would be legal, he would use every exertion to make it as equal as possible upon all citizens. The Governor's remarks were well received."

The mob did not hear the Governor, for it was rioting several miles uptown. But Greeley's *Tribune* seized a favorite salutatory phrase of the Governor—"My Friends"—and proclaimed that the State's chief executive "called these savage rioters his 'friends'—as indeed they are." Greeley inferred that the Governor was part of a Copperhead fifth-column conspiracy, and that the Federal Government must declare the city "in a state of revolution."

Actually, apart from his mistimed phrase, Seymour had been temperate, as usual, and had urged his hearers "to take good care of all property as good citizens, and see that every person is safe. The safekeeping of property and persons rests with you and I charge you to disturb neither. It is your duty to maintain the good order of the city, and I know you will do it. I wish you now to separate as good citizens, and you can assemble again whenever you wish to do so."

Bystanders on the spot at the time thought this a speech counseling law and order. Had the rioters been present, it is doubtful if these temperate words would have exercised any effect upon them. The active Radical press began to belabor the Governor, and to try to make him a victim, if not the culprit, of the whole outrageous affair. That night and the next day, high tension reigned throughout the city.

Except for the *Daily News* and the *World,* the press of the city bitterly reprehended the outrages. None more so than Horace Greeley, whose pen was doubly dipped in acid after the attempt to break into his office. Henry J. Raymond's *Times,* the stoutest straight Administration organ in the city, took strong lines against the rioters. "The mob is not our master," thundered an editorial the day after Seymour's speaking. "It is not to be compounded by paying blackmail. It is not to be supplicated and sued to stay its hand. It is to be defied, confronted, grappled ,with, prostrated, crushed."

Much of this heavy rhetoric was directed at rioters whose favorite paper was the *Daily News,* owned and directed by Fernando Wood, the former mayor and present Congressman who advocated peace at any price. They did not even know of the polemics of the *Times.* But it was also a blast against the Governor.

The management of the *Times* feared, however, that the mob would turn on them just as it had sought to invade Greeley's *Tribune* the preceding day. Therefore Raymond's paper made hasty preparations to defend its quarters. In some way, three Gatling guns were procured from the authorities at Washington—the tradition of the paper has it to this day that Raymond's friendship with the President led the latter to have them sent.

These Gatling guns had been invented in 1862 by a genius in Indianapolis, Dr. Richard J. Gatling, who offered them to the War Department, with indifferent results. The weapon itself was the father of the machine gun of the First World War, and even at the time was an effective instrument for massing fire power. But the Ordnance Department of the army turned a cold shoulder upon this brilliant new weapon, the tactical need for which had already been discerned by many field commanders out of grim experience of the lack thereof. On July 13, 1864, almost a year to a day after the riots just described, Colonel James A. Hardie, an Inspector General in Secretary Stanton's office, answered an inquiry from General Carrington, at Indianapolis, concerning the gun in these words: "I am directed to inform you that the Ordnance Department have never purchased any of the 'Gatling guns' and that only very few are in use in our Navy. The gun does not enjoy a high reputation." Carrington's inquiry, incidentally, arose from the fact that by 1864 Dr. Gatling had become a first-rate fifth-columnist, and was negotiating with the Confederate Army for the employment of his epoch-making new tool of war.

In any event, it was said the President managed to smuggle three of these army rejects to the *New York Times*. One of them was mounted on the roof, so that its field of fire could sweep the street in either direction. The others were set up just inside the business office. The entire staff was armed with rifles. Any rioters seeking to break into the plant would have had a hot reception.

By July 15, the mob fires were dying down. On that same day, Secretary Stanton reluctantly ordered a temporary suspension of the draft lottery, and the publication of the names

[*149*]

of men drafted, in New York and Brooklyn. About that time, State troops which had been sent to Gettysburg were released by Meade and came back to Manhattan. They were accompanied by some regiments of Federal soldiers. Thenceforward, troops were on hand to control any new outbreaks, and the danger was at an end.

The New York Municipal Legislature promptly passed an ordinance, in the hope that it would remove some of the resentments which might have caused, or occasioned, the troubles. The measure instructed the City Treasurer to pay the $300 required for the exemption of any drafted man "who shall be found unable to pay" it. If he were willing to volunteer, the same sum would be given him. Mayor Opdyke vetoed the bill because he felt it to be both unwise and unnecessary. In this, the Mayor's judgment proved correct. After this, the Manhattan hoodlums did not riot any more against the Enrollment Act and its lottery.

The New York riots completely overshadowed two other disturbances in the region at the same time, one at Troy, almost across the river from Albany; and the second at Boston. On July 14, a mob in Troy attacked and destroyed the printing plant of the *Troy Times,* then demolished a Negro church, and opened the jail. The authorities at Albany were slow in suppressing the outrages. The next day, however, militia from Albany crossed the river, dominated the town, and the mob dissolved.

The Boston trouble, which came to a head on July 15, was occasioned by the rage of bystanders when an officer slapped a woman. Her friends attacked the assailant and the police quelled the disturbance. The city authorities promptly prepared to cope with further trouble, they had militia on hand, and posted squads of police and militia all over the city. A

[*150*]

little after eight that evening, a mob of from 500 to 1,000 men, women and boys gathered in front of the Cooper Street Armory and undertook to batter down the locked doors.

At length they broke into the enclosure, where soldiers were under arms to protect it. The mob attacked, the soldiers fired on them, and made a bayonet charge which put the rioters to flight. Six or eight people were killed, including one woman. At the same time another mob tried to loot a gun store, but was checked. The police and soldiers kept matters from getting out of hand, and by midnight, Boston was quiet again.

The reader will wish to know the losses due to the New York riots. Unfortunately, the actual damage to persons and property during the three days was not accurately determined at the time, and to this day has remained a controversial matter.

Greeley's *Tribune* reflected the point of view of those who hoped President Lincoln would become sufficiently alarmed to order martial law for the city. On July 20, that paper printed a "list of persons killed in the late riots, for whom burial certificates have been obtained." This gave 74 names, of which nine were those of children between two and sixteen. The article alleged that many corpses remained concealed in boxes in cellars uptown, "awaiting removal." Four days later, the *Tribune* estimated the death list at between 300 and 500. Later, Greeley doubled the figures, and charged that hundreds of bodies had been buried in back yards, or "smuggled across the ferries." The New York Metropolitan Police put the figure at "about a thousand." In 1891, in a book about New York, Theodore Roosevelt swelled the total to 1,200.

Recent investigators of the subject have studied the death records of New York City from 1853 to 1867, and declare there is no basis for these large figures. "If anything like a thousand people died in New York during the week of July 13 to 20, 1863," says Stewart Mitchell, a painstaking historian of the period, "their corpses must have disappeared in some miraculous manner. . . . There is no evidence that any more than seventy-five possible victims of the violence of three days died anywhere but in the columns of partisan newspapers." *Valentine's Manual of New York* gives New York City deaths for all July, 1863, as 2,683; the 1864 figure was 2,552; that for the next year, 2,624; and in 1866 the total mounted to 3,903. The statistical evidence does not sustain the large figures of deaths in the riots.

Claims for property damage flooded the local authorities as soon as the fact became known that New York County must pay the damages. The *Times* on August 4, 1863, estimated the expected money cost of the riots at $1,100,000. The County Supervisors established a special committee to examine the requests for riot dividends. Through the rest of that year and during 1864, New York County paid out $1,356,669.61 for riot expenses. Belated claims paid in 1865 brought the total to $1,516,423.99. These warrants were met out of the sale of Riot Indemnity Bonds of the County of New York. There was an offset, a credit entry on the books for $457.52, which sum had been realized through the sale of "property taken from rioters."

But payment for property damage did not make up all the million and a half last mentioned. In addition to the $1,216,-209.55 paid these claimants, the county met a variety of other riot expenses. The "State Militia on duty" had cost $261,-757.50; the salaries of clerks and examiners of the claims amounted to $13,729; meals and supplies called for $10,006.18. Furniture for the "Riot Committee" was listed at a picayunish $86.73.

Nor is the effort to allocate responsibility for the uprising especially fruitful in other than subjective inferences. At the time, Confederate agents were charged with the chief responsibility. Governor Seymour and Fernando Wood were the targets of broad hints of complicity with the intrigues of secret agents of the Richmond authorities. Little evidence is accessible to sustain any of these inferences.

The Confederates made what capital they could of the riots; they needed some salve, however pitiful, for their wounds of Gettysburg and Vicksburg. But at that juncture their staff of secret agents in Canada was as incompetent as it was loquacious. George N. Sanders, then the leader of the group, could neither see nor seize hidden opportunities. Jefferson Davis had so little confidence in the eccentric Kentucky marplot that he made slight use of him in matters of importance to be undertaken on and from Canadian soil.

At the moment, the Richmond hopes were set on releasing Confederate prisoners from Johnson's Island, Camp Douglas, and other Union military prisons in the West. The secession President had sent picked groups of officers to Canada to undertake these tasks. They concentrated on the specific assignment and, as will be seen a little later, returned to the Confederacy when their efforts failed. The available evidence indicates in no way that they had any hand in the New York draft riots.

We have already seen the part that Governor Seymour played. His faults were serious—an obstinate attachment to verbal forms which did not fit realities; a reluctance to take drastic action; overconfidence in the trustworthiness of political associates. Yet the truth of his loyalty to the Union cannot be gainsaid. Before Gettysburg, Seymour had displayed extraordinary energy in meeting frantic appeals from Washington for every possible battalion of State Militia to help Meade check the invasion. After the riots, Secretary Stanton wrote the Governor in terms of the highest appreciation of the great services he had rendered during the Gettysburg invasion emergency.

Fernando Wood's status was somewhat different. The career of this extraordinary character is described in detail later in this volume. Suffice it to say now that he had been Mayor of New York in 1860, at which time his secession sympathy was frequently expressed, both in official acts and in the columns of the *New York Daily News,* which he and his brother Benjamin controlled. In the fall of 1862, Fernando had been elected to Congress from a district that he dominated.

At the time of the riots, however, the Congress was not in session and Wood was in New York City. The Congressman had already made himself an advocate of peace at any price, looked with favor on the Knights of the Golden Circle and similar anti-Union secret societies, and had denounced Lincoln's conduct in the Vallandigham case in the severest terms. But any direct connection of this New York Copperhead Congressman with the start of the riots is not revealed by the available material. He was a master of secret politics, and had he been at the focus of such a conspiracy, his agency in it would have been verbal only—no scrap of paper would have remained to damn him. The evidence of attitude, supplied by the columns of the *Daily News,* was not so much of incitation to riot as it was of extenuation of the misdeeds of the rioters after they had begun.

The likelihood is that this scandalous disturbance was symptom, not conspiracy. The labor sections, where it first broke out, were feeling the pinch of a cost of living that increased far more rapidly than did the workers' wages. This was

[*154*]

about the time gold reached its highest quotation. Among the recent Irish immigrants, as yet unassimilated, were hundreds of young men seduced overseas by Union recruiting officers in Ireland. The latter made grandiose promises, which the War Department did not always honor. The *Daily News,* the *World,* and the *Journal of Commerce* had pointed this out repeatedly. The tinder was ready for the spark.

The disaffection against the draft, and the controversies over its constitutionality as well as its administration, continued long beyond the end of the war. In 1863, the Supreme Court of the State of Pennsylvania, by a vote of three justices to two, declared that the Federal act was unconstitutional. The Court's personnel was changed by the 1864 election, and the new Republican majority promptly reversed the decision. Two United States Circuit Courts upheld the act. It was not presented to the Supreme Court of the United States then or thereafter.

Governor Seymour continued his challenge of the constitutionality of the measure, of the existence of any practical need for it, and of the fairness of its application. Beginning the month after the Manhattan riots, he engaged in an exchange of letters with President Lincoln which gave each of the men the chance to state and justify his position. The conflict of view between them was not of good and bad, or right and wrong—it was of rival and contending goods. In the correspondence, Lincoln showed to better advantage, but there can be little doubt that Seymour's views had weight.

The story of the draft has a useful epilogue. When Abraham Lincoln was confronted with the need for it, he had no experience of the past to guide him. The Commander in Chief of the nation during the Civil War was obliged to pioneer along an unknown path. He must improvise, without time and under pressure. He must use weak and untried tools to break down a sturdy inheritance of traditions—to say nothing of disloyalties.

When the nation confronted another great war crisis, the Civil War wrote the prologue for improved performance. It had happened that after Appomattox, Provost Marshal General Fry had written and filed an elaborate, argumentative report and justification of his handling of the draft. This was deposited in the records of the War Department. In 1917, to meet the challenge of the First World War, Woodrow Wilson sought a democratic method to secure a greater equality of sacrifice among the men of America. The President was historian and political scientist as well as statesman and world figure. On his suggestion, General Enoch Crowder, the new Provost Marshal General, dug out General Fry's report from the dusty files, and studied it.

This enabled him to ascertain the errors Fry had made, the first need in the effort to avoid repeating them. As a result, the selective-service structure which the United States employed in the years 1917-19 bore, and deservedly, a high repute.

In 1940, President Roosevelt examined the experience of both of these conflicts. The selective-service structure for our part in the Second World War constitutes a further forward step of enlightened war policy.

Chapter 8

VALLANDIGHAM AND GENERAL ORDER NO. 38

THE year 1863 had been full of strange contrasts on the battlefield. Militarily, the year had given proof positive that the Confederacy could not defeat the Union. The mistakes of Chancellorsville were erased at Gettysburg, those of Chickamauga at Missionary Ridge, and the fall of Vicksburg let the Father of Waters flow unvexed to the sea. Thereafter it was not open to question that the Loyal States of the Union could continue to pay the price of blood and taxes to crush the Confederacy. The question was: Would they?

The answer to this depended on the outcome of the struggle on the hidden front at home. In this field the year brought no real decision. Indeed, it was not until late in 1864 that Lincoln crushed the Copperheads, temporarily routed the Radicals, and ensured the doom of secession. All through 1863 civil strife blazed north of the theater of war. Perhaps the strangest of its struggles—one containing the elements of high drama, with incidental comic relief—was that over Clement Laird Vallandigham.

The story of this high priest of peace at any price cannot be understood without a knowledge of his background. He was born in New Lisbon, Columbiana County in central Ohio, in

1820. After log-cabin schooling, he did some college work in Pennsylvania. Then he taught school ("preceptor" was his title), returned to New Lisbon and read law, and was admitted to the bar at the age of twenty-two.

Young Vallandigham's mind and energy made him a successful lawyer, but he quickly developed a passion for politics. In 1844 he was elected to the Ohio House, its youngest member, and the next session became its Speaker. This was followed by a few more years of law. His hunger for politics led to an unsuccessful race for Congress in 1854. Two years later he seemed defeated, contested the count, and in May, 1858, was seated. He won the next two elections but, as has been noted, a Republican stalwart nosed him out in the fall of 1862, thanks to a gerrymander.

A man of good presence, Vallandigham was handsome, high-spirited, and self-willed. He had a voice of fine tone, which would carry out of doors as well as in. His political attitude was curiously compounded. On issues he was unchanging, but often he would support a man with whose views he disagreed. So it was that, although he did not espouse the Douglas doctrine of Popular Sovereignty, yet in 1860 he supported the Little Giant for the Presidency rather than John C. Breckinridge. After the fall of Sumter, his strict-construction views pushed aside his Union interests.

Another aspect of the man foretold the course he would take under mounting war pressures. In addition to being an able lawyer and a persuasive speaker, he was almost a fanatic. This trait he had through direct inheritance, for his father came of French Huguenot stock impressed with Calvin's narrow zeal, while his mother was of a Scotch-Irish family which clung to the unyielding tenets of John Knox.

As a youth, Vallandigham had so strongly espoused what

[*158*]

MAJOR GENERAL AMBROSE BURNSIDE
who issued General Order No. 38

CLEMENT L. VALLANDIGHAM

*Zealot, mystic, and Copperhead
extraordinary*

A RARE OLD GAME OF "SHUTTLECOCK."

JEFF—"*No good sending him here. I'll have to send him back.*"
ABE—"*He's none of mine, anyhow.*"

VALLANDIGHAM'S PLIGHT—THE FATE OF EVERY TRAITOR

From Leslie's Weekly, 1863

then they called temperance—by which the true believers meant total abstinence—that on one occasion he said he would commit suicide rather than let liquor pass his lips. While in college, he fell out with its president over a point of constitutional law, and refused to take an earned diploma offered him. His hatred of the doctrine of force led him to despise the Maine and other prohibition laws of the 50's so much that, despite all his temperance views, he quit that cause.

The inflexibility of his will was shown by his actions after his defeat for re-election in 1862. He returned to Washington for the last term of the "lame duck" Congress with the belief that the Seymour success in New York, and other Administration upsets, attested the rightness of his own course.

During the late winter term, he frequently took the floor of the House to denounce Lincoln's conduct of the war, and particularly the Emancipation Proclamation and the suspension of the writ of habeas corpus. Soon after the Congress adjourned on March 3, 1863, he went to Albany, New York, to confer with Governor Seymour.

This brought together the leader of the Democrats of the West and the head of the Eastern Democracy. Thus far these two men had been in close harmony on most party matters. Both had supported Douglas in the late 50's; both sought his election in 1860; and both looked askance at the lengths to which Lincoln had gone to carry on the war.

The discussion, which lasted several days, focused on two points: the immediate issues of emancipation, conscription, and the suspension of habeas corpus; and the more general problem of outlining a common policy by which the Democrats on both sides of the Appalachians could agree, so as to put up a united front against Lincoln's resort to devices beyond the Constitution.

[*159*]

Seymour agreed with his visitor's dislike of the two immediate issues, and seemed pretty much in accord on the general party program. Apparently neither man yet realized that the major body of the Eastern Democracy would line up behind Seymour, in favor of Union victory as the prime objective, with insistence on maintaining the Constitution as a minor theme; while in the Northwest, the Copperheads and the Butternuts would increasingly back Vallandigham's determination that the paramount issue was constitutional methods—even if these meant the defeat of the Union armies and the independence of the Confederacy.

About two weeks after Vallandigham reached his home in Dayton, President Lincoln and Secretary Stanton assigned a new general to the command of the Military Department of the Ohio. The new commander reached Cincinnati March 25, and began issuing orders which stirred the Democratic leaders to wrath and action.

The military firebrand was Major General Ambrose E. Burnside, who now became a new and, for a time, most important actor in the drama.

Burnside, who hailed from Rhode Island, was a small man —small in body, mind, and soul. Personally amiable and a good talker, he had the reputation of having one of the best seats in the saddle in the Regular Army. Nowadays his name is best preserved by the cheeky semibeard adornment that he made popular, still called "burnsides" as well as "sideburns."

A West Point graduate, he had been in civil life most of the 50's. He was a New England Democrat, and at one time he ran for Congress on that party's ticket, but was defeated. His friend George B. McClellan got him a job with the new Illinois Central Railway, and he tried his hand at other business essays, with indifferent results. When the war broke out, Burnside returned to the army, and during the Peninsula and Antietam campaigns was one of McClellan's corps commanders and personal intimates.

When Lincoln dismissed the "Napoleon of the West" from command of the Army of the Potomac, for successor he picked Burnside. The latter took the place with reluctance, saying that he did not feel equal to the task. As a matter of fact, Lincoln is supposed to have selected him chiefly because at that time Burnside was a stanch follower of "McNapoleon"—as the Radicals irately termed McClellan—and his political conservatism. Therefore Burnside's choice might help to keep the conservative Democrats on the President's side.

But be that as it may, the correctness of the General's self-analysis was attested by his winter campaign; it culminated in the hideous carnage of Fredericksburg, December 13—the Federals' most stupidly planned battle until June, 1864, when Grant topped it at Cold Harbor.

Immediately after the retreat across the Rappahannock, the Radicals in Congress, and particularly the Joint Committee on the Conduct of the War, began looking for a burnt offering to sacrifice. In view of the believed sameness of view between McClellan and Burnside, they hoped the latter would be the man. But when the committee visited the uneasy camp at Falmouth, imagine their surprise to find the beaten General now out-Heroding Herod. The army must purge itself of all officers of doubtful views. They must entrust command only to true believers.

Amazed and delighted, the committee picked another victim, and urged Lincoln to save Burnside's scalp by giving him a cushy job in the West. On January 25, the General was relieved, "at his own request," the order said.

In a few weeks Stanton picked this new Radical for another post. The head of the War Office had been stirred to action not only because of the general problem of the draft in the Ohio Valley, but also by a secret report from Carrington. Writing from Indianapolis on March 19, that worthy transmitted alarming reports from his spies in the castles of the Knights of the Golden Circle in Indiana and Ohio. These claimed, as we already know, that they had "the co-operation of the fraternity in Kentucky, Tennessee, etc. That at the next raid of Morgan, he will leave the command and quietly appear, to raise the standard of revolt in Indiana."

Likewise alarmed by Vallandigham's return to the region, and his immediate incitement of the people, Carrington asked the excitable Secretary of War for authority to arrest the Democratic firebrand. Stanton immediately issued an order putting Burnside in command of the Department of the Ohio, and shipped him West.

There were busy days in Cincinnati when Burnside took over. The zone of his command was Ohio, Indiana, Illinois, and Kentucky. Operating under the claimed authority of an act of Congress of 1862, he proceeded to issue a swift stream of orders telling citizens what they could and could not do. Some of these came from the press after interchange of telegrams or letters with Stanton, Halleck, or the Adjutant General's Office at Washington. Others were issued first and explained to the authorities at the capital later on.

And they were quite embracing. General Order No. 9 prohibited citizens from criticizing the military policy of the Administration—and the civil policy too. No. 15 forbade the people to keep or bear arms.

But No. 38 was the most extraordinary of them all. It laid down a number of new rules to govern not only the citizen's conduct, but also his expression of opinion—almost his secret and unuttered thought. One paragraph declared that "the habit of declaring sympathy for the enemy will not be allowed in this Department. Persons committing such offenses will be at once arrested, with a view to being tried as above stated, or sent beyond our lines into the lines of their friends." This same section repeated that "it must be distinctly understood that treason, expressed or implied, will not be tolerated in this Department."

This new turn of affairs had the expected effect on Vallandigham, who made plans to take his protest to the people. In doing so, he had an added personal purpose. He loved politics, both the quest for the suffrage of the people and the holding of public office. Ohio would elect a new Governor that October —at that time, she held her State elections in the off years— and with the backing of the Democratic chieftains, Vallandigham had determined to run for the Governorship.

A week after his return to the State, he had broken the ice by a talk at Hamilton. On April 30, after the issuance of General Order No. 38, he went to Columbus, and there sharply criticized the order, the General, and the President. He was billed for an open-air meeting at Mount Vernon, Ohio, the next day.

At this point, there is need to shift attention to Burnside's developing plans. As soon as Order No. 38 was out, he set up machinery to enforce it, the central element of which was a Military Commission to try citizens accused of violating it.

Burnside knew that Vallandigham would be the first real morsel for the commission to chew upon, and undertook to give it a personnel which would, to some extent, offset the charge sure to be made that this great Democrat, friend of the lamented Douglas, had been tried by rabid Radicals. So one member named in the Special Order of April 21 establishing the commission was Colonel James L. Van Buren, a relative of the late President. The Colonel, an aide on Burnside's staff, carried over from the General's days and gave a Democratic flavor to the commission.

Then for its Judge Advocate, Burnside named Captain James Madison Cutts, brother of Adèle Cutts, Douglas's second wife. From 1857 until the Little Giant's death in 1861, young Cutts had served as personal secretary to his brother-in-law. As Judge Advocate, he would seek to convict of treason a Douglas supporter who quoted the Little Giant in almost every speech he made. As ordered, the commission met in Cincinnati the day after its creation, but contented itself with minor cases until Vallandigham's arrest.

Vallandigham was at Mount Vernon May 1, according to plan. He spoke in the open, to an enormous and applauding crowd, nearly all Democrats. Leaning on the speaker's platform, just six feet from the speaker, was an officer from Burnside's staff, young Captain H. R. Hill, of the One Hundred and Fifteenth Ohio Volunteers, who took copious notes of the firebrand's words.

There was no doubt about it, the speaker was aflame. He termed the President "King Lincoln" and appealed to the people to remove him from the throne by going to the ballot box. He denounced General Order No. 38, and spat upon it. The crowd shouted agreement throughout the eloquent invective. Vallandigham then returned to Dayton, and Burnside's Captain sped back to his chief.

The next day Burnside listened to the young man's report, then acted swiftly. That night he sent a special train to Dayton, with a company of Ohio Volunteers. They debarked in the dead of night; the troops marched to Vallandigham's home and demanded entrance. He refused, and fired a signal pistol from an upstairs window. The soldiers immediately burst into the house, forced their prisoner to dress, took him to the train, and sped for Cincinnati. It was well that they moved so swiftly; otherwise there might have been an attempt to rescue him.

The captive was thrown into a military prison in Cincinnati, supposedly in close confinement. Nonetheless he managed to smuggle out an address to Ohio Democrats, which was published widely. "I am here in a military bastile," he wrote "for no other offense than my political opinions, and the defense of them, and of the rights of the people, and of your Constitutional liberties. . . . I am a Democrat—for the Constitution, for law, for Union, for liberty—this is my only crime. . . . Be firm, be true to your principles, to the Union, to the Constitution, and all will yet be well."

The day after his incarceration, Vallandigham was brought before the Military Commission; its president, Brigadier General R. B. Potter, was in the chair. The first order of business was the reading of the charge and its specifications. The charge was that the prisoner had uttered public expressions in violation of General Order No. 38, the Department of the Ohio, voicing sympathy for those in arms against the Government of the United States. The specifications were that he had said publicly that it was:

"A wicked, cruel and unnecessary war . . ."

"A war not being waged for the preservation of the Union . . ."

"A war for the purpose of crushing out Liberty and erecting a Despotism . . ."

"A war for the freedom of the blacks and the enslavement of the whites . . ."

This done, the prisoner was asked to plead. He asked delay, in order to obtain counsel. The commission cleared the room,

[*165*]

conferred, then announced he must plead first, then he could have half an hour to get a lawyer. But Vallandigham, denying the jurisdiction of the military tribunal, refused to plead guilty or not guilty. Thereupon the commission directed the Judge Advocate to enter, in the prisoner's behalf, a plea of not guilty to both charge and specifications.

This done, young Captain Hill, the prosecution's star witness, took the stand and repeated the story of the Mount Vernon speech. Acting as his own counsel, Vallandigham cross-examined the Captain in an effort to bring out the constitutional foundation of his speech. Hadn't the witness heard him endorse the principles of the Crittenden Compromise, for which Douglas had labored? Had Hill not heard the accused quote Stephen A. Douglas? Cutts promptly objected to this question bringing in his brother-in-law, and the commission promptly excluded it.

Hill's evidence was all the prosecution wanted. The prisoner put on "Sunset" Cox, a prominent Cincinnati Democratic Congressman, who had heard the speech, and thought it completely protected by the Constitution. After vigorous argument of guilt by Judge Advocate Cutts, the officers had the grace to recess a day, for the prisoner to draft a formal protest of the right of the commission to try him. On assembly the next day, its members caucused three hours, and brought in the verdict of guilty, but took the sentence under consideration. No one died of shock at the unexpectedness of the outcome.

Vallandigham had already found the United States courts unwilling to intervene in his behalf. Shortly after the trial opened, George E. Pugh, able conservative Democratic lawyer and former United States Senator, applied to Judge Humphrey H. Leavitt of the United States Circuit Court for a writ of habeas corpus for Vallandigham. The application was heard May 11. On the Judge's invitation, A. F. Perry appeared for General Burnside, and the latter presented to the court a written address defending General Order No. 38.

"If I were to find a man from the enemy's country," declared the General, "distributing speeches in camps, speeches of other public men that tended to demoralize the troops or to destroy their confidence in the constituted authorities of the Government, I would have him tried. . . . Why should such speeches from our own public men be allowed? . . . They create dissension and discord which, just now, amounts to treason. . . .

"We are in a state of war, and an emergency is upon us which requires the operations of some power that moves more quickly than the civil. There never was a war carried on successfully without that power."

Such men as Vallandigham, he continued, "must not use license, and plead that they are exercising liberty." Burnside's duty required him "to stop license and intemperate discussions which tend to weaken the authority of the Government and the Army." For these reasons he had issued the General Order, for violating which the prisoner had been brought before the Military Commission.

Whether or not persuaded by Burnside's logic, on May 11 Judge Leavitt refused the writ. His opinion said he did not know the General's authority, but he assumed that the President, as Commander in Chief, had clothed him with the necessary power to act. The Judge did not indicate what he deemed the limit, under the Constitution, of the powers of the Commander in Chief.

The commission convened again on May 15, and sentenced Vallandigham "to be placed in close confinement in some fortress of the United States, to be designated by the Commanding Officer of this Department, there to be kept during the continuation of the war." Approving it the next day, Burnside designated Fort Warren, in Boston Harbor, as the place of confinement.

There was immediate, and explosive, reaction to the dispatches from Cincinnati. The day of the conviction, Governor Seymour wrote an Ohio friend the affair was "cowardly, brutal, and infamous." The day of the sentence, in a letter to a mass meeting in Albany, he charged that the transaction involved "a series of offenses against our most sacred rights. It interfered with the freedom of speech; it violated our rights to be secure in our homes against unreasonable searches and seizures; it pronounced sentence without trial, save one which was a mockery, which insulted as well as wronged. The perpetrators now seek to impose punishment, not for an offense against law, but for the disregard of an invalid order put forth in the utter disregard of the principles of civil liberty."

The chief executive of the Empire State went on to express the gravest concern at the situation. "The people of this country," he warned, "now wait with the deepest anxiety the decisions of the Administration upon these acts. Having given it a generous support in the conduct of the war, we pause to see what kind of government it is for which we are asked to pour out our blood and our treasures."

What Lincoln did, he went on, would "determine in the minds of more than one half of the people of the Loyal States, whether the war is waged to put down rebellion at the South, or destroy free institutions at the North."

The mass meeting went wild over the letter. It adopted resolutions to the same effect, addressed to Democrats throughout the nation, and carefully forwarded a copy to the President.

[*168*]

Burnside's action of May 16 had thrown the whole mess right into Lincoln's lap. As Commander in Chief, he alone could review, approve, modify, or set aside the General's order. As Chief Executive of the civil government, he alone could cope with the swelling protest of the outraged conservatives. What hand had he taken in the case so far? What would he do about it now?

At the time, some voiced suspicion of Lincoln's secret agency in Burnside's bold course. But the only remotely close approach to this to be found in the record is the episode, already decribed, of Carrington's appeal to Stanton for authority to seize Vallandigham, and the Secretary's quick action in sending Burnside to command the Department of the Ohio. No evidence has been found to show that Stanton talked to Lincoln about the new appointment, and in view of his secretiveness, it is likely he did it on his own.

In their official history of Lincoln, Nicolay and Hay make the plain statement that the trial was a *fait accompli* before Lincoln knew about it. Burnside's department letter book contains no word from Washington on it until after the sentence was pronounced. Halleck, the General in Chief of the Army, kept a careful file of pressed copies of his confidential letters. His first to Burnside on this subject was four days after the event. "Father Gideon" Welles, who relished such tidbits for his diary, made no entry on the case until May 19, when it came up at a Cabinet meeting. The evidence is impressive that it took the President by surprise, and greatly embarrassed him.

Nor was this strange, for he had weighty matters on his mind and heart. On April 27, "Fighting Joe" Hooker, Burnside's successor in command of the Army of the Potomac, had moved boldly up the Rappahannock, crossed it handsomely, and found a clear path to Richmond. But soon the stream of good news became a trickle. The day Vallandigham spoke at Mount Vernon, Lincoln was haunting the telegraph office at the War Department, and Welles took note of his great uneasiness, his complaint that "nothing reliable came from the front," and his "feverish anxiety to get facts." Burnside's raiders seized the Ohio Copperhead the day after Stonewall Jackson routed Hooker's right. The Military Commission concluded its trial about the time the White House heard that the army had retreated and was "on this side of the river again." No wonder Nicolay and Hay declare that the news from Cincinnati "took the President somewhat by surprise," and insist that had he been consulted in advance, he would not have authorized the arrest.

This makes sense. The master politician of the war would have made no such blunder. But now he was torn between two courses, either of which might be harmful. Were he to disapprove the proceedings, it would greatly weaken Burnside's authority, and that of every other commander of a military department, and would encourage the Copperheads everywhere. But his approval would be the signal for even more bitter attack. Vallandigham would be in a Northern prison, a fact sure to lead to increasing demands for his release.

Lincoln saw himself in danger of being impaled on one or the other of the sharp horns of this dilemma, and determined to be gored by neither. As so often is the case with great men confronted with disaster, his capricious sense of humor and zest in jocund relief of tension supplied the remedy.

In examining Burnside's Order No. 38, he came across the provision of an alternate punishment to either death or prison. Persons so arrested would be tried *"or sent beyond our lines into the lines of their friends."* Here was his escape made to order for his mood. He would send Vallandigham not to

Fort Warren, but to the Confederacy. This would make him so ridiculous that he could hardly wear the robes of martyrdom.

On May 19, he put the matter before the Cabinet. Welles noted that all the members regretted the arrest, held it a bad Burnside error, and wished the prisoner had been sent across the lines. Right after the meeting, the War Department sent this telegram to Burnside:

"The President directs that without delay you send C. L. Vallandigham under secure guard to the headquarters of General Rosecrans, to be put by him beyond our military lines; and in case of his return within our lines, he be arrested and kept in close custody for the term specified in his sentence."

Then the President and Stanton summoned General Halleck, who sent along the bad news to Burnside. There were many, Halleck's confidential letter said, who feared the case might do more harm than good. As he himself had not read the testimony, he offered no opinion whether or not the findings were justified. Nevertheless, in the Loyal States "it is best to interfere with the ordinary civil tribunals as little as possible. Treasonable acts, in those States, unless of immediate and pressing danger, should be left for trial by the courts, as provided in the Act of Congress." He wrote simply to put Burnside on his guard "against inciting opposition to the Government by unnecessary arrests and military trials."

To this he added a general lament concerning generals commanding districts outside the theater of war. "It seems difficult," he complained, "to find military commanders of sufficient judgment and discretion to avoid conflict with civil authorities" in the Loyal States. "In many of these conflicts the officers have been entirely in the wrong, assuming powers

[*171*]

which do not belong to them." He concluded his letter by insisting that General Burnside get ready to take the field.

A few days afterward, the President began work on his response to the Albany resolutions. He realized the importance of an effective answer. Perhaps he likewise had begun to regret his quick-flash essay in avoidance of the Vallandigham dilemma. The shift of sentence from prison to exile had not met the statement of the Democrats that "the blow struck at a citizen of Ohio is aimed at the rights of every citizen of the North"; neither did it reverse the action of Burnside's commission, nor restore Vallandigham's liberty in the Union States.

Lincoln pondered the matter, made rough notes, and consulted intimates about it. He knew the disapproval with which such conservative Cabinet members as Blair, Bates, and Welles regarded Burnside's acts.

The General, on June 3, compounded his Vallandigham blunder by another General Order, suppressing a paper in Chicago. Welles noted, on that day, that "the President—and I think every member of the Cabinet—regrets what has been done." They knew that such a course "gives bad men the right of questions, an advantage of which they avail themselves. Good men, who wish to support the Administration, find it difficult to defend these acts." These were Burnside's own, he insisted, without any hint from Washington. Nonetheless "the responsibility is here, unless they are disavowed and called to account, which cannot be done."

He went on to say that "the constitutional rights of the parties injured are undoubtedly infringed upon." But still the question remained: "Should the Government, and those who are called to legally administer it, be sustained, or those who are striving to destroy both?"

A little later, the President read the Cabinet a further draft of his letter, and they thought it had "vigor and ability." On June 12, it was dispatched.

The President's letter began by noting with appreciation that the resolutions showed that their makers had supported the Union, in spite of the policy of the Administration. Then he reviewed the insistence that the guarantees of the Constitution must not be flouted, and in particular those of "liberty of speech," "liberty of press," and "habeas corpus." But the fact was that these were made the cloak for aiders and abetters of secession and treason. Worse than that, the civil courts of the country, as might have been expected, had proven "utterly incompetent" to punish those who committed such crimes.

This was because civil courts are organized chiefly for trials of individuals in quiet times, on charges of crimes well defined in the law. Even then, bands of highwaymen frequently grew too powerful for the ordinary courts. But what comparison do such bands bear to the insurgent sympathizers in some of the Loyal States? "Again, a jury too frequently has at least one member more ready to hang the panel than to hang the traitor. And yet again, he who dissuades one man from volunteering, or induces one soldier to desert, weakens the Union cause as much as he who kills a Union soldier in battle. Yet this dissuasion or inducement may be so conducted as to be no defined crime of which any civil court would take cognizance."

This state of affairs forced a new governmental approach, particularly for purposes of prevention. The President called attention to the small value of constitutional procedure if arrests could never be made until definite crimes had been committed, and illustrated this by a few notable examples, such as those of Generals Robert E. Lee and Joseph E. Johnston, now occupying the very highest places in the rebel service, who had

[*173*]

been "within the power of the Government since the rebellion began.

"Unquestionably if we had seized and held them," the letter continued, "the insurgent cause would be much weaker. But no one of them had then committed any crime defined in the law. Every one of them, if arrested, would have been discharged on *habeas corpus* were the writ allowed to operate."

Then he came to the Vallandigham case. He had been arrested, not "because he was damaging the political prospects of the administration or the personal interests of the commanding general, but because he was damaging the army, upon the existence and vigor of which the life of the nation depends. He was warring upon the military, and this gave the military constitutional jurisdiction to lay hands upon him."

Had Vallandigham's arrest been made on a mistake of fact, Lincoln would gladly correct it. But this was not the case, and, he continued: "Long experience has shown that armies cannot be maintained unless desertion shall be punished by the severe penalty of death. The case requires, and the law and the Constitution sanction, this punishment. Must I shoot a simple-minded soldier boy who deserts, while I must not touch a hair of a wily agitator who induces him to desert? This is none the less injurious when effected by getting a father, or brother, or friend into a public meeting, and there working upon his feelings till he is persuaded to write the soldier boy that he is fighting in a bad cause, for a wicked administration of a contemptible government, too weak to arrest and punish him if he shall desert. I think that, in such a case, to silence the agitator and save the boy is not only constitutional, but withal a great mercy."

Now the President made a shrewd political counterthrust. The Albany resolutions had been addressed to "Democrats."

COLUMBIA: *"Where are my 15,000 Sons—murdered at Fredericksburg?"*
LINCOLN: *"This reminds me of a little joke—"* COLUMBIA: *"Go tell your
Joke at SPRINGFIELD."*   *A cartoon from Harper's Weekly, 1863*

ONE OF THE MANY VICIOUS ANTI-LINCOLN CARTOONS

*Lincoln is represented as saying: "Now, my friends, I'm almost in and the
millennium is going to begin, so ask what you will and it shall be granted." The
Negro says: "De white man hab no rights dat cullud pussons am bound to
respect! I want dat understood." One follower says: "I represent the free love
element and expect to have free license to carry out its principles." Other
followers demand women's rights, abolition of private property (and of police-
men), suppression of religion, etc., etc.*

A Currier and Ives contribution toward national unity

GENERAL GEORGE B. McCLELLAN

"MacNapoleon" in a characteristic pose

He countered that Burnside, who had had Vallandigham arrested and tried, was a Democrat, "having no old party affinity with me, and the judge who rejected the constitutional view expressed in these resolutions, by refusing to discharge Mr. Vallandigham on *habeas corpus,* is a Democrat of better days than these, having received his judicial mantle at the hands of President Jackson."

He closed with a remarkable admission that "it gave me pain when I learned that Mr. Vallandigham had been arrested (that is, I was pained that there should have seemed to be a necessity for arresting him), and it will afford me great pleasure to discharge him so soon as I can by any means believe the public safety will not suffer by it. I further say that, as the war progresses, it appears to me opinion and action, which were in great confusion at first, take shape and fall into more regular channels, so that the necessity for strong dealing with them gradually decreases. I have every reason to desire that it should cease altogether, and far from the least is my regard for the opinions and wishes of those who, like the meeting at Albany, declare their purpose to sustain the government in every constitutional and lawful measure to suppress the rebellion. Still I must continue to do so much as may seem to be required by the public safety."

This is more than an adroit avoidance. It deserves rank as a great state paper. In it, Lincoln truly showed that, with the nation in danger, the safety of the people is the supreme law.

Chapter 9

CANDIDATE IN EXILE

THE President's instructions reached Burnside's head-quarters the late afternoon of May 19, the day of their issuance at Washington. The rebuked General immediately started Vallandigham on his journey south to exile.

That evening, the former Congressman was moved from his cell in the military prison to a cabin on a flat-bottomed side-wheeler, the United States gunboat *Exchange,* which was to convey him down the Ohio to Louisville.

Orders for instant departure were countermanded, but the gunboat left three days later, and arrived at the Louisville wharf at noon on Sunday, May 23. Vallandigham was put in an open omnibus and carried to the railroad depot; the report of the Master of the *Exchange* added that "not the slightest manifestation of public sentiment was observed." The transit from Louisville to Nashville, and that from the Tennessee capi-tal to General Rosecrans' headquarters at Murfreesboro, were also uneventful.

At that point, Major William M. Wiles, Provost Marshal General of Rosecrans' army, conducted Vallandigham to his office and "furnished him with refreshments." The prisoner's next move, guarded by a troop of cavalry, was to a pleasant mansion on the Shelbyville Pike, five miles southeast of Mur-freesboro.

[176]

When it was daylight, the party trotted forward to the last cavalry vidette of the Federal lines. Then Rosecrans' Provost Marshal sent a note, under flag of truce, to the nearest Confederate outpost, advising the enemy of the object of the visit. After a while, a Colonel Webb, commanding an Alabama cavalry regiment, approached, to inform the Federal officers that "Mr. Vallandigham would not be received under a flag of truce, or in any official manner, but that if he were set beyond our lines, and approached those of the Confederate Army to request admittance, he would be received and treated as would any other citizen."

There is dispute over the exact manner in which the Confederates received him. Rosecrans' Provost Marshal insisted in his official report that he carried Vallandigham out to the Confederate lines and delivered him to an orderly sent out to receive him. According to this version, Vallandigham then, in the presence of two Federal officers, "delivered himself up as a prisoner, stating that he was a citizen of the State of Ohio and the United States of America."

But the Confederate account did not correspond. Lieutenant Colonel Sir Arthur J. L. Fremantle of the British Army, who was on tour over the Southern theaters of war, made a diary entry May 28 that at the headquarters of General William J. Hardee, one of Bragg's corps commanders, he had met the exile. The entry continued that Vallandigham "was, as General Hardee expressed it, 'dumped down' in the neutral ground between the lines and left there." A little later, Colonel Webb showed the British visitor "the house where Vallandigham had been 'dumped down' when they refused to receive him by flag of truce."

The Ohio Democratic leader "then received hospitality from the Confederates in the capacity of a destitute stranger." Fremantle was careful to point out that "they do not in any way receive him officially, and it does not suit the policy of either party to be identified with one another."

Vallandigham, who impressed the diarist as "a good-looking man," stayed at Hardee's headquarters near Wartrace for a few days while plans were made about his disposal. Neither he nor the Confederate authorities relished the new relation.

Nor was this to be wondered at. In Vallandigham's case, whatever might have been the inferential effect of his strict-construction views, up to the time of arrest he had not flatly favored the success of the Southern revolution. Then Burnside had almost made a martyr of him, only for Lincoln to make him a comic character. He wanted to get off secession soil as soon as he could.

Equally interesting was the change in the Confederate attitude. During the trial, Dixie had exulted. Now at last the Northwest might raise the standard of rebellion. The mercurial Beauregard saw visions of a great invasion, perhaps with himself in command of the Army of Tennessee, in place of Bragg. It was Vallandigham in Ohio, however, over whom they had exulted. He might have been an asset there, but both Bragg at Shelbyville and Davis at Richmond knew that in Tennessee he was a liability to the Southern cause.

Be that as it may, the proprieties were preserved. The visitor was sent to Chattanooga, Knoxville, Bristol, Lynchburg, and Richmond. He had several interviews with Robert Ould, the Confederate Government's official Commissioner of Exchange of Prisoners, who met him at Bristol and conducted him to Wilmington. Ould reported to President Davis the details of their discussion. John B. Jones, clerk in the Confederate War Department, made a diary note of Ould's communication.

The exile's view seemed to be that if only the South could

hold out that year, the peace party of the North would sweep the Lincoln dynasty out of existence. He urged against the planned invasion of Pennsylvania, warning that any such move would unite all parties in the North, thus so strengthening Lincoln's hands that he would be able to crush all opposition. On this last, Davis had endorsed his dissent. Ould's memorandum contained another interesting remark, that "Mr. Vallandigham had said nothing to indicate that either he or the party had any other idea than that the Union would be reconstituted under Democratic rule."

Early in June, Vallandigham reached Wilmington, North Carolina, where he took the fast blockade-runner the *Lady Davis* for Bermuda, arriving there on June 22. This was a brief stopping-point, from which a British steamer took him to Halifax, where he landed July 5.

He soon went to Quebec. There the officialdom of the province greeted him as a hero, giving him an elaborate reception at the exclusive Stadacona Club. He left July 15 for Niagara Falls, to meet his family and confer with Ohio associates upon the future cause. For the journey, the Managing Director of the Grand Trunk Railroad provided, with his compliments, a sumptuous private car.

Vallandigham remained at the Clifton House, on the Canadian side of the Hanging Bridge, for about two weeks. He was soon joined by his wife and daughter, and by his devoted friend and political associate, Congressman George H. Pendleton of Cincinnati.

Ohio politics was the chief matter which had brought Pendleton to Canada—to be exact, the extraordinary fact that the Democracy of the Buckeye State had named Vallandigham their candidate for the governorship, and the campaign was already going forward at high heat.

[*179*]

The Democratic delegates had gathered at Columbus on June 11, already determined on Vallandigham as the issue for the canvass, and as the man to be put in the governor's chair. The opening session of the convention showed this to be the general feeling. The leaders promptly determined that the State, and the nation, could have no more persuasive testimony of the issue than the exile's nomination by acclamation. This was done immediately, and with great enthusiasm.

Not only was he candidate, but platform too. The party's resolutions reaffirmed the devotion of its members to the Union. They recited the purpose of the party, obvious weeks before, to select Vallandigham for their candidate for the governorship. This had made his arrest a direct insult to the sovereignty of the people of Ohio, for it was an effort to prevent their choice of chief executive at the ballot box. Therefore the convention had demanded that President Lincoln redress these wrongs, and restore their leader's right to live in his home State.

A distinguished committee was designated to bear this protest to Washington. Before doing so, it drafted an elaborate letter reciting the wrongs that must be righted. Likewise it undertook to answer Lincoln's reply to the Albany Democrats. The Ohio letter denied that Vallandigham had made war on the military. It disagreed completely with the President's strictures on the danger of the writ of habeas corpus in time of war.

"If an indefinable kind of constructive treason," it asked, "is to be introduced and engrafted upon the Constitution, unknown to the law of the land and subject to the will of the President, whenever an insurrection or invasion shall occur . . . what safety or security will be left for the liberty of the people?"

The letter was circulated over the State, and practically every prominent Democrat signed it. The committee carried it to Washington and presented it to the President, who answered them in a letter dated June 29.

The question they had raised, he wrote, was "simply a question who shall decide, or an affirmation that nobody shall decide, what the public safety does require in cases of rebellion or invasion."

The Constitution, he went on, "contemplates the question as likely to occur for decision, but it does not expressly declare who is to decide it. By necessary implication, when rebellion or invasion comes, the decision is to be made from time to time; and I think the man whom, for the time, the people have, under the Constitution, made the Commander in Chief of their army and navy, is the man who holds the power and bears the responsibility for making it."

This is a deep and penetrating judgment of the location of the mainspring of power in the no man's land of the Constitution. Whenever our nation is at war, the question is mooted again, the President's power as Commander in Chief is attacked, and he is assailed as a despot. The Lincoln view just quoted remains to this day the most succinct and satisfactory one ever put in words. Those who in times of high crisis, with the nation in peril, have had responsibilities similar to those he shouldered have acted upon the identical conception of their job. It must be so.

He did not give much space to other points of controversy the Ohio disputants had sought to raise against his Albany letter. Instead, he took up the chief demand, that Vallandigham be brought back from exile, and sought to turn it upon his critics. This he did by making an offer to the signers of the letter. If they would accept it, their nominee for the governorship could come back to his native State.

There were three prongs to the proposition, seemingly logical enough. These were:

1. That the Federal Union was then confronted with an insurrection, and that the army and navy of the United States were a constitutional means of its suppression.

2. That no one of the committee would do anything which, in the member's own judgment, would "tend to hinder the increase, or favor the decrease, or lessen the efficiency of the army and navy, while engaged in the effort to suppress the rebellion."

3. "That each of you will, in his sphere, do all he can to have the officers, soldiers, and seamen of the army and navy, while engaged in the effort to suppress the rebellion, paid, fed, clad, and otherwise well provided for and supplied."

If the committee, he continued, or a majority of its members, would write their names on the back of his letter to them, he would publish the letter and the names. This would mean revocation of the sentence against Vallandigham. He emphasized that this would pledge the signers, not their nominee—that Vallandigham would return to the country unpledged.

Then he went on to allege that he made this offer because any such undertaking on the part of these leading Ohio Democrats would be powerful moral reinforcements for the successful prosecution of the war. Indeed, this would much more than offset the damage that would result from Vallandigham's return.

This may have been a purpose; it might even have been a faint hope; but by no stretch of the imagination could Lincoln have expected its acceptance. His real reason for the proposal must have been to turn the argument in such a way that his assailants would be hoist by their own petard.

The apparent open candor, almost naïveté, on the surface of the offer barely masked the shrewd politics at its core. The Ohio Democrats, undeceived by it, promptly refused. Its acceptance would involve an imputation of the sincerity of their Union sentiments, they charged, together with an implied concession by them of the legality of their hero's banishment.

These things had occurred during Vallandigham's journey from Shelbyville to Niagara Falls. Most of them he had learned of while traveling; the rest Pendleton discussed there at the Clifton House. The candidate and his campaign manager planned the next steps to take.

One item decided on was the renewal of the effort to get the civil courts to intervene. As has been seen, on May 11 Judge Leavitt of the United States Circuit Court at Cincinnati had declined to issue a writ of habeas corpus. Incidentally, former Senator Pugh, who had presented the application, had been nominated by the Democrats for the lieutenant-governorship, and was active on the stump seeking votes for his exiled running mate. He soon appealed the Circuit Judge's action to the United States Supreme Court.

Despite the fact that the venerable Roger Brooke Taney was still Chief Justice, the high court would not act upon the appeal. The issues presented were the same as those to come before the court two years later, in the famous Milligan case. But this was after Appomattox, when the court no longer felt the pressure of the war emergency. Now it said it had no jurisdiction over such a tribunal as a Military Commission.

Vallandigham likewise made immediate appeal to the Government at Washington, to be allowed to re-enter the United States. Doubtless this was done merely for the record, in the hope that it might have some slight weight in the Ohio campaign. Seward paid no heed to the request.

The candidate in exile issued from the Canadian side of Niagara Falls, an "Address to the People." It was a masterpiece, particularly in the way it sought to transform the liability of banishment into an asset of appeal.

"Six weeks ago"—so ran its theme—"when just going into banishment because an audacious but most cowardly despotism caused it, I addressed you as a fellow citizen." Now, while still in exile, "though almost in sight of my native State, I greet you as your representative." He gave warm thanks to the Ohio Democracy for nominating him. They had been sound in judging that his arrest was the only real issue in the campaign. Furthermore, his journey through the Confederacy had convinced him that the war could not be won by conquest.

Like the summer soldiers and sunshine patriots of a later day, Vallandigham contended, before the nation had made a supreme effort to win the war, that it could not be won on the battlefield. "If this civil war," continued his address, "is to terminate only by subjugation or submission of the Southern force in arms, the infant of today will not see the end of it."

This proved an effective appeal in Ohio. The Administration forces did their utmost to make fun of it, and to ridicule its author. But Lincoln's intimates in the White House privately admitted its political force and persuasiveness.

Now we turn to the other side of the Ohio campaign—the steps the Administration men took to thwart Vallandigham's candidacy. The events of May and the Democratic indignation over them had caused consternation among the Republicans. They saw all too well the way Burnside's impetuous course, and Lincoln's reluctant endorsement of it, had given the opposition a real battle cry.

Their concern increased when the Democrats nominated Vallandigham and Pugh. They began to fear defeat at the ballot box in October. Some of the shrewder heads among them determined that they could best meet this threat by choosing a War Democrat for their own candidate. The Republican State Convention met in Columbus late in June. A few days before the delegates gathered, their attention had been arrested by a ringing speech which John Brough, a Democrat and a supporter of Lincoln's war policies, made to a mass meeting at Marietta.

Brough was a gallant and interesting character. He had been born in Ohio in 1811, became a devoted follower of Old Hickory, went to the Ohio Legislature in the 30's, and did well there. During the next decade his fame grew as the best Democratic orator in the State. In 1844, he bought a paper at Cincinnati, changed its name to the *Enquirer,* and started it on its long career. With the outbreak of the Civil War, he promptly ranged himself with Lincoln and gave stalwart support to the Administration's conduct of the war. His Marietta speech had thrilled the loyalists throughout the State.

The Republican State Convention soon turned to him as its choice for the governorship. Brough accepted, as a War Democrat, and plunged into an extraordinary campaign. This carried him to every section of the State, and everywhere he spoke his strength and his influence grew.

Two military events operated to strengthen Brough's appeal to the Ohio voters. One was the general elation among the people of the region over the twin victories of Vicksburg and Gettysburg. These showed that the Boys in Blue could fight just as well as Johnny Reb—victory might be slow, but it was by no means impossible.

Then again, the Confederate invasion of Pennsylvania had irritated most of the people of all the Loyal States. In addition, John Morgan's raid into Indiana and Ohio had angered the inhabitants of the Ohio Valley, including even the Copperheads themselves.

This raid was perhaps John Hunt Morgan's most ambitious enterprise as a *beau sabreur,* and its outcome was most unfortunate. It came at a time when he thought some daring exploit was needed to complete his personal re-establishment with his own followers. In December, 1862, the dashing young General had married for the second time, his new bride being the daughter of a well-to-do Middle Tennessee family who lived at Murfreesboro. Morgan's new adventures in matrimony interfered with his attention to his command, to the extent that such devoted friends and subordinates as Basil W. Duke, George St. Leger Grenfel, Thomas H. Hines, and others felt that the rebel raider was neglecting his command, and sacrificing his career and their military reputation.

At length the General heeded this disapproval and undertook to redeem himself. In February he tore himself from the arms of his bride, to embark upon a series of extraordinary military exploits. Some of these were so successful that on May 1, 1863, the Confederate Congress passed a resolution to express its thanks for his "varied, heroic and invaluable service."

Spurred on by this praise, and also by the fact that he greatly preferred adventures beyond the lines to the usual tasks of cavalry covering a fighting army, Morgan began pressing his superior commander, "Fighting Joe" Wheeler, for permission to ride north to the Ohio River. Wheeler gave it reluctantly, and on July 2 Morgan set out with about 2,500 men. They made rapid progress, and were on the south bank of the Ohio, ready to cross, six days after his start. They had covered from fifty to sixty miles a day without undue laming of the animals or straggling of the men. There was little fighting en route, the most conspicuous incident being at Mt. Sterling, near the Ohio River. There some of Morgan's men broke into the Mt. Sterling State Bank and seized its cash on hand. This exploit reverberated in Kentucky for many years thereafter, and is still debated.

The Confederate column crossed the river the night of July 8, into Indiana. The Union authorities had been advised of the approach of the raiding party. The Department of the Ohio collected a substantial body of cavalry and other arms. As soon as Morgan was reported north of the river, the Federal forces concentrated and took up pursuit. Morgan and his men rode east for several days, with the pursuers hard on their heels. It was touch and go, and many legends lingered of a nocturnal dash of the fleeing Confederates through Cincinnati's suburbs.

They were brought to battle at Buffington Island, where strong Federal forces conclusively defeated them. Morgan and 1,200 men escaped and fled northeast. On July 26, at Saline-ville, a hamlet near New Lisbon, Ohio—incidentally, the birth-place of Vallandigham—the Confederates were surrounded, and surrendered.

The Knights of the Golden Circle might have been looking forward to the advent of the Confederate General, but they wept no tears at his disaster. Many homes along the expected path of his passage had five-pointed stars affixed to the win-dows as recognition symbols. But such signs made no difference to the General or his raiders. They seized horses, took food and supplies, burned habitations, without the slightest con-cern over whether the owners of the property thus seized were friendly to the Confederate cause or loyal Unionists. The conduct of the raiders, together with their defeat and capture, hurt the cause of the Democratic nominee for the governorship.

The raiders were taken to the Ohio State Penitentiary at Columbus, and imprisoned there. On November 26, exactly four months after their capture, Morgan and six of his fellow captives escaped from their confinement. At the time it was reported that they had escaped by tunneling under the walls of the prison. But then, and later, many believed that well-placed bribes procured the release.

Throughout the summer and the fall, former Congressman Vallandigham was advised of these developments, good and bad, in his native State. The candidate and his party remained at Niagara Falls only about a fortnight. Early in August, the Vallandighams and George H. Pendleton went to Quebec. After a few days there, on August 21 they took train for western Canada. Windsor, just across the border from Detroit, was their destination. The candidate in exile went there determined to make the best of things, to settle down on British soil and campaign from a distance.

The Federal authorities, however, feared the worst. They felt sure that he planned to smuggle himself across the border, make his way to Ohio, and take the stump. Now they were in the greatest apprehension. When word of his arrival at Windsor reached the Commander of the Military Department, at Cincinnati, he telegraphed to the Provost Marshal at Detroit: "If Vallandigham crosses into Michigan, arrest him, and at once send him under a strong guard to Fort Warren."

Vallandigham, however, did not take the chance. Soon he acquired a comfortable home at Windsor, and lived there with his family for the next ten months. Nonetheless, his heart was in the Ohio campaign. He sent many messages, statements, and speeches to his supporters, and these were read and quoted from on the stump all through the State.

It was an extraordinary canvass. Both sides put forth their utmost efforts. Pugh, Pendleton, "Sunset" Cox, and others made effective use of the whole Burnside episode. At the start, the Ohio conservatives were aghast at the high-handed tactics of the Administration. As James Madison Cutts had written Lincoln late in July, Order No. 38 had "kindled the fires of hatred and contention."

Lincoln acted on this timely hint, insisted that General Burnside get into the field, gave him a corps, and sent him through Cumberland Gap into East Tennessee.

October 13 was election day, and more Ohio men went to the ballot box that day than ever before in the history of the State. Furthermore, the count of the ballots showed what a hold Vallandigham had upon Democrats, conservatives, and Copperheads. He received the largest number of votes a Democratic candidate for the governorship had ever had before that year. But Brough had 100,000 more!

Actually there were two different elections—the normal one in Ohio itself, and that conducted by the State authorities for Ohio soldiers, wherever these might be upon the war front. There was much voting, for example, in Chattanooga, to which the Army of the Ohio, along with other Rosecrans forces, had retired after Chickamauga and was now hemmed in by Bragg.

Of the civil vote, Brough received about 247,000, against Vallandigham's 185,000. With the troops, however, the War Democrat had nearly all of them—almost 43,000, to fewer than

[*189*]

2,500 for the peace candidate. Altogether, Brough's majority was 100,099 in the total of 432,000 votes cast.

Despite the impressive total of dissent, Ohio had put its trust in Lincoln, and refused to leave the ranks of the Loyal States.

BRIGADIER GENERAL JOHN HUNT MORGAN

The Confederate raider on whom the hopes of the Copperheads were centered

OLIVER P. MORTON

Governor and dictator of Indiana

HORATIO SEYMOUR

Governor of New York and leader of the Loyal Opposition

Chapter 10

MORTON: DICTATOR OF INDIANA

LINCOLN needed the comfort of Brough's victory, for elsewhere in the Ohio Valley the year had been one of even greater tumult and distress than that in Vallandigham's State. Neither in Missouri, Illinois, nor Indiana had there been effective offset against the resentment of the Butternuts and the Copperheads.

An odd, disturbing symbol of the situation was that the disaffected did not regard these titles as fighting words. They had been coined in malice; the Union men employed them as expressions of contempt. But the fifth-columnists refused to take them as words of disgrace. The Tories of the Revolution and the early Methodists of Asbury's time had proudly adopted the slurs applied to them as badges of honor. Now Butternuts and Copperheads sought to profit by their example.

"Butternut" originally had been used to describe a farmer so poor that his outer garments were dyed with the bark of the butternut tree. The peace party in the Ohio Valley adopted the sneering word as their name, and contrived an emblem to fit it. A pleasing one was to cut a butternut transversely, remove the kernel, and thus leave the outlines of two perfect parts joined together. Wearing these badges, they represented the Northern and Southern hearts which not even war could tear apart.

"Copperhead" had undergone a similar transformation. The stealthiest, most venomous serpent of the prairies was known as the copperhead. He lay in hiding, struck without warning, and his sting was death. The anti-slavery men and other ardent Unionists employed the title of the reptile to denominate the enemies they deemed traitors.

But the men so reprehended would not accept the definition. The head of the Goddess of Liberty was minted on one side of the large copper penny the Treasury had coined for many years. The men termed "Copperheads" regarded themselves as lovers of liberty. They determined to cut the Liberty head out of the penny, affix a pin to it, and wear the copper Liberty head on lapel or shirt as a badge of true respect for the Constitution and the Union.

The winter and spring of 1863 saw the passing of the Knights of the Golden Circle as the secret agent of disaffection. In part, this resulted from the 1862 exposures and arrests. But the chief reason was the loose-knit character of K.G.C. It had no real central command, the liaison between the various States was poor, and in no sense could it promise effective general action to aid the Confederate cause. The need for a better agency led to the Order of American Knights.

Phineas C. Wright, a St. Louis lawyer, established the new order early in the year. We have already alluded to his pre-war background in New Orleans. After his move to the Missouri metropolis, Wright became active in the Corps de Belgique, a local subversive order, and pamphleteered against the Union program. He was an addict to meaningless ritualistic phrases, and a visionary burning with zeal. He determined to be the Moses of the secret, sacred bands of brotherhood with the Confederate cause.

The instructions and oaths of the O.A.K. were as shallowly impressive as those of its predecessor. For the other's three degrees, the American Knights substituted five. Only high officials could take the two top degrees. The principles were States' Rights which would have pleased Calhoun. Negro slavery was indorsed, because the society "should promote the advancement of both races, and [slavery] is approved by the sanction of Divine economy."

The American Knight took oath "at all times, if need be, to take up arms in the cause of the oppressed—in my country first of all—against any monarch, prince, potentate, power or government usurper, which may be found in arms waging war against a people who are endeavoring to establish . . . a government for themselves of their own free choice."

The order had a military department, which its leaders designed to employ in setting up a Northwest Confederacy, to ally itself with that of the South. But this was not set forth in the written ritual of any of the degrees, and was communicated verbally only to the select conspirators who were admitted to the top command.

The founder and organizer himself took the title of Supreme Grand Commander. He was responsible to a Supreme Council. There was a Grand Commander in each State, who was selected by the State Council. Every county had a Grand Seignior. The central organization had a Grand Missionary, whose duty was to organize and supervise the township lodges.

Wright undertook to make the overhead structure efficient. He himself set up the State Councils in Missouri, Illinois, and Indiana, and perhaps other States as well. The Missouri organization grew rapidly over the northern part of the State; practically every ward in St. Louis established a local lodge, and scores of counties followed suit. Arms and ammunition were purchased in the metropolis and shipped to the outlying units. By the end of the year, the Missouri O.A.K. seems to have grown most formidable.

The promoter general soon became a traveling missionary of treason, and for several months journeyed through Illinois, Indiana, Ohio, and other States. In the first two of these he was unusually successful. The Ohio outcome was less so, owing to the backwash of Morgan's bootless raid and to the charges and countercharges of the Vallandigham campaign.

The Illinois election in the fall of 1862 had warned Governor Richard Yates of the stormy future. His annual message to the new legislature soft-pedaled emancipation and other Union measures. The solons ignored this olive branch, and elected William A. Richardson, a sharp critic of the war program, to Douglas's vacant seat in the Senate. The Illinois House then passed some extraordinary resolutions which urged an armistice, so that a convention of the States could be held in Louisville. They declared that "further prosecution of the present war cannot result in the restoration of the Union and the preservation of the Constitution as our fathers made it, unless the President's Emancipation Proclamation is withdrawn." This passed the House by a large majority, and failed in the Senate only because of the death of a Democratic member, which left that chamber evenly divided. Yates finally had to employ a legislative trick to get rid of the hurtful general assembly. Under the Illinois constitution, if the two houses would not agree on a period for adjournment, he could fix the day. They did not so agree, and he adjourned them until the last day of their terms, the Saturday before the first Monday in January, 1865!

This highhanded trick brought a mass meeting of protest, held at Springfield and said to have been attended by 40,000.

It also awakened the Douglas Democrats, who insisted that the errors of the Government at Washington "form no excuse for any loyal citizen to withhold his support from the Government." Because the protest was portrayed as the expression of the Democracy of Illinois, though only of the Copperhead portion, many of the Democratic generals at the front repudiated the party organization and publicly resigned from the party. Among these were John A. McClernand, a Douglas friend, and John A. Logan, a former foe.

What the generals said did not check the subversive influences in the Illinois soldiery—even at the front. The One Hundred and Ninth Illinois regiment, most of whose men came from Egypt, had so many desertions, and indulged in such fraternization with the Confederates, that Grant was forced to disarm the men in Mississippi and send them home in disgrace. Another regiment, the One Hundred and Twenty-Eighth Illinois, stationed at Cairo, had so many desertions that in March, 1863, only thirty-five soldiers remained present for duty. Guerrilla bands ranged southern Illinois, particularly in the disaffected northeast Missouri region.

The draft enrollment precipitated bitter rioting, as when a mob of several hundred besieged the hamlet of Olney for several days, and threatened to burn it unless the enrollment lists were turned over to them. A Federal Provost Marshal received the report that the sheriff of one county was an American Knight, and that no jury would convict for any draft or desertion charge.

The Knights of the Golden Circle did not develop the armed organizations in Illinois that they had in Indiana. But when, early in 1863, Wright visited Springfield and Chicago, he proposed the replacement of the Knights of the Golden Circle by an integrated order with a strong central command.

[*195*]

The Illinois K.G.C. group liked the change, and organized lodges of the American Knights with great alacrity. For these, they did not hesitate to recruit and drill large bands of men from Bloomington to Cairo, with quite a number of scattered units in Chicago, and a few around Quincy.

The new anti-Lincoln drive in Chicago received aid and comfort from a bold and enterprising newspaper of that metropolis, the *Chicago Times*. During the spring and early summer of 1863, this journal's criticism of the Lincoln policies, especially of the draft, were vigorous and effective.

Burnside's trial of Vallandigham had enraged the conservative press all over the country, the *New York World* and the *Chicago Times* being conspicuous in their assaults on the bombastic but thin-skinned General. Within a week of the Ohio Democratic leader's departure on his personally conducted trip to the Confederate lines, Burnside could contain himself no longer. The *World* was published outside the territory of his military department, and he could not send troops to suppress it, although he could and did forbid its circulation in the department. But he sent soldiers to stop the publication of the *Chicago Times*.

General Order No. 84, which he issued on June 1, charged the New York paper with creating distrust of the Administration's war policy, and declared "its circulation in the theater of war is calculated to exert a pernicious and treasonable influence, and is therefore prohibited" in his department. "Any person detected in forwarding, selling or in any way circulating the paper . . . will be promptly arrested and held for trial.

"On account of repeated expression of disloyal and incendiary sentiments," the order continued, "the publication of the newspaper known as the *Chicago Times* is hereby sup-

[*196*]

pressed." Brigadier General Jacob Ammen, commanding the District of Illinois, was charged with the execution of the fiat against the *Times*.

Soldiers occupied the plant on June 3, and destroyed part of the issues for that day. No effort was made the next day to put out a paper. But Wilbur Fisk Storey (of whom more later) and his cohorts demanded instant withdrawal of the order. Even more important, several Illinois friends of the President reprehended the General's action. The President took early action and on June 5 the embittered and undaunted *Times* resumed publication, its circulation and advertising greater than before.

The *Chicago Times*, victim of this new Burnside blunder, had an interesting background. Stephen A. Douglas had set it up in 1854, as an instrument to promote his fight against his political enemies. Under its able editor, James W. Sheahan, it did this exceptionally well. The journalism of that day was frankly partisan, but the *Times*'s accounts of the 1858 senatorial campaign were decidedly less biased than those in the Lincoln organs. But it had perennial business-office troubles, Douglas was so pressed by land, campaign, and other money needs that he could put up no more cash for it, and in July, 1860, Cyrus H. McCormick bought its debts and took the paper over.

The new owner was striking in other ways than as the inventor of the Virginia reaper. A ruthless rule-or-ruin man, he was one of the first millionaire manufacturers who wanted a political career. From 1860 to 1880, McCormick sought office from the people, only to be thwarted because of public resentment against his domineering, unyielding attitude. Though he had been away from his native Valley of Virginia for two decades, so pronounced were his slavery views that Medill's

Chicago Tribune felt entitled to say that "the prejudices of his youth have built upon a defective education a perfect monomania in behalf of man-stealing."

In addition to being pro-Southern, McCormick believed in peace at any price, and his paper worked hard for the Critten-den Compromise. His loyalty was so doubted that after Sumter he felt it necessary to publish a signed editorial, to declare that "though a native of the South, I am a citizen of Illinois, and of the United States, and as such shall bear true allegiançe to the Government." This he would do "without considering whether my country is right or wrong."

The criticism of the *Chicago Tribune* and other Radical papers irked him, to the point that in June, 1861, he sold the *Times* to Wilbur F. Storey, who was proprietor of the *Detroit Free Press*. Storey, an able publisher, soon had the *Times* on a money-making business. But he did not change Cyrus McCor-mick's policy about the war; rather, he stiffened it. By the summer of 1862 his was the leading Copperhead sheet in the West. The *Tribune* refused to heed the shift of ownership to Storey; to almost the end of the war it sneeringly referred to the *Times* as "Mr. McCormick's paper."

At this particular juncture, the *Tribune* approved of the Burnside action, albeit a little shamefacedly. Throughout the country, however, conservative papers and political figures watched these extraordinary military suppressions of free speech and free press with anxious attention. Governor Sey-mour wrote a friend in Chicago a letter which the *Times* pub-lished in justification of its own course. "Our friends in Chi-cago," the Governor's letter declared, "bore themselves nobly during the trials and excitements growing out of General Burnside's insane conduct. They won a victory for themselves and the country. I believe the aroused spirit of the American people, in behalf of their 'home rights,' will yet save us from despotism." This well expressed the general Democratic view.

Ohio subversionists manifested no such organizing skill as those in Illinois had done. Yet throughout the first six months of 1863 "an unusual degree of excitement, disorder and violence" existed throughout Ohio. In Noble County, a mob sought to force a provost guard sent to arrest a deserter to surrender to it, and then paroled both as though prisoners of Confederate soldiers. In Holmes County, captured deserters were freed by an armed band, and the arresting soldiers had to use stone walls as breastworks. The legislature was not in session, but the stage had been laid for an exciting State campaign. As has been seen, in the spring the peace party had believed that it could put Vallandigham, its chosen leader, in the governor's chair that fall.

Of all the States of the Ohio Valley, Indiana displayed the most active and determined opposition to the Lincoln program for the conduct of the war, and the means employed to check it were the most extreme used in the West. In 1860, Oliver P. Morton had been elected to a four-year term as Governor, and hence he had not been forced to a re-election campaign in the fall of 1862. But, as has been noted, the Democrats dominated the canvass and the ballot box that October; their candidates won important gains in the congressional delegation, carried the minor State offices, and swept the legislature. This had been done despite the Morton-Carrington-Grand Jury exposure and indictment of sixty Knights of the Golden Circle. The majority of the voters of the State quite definitely repudiated the Lincoln-Morton regime.

The Governor suspected that he was in for stormy days. But he did not realize how hostile the legislature would prove to be. It met right after New Year's Day, organized with Democratic control of both houses, and then signalized the beginning of the session by refusing to receive the annual message which the Governor submitted to it.

To make this contempt for the chief executive of the State even more conspicuous, the Indiana Legislature passed resolutions praising Governor Seymour of New York for his message to his own legislature, particularly his reprehension of the emancipation plan, which criticism they termed "clear, forceful and patriotic." The Indianians denounced the arming of Negroes, began investigations into Morton's financing of the State government, and came so close to putting over two Democrats for the United States Senate that the Republicans had to flee from the State capital to break the quorum. The hegira continued for several days.

The antiwar majority made up its mind to take the whole enlistment power out of Morton's hands, and put it under the charge of a commission of certain Democratic State officials. They announced that they would refuse to consider any other legislative measure until such action was taken. The Republicans withdrew again, this time to Madison. Eventually the legislature, lacking a quorum, adjourned without having made any appropriations at all.

While this was going on, the efforts of both Morton and Carrington to get useful service from Indiana courts, either State or Federal, to punish inciters of desertion or resisters to the draft, proved almost hopeless. The situation appalled General Carrington, who wrote despairingly to Stanton that military law was the only recourse. There were riots over the State, desertion was growing at a rapid pace, and throughout the spring and summer armed hostilities broke out in many places.

Wright visited several cities in Indiana in the spring of

1863, to promote his plan for the O.A.K. succession to the Knights of the Golden Circle. The Indiana leaders embraced it with relish. They realized that there had to be an effective central control; otherwise the South could never get the aid it needed. So Dr. Bowles, Harrison H. Dodd, and their cohorts enthusiastically made the switch. A new Military Department was established, and active arrangements made for arms and ammunition to be imported, both surreptitiously through Kentucky, and in the guise of merchandise by open freight from New York.

The legislature confidently expected that the lack of appropriations would force Morton to call a special session. And when he did so, before they would appropriate a penny for this man they thought a fiend incarnate, they would pass their bill, and override his veto, for a Military Commission in Democratic hands. This would put the Governor in solitary confinement, so far as the continuation of his usurpation of power was concerned. For them, he was the enemy—not Johnny Reb.

Superficially, this was good logic, good calculation of the normal expectancy of State politics. But the Democratic cabal which had made up its mind to take the Governor's power away from him did not know the full nature of the intended victim.

Oliver Hazard Perry Throck Morton, to give him his entire christened name, was forty years old at the time of this new crisis. He was born in Wayne County, Indiana, in 1822. As a child he was taken to Springfield, Ohio, where some Scotch Presbyterian aunts helped teach the young idea how to shoot. At fifteen, back in Indiana, he worked as a drug clerk, then was apprenticed as a hatter, and turned from this youthful trade to Miami University, where he made a mark in mathematics and in debates. Next he read law, practiced a little, and in 1848 was unsuccessful Democratic candidate for prosecuting attorney. A little later he was appointed circuit judge to fill an unexpired term, then went to the Cincinnati Law School to learn more about the functions of the judge.

With the repeal of the Missouri Compromise in 1854, Morton saw a chance to get ahead in agitation and in politics. He took a lead in the new Republican party in Indiana, forged along rapidly in the public eye, and wanted to go to the United States Senate. His hope was thwarted, but he was given the promise of the 1860 Republican gubernatorial nomination as a consolation prize. The Democratic split that year put him in office at the State House.

Upon the outbreak of the war, Morton promptly went to the farthest extreme for its prosecution. He believed in total war, and desired to make it "instant and terrible." From the start, he set up the State machinery for volunteering and recruitment which operated under forced draft until the end of the war. He was not satisfied with furnishing the number initially requisitioned by the President in his proclamation of April 15, 1861. Instead, Morton raised twice as many as in the call, and sent the number summoned. But he kept the others in reserve, drilled them in the State, established camps, set up a State arsenal and ordnance factory, and laid the groundwork for a huge, highly political, rather efficient Indiana State military establishment. The Republicans controlled the legislature during the two first years of his term, and it obediently passed the enabling legislation that he demanded. From the start, the whole process of enrollment and recruitment was tightly held in his grasp.

The Governor had a sturdy frame, a loud and far-reaching voice, and an emphatic personality. He was fanatical in his views, ruthless and ferocious in his methods, and would let nothing turn him from whatever purpose he might hold. There was some talk about his conduct of financial matters, but no proven instances of his greed for or misuse of funds.

This was the man whom the Democratic legislators expected to kneel to them in order to get the appropriations to run the State of Indiana from January, 1863, for the next twenty-four expensive months.

The Democratic leaders had calculated shrewdly. There would seem little question that once the Copperhead legislature was called back into special session, it would force through its measure to take over the control of Morton's military establishment. But there was no special session. The Governor did not announce that he had no intention of summoning one. But the weeks passed, and then the months, and the anti-Morton solons were still at home.

What the Governor had done was to abandon the normal pattern of constitutional government in the State of Indiana. The reason he gave for this was that it was the only way to save the Union cause. Once let the Butternuts and the Copperheads emasculate his authority and Indiana would become worse than neutral. Therefore Oliver P. Morton ruled the State as a despot, subject to control by neither legislature, nor court, nor public opinion. From the spring of 1863 until January, 1865, when a new and Radical legislature assembled, Morton was the dictator of Indiana, and did whatever he willed.

This was an extraordinary development for an Anglo-Saxon political society. From time immemorial it had been almost a sacred maxim of this race of free people under representative government that the power of the purse must control. The safeguard of the people's liberty had ever been regarded as their right to grant, or refuse to grant, moneys sought by the executive—whether king, or President, or governor. Now, for the first time since the days of James II, an Anglo-Saxon community was conducted without obtaining the approval of the legislature for taxes raised and money spent.

There seemed no limit to which this Radical dictator would not go to effect his ends. The State had to have money, and Morton used every conceivable device to drag it in. The State arsenal he had set up had never been legislatively authorized or adopted, so in a technical sense it remained his private personal property. He sold large quantities of its production of weapons and ammunition to the Federal Government, and it returned a profit of about $75,000 a year. The State treasurer, a Democrat, demanded that these funds be put in the official treasury. Morton refused, and instead put them in a private safe in his private office.

He harassed the county governments wherever the Republicans had the control, to get them to appropriate from county funds for the purposes of the State. A good deal of money came in this way, and went into his own strongbox.

But it was far from enough, so the money-seeking dictator journeyed to the capital on the Potomac again and again, club in one hand and empty purse in the other. His appeals to Chase, and to Fessenden when the latter succeeded as Secretary of the Treasury, ran into the stone wall of a bureaucratic conception of public funds. They refused his pleas, saying that it was patently illegal to pay out Federal funds to a State. He appealed to the White House, but an Abraham Lincoln who had not hesitated to employ the draft felt that he could not stretch his powers as President—either the great residual group or the almost illimitable powers as Commander in Chief under which he had freed the slaves—to send Treasury funds into the Governor's private care.

But not so Edwin M. Stanton, who made short shrift of matters of constitutionality, and issued orders to send $250,000 to Indianapolis. Morton gave him a jubilant and hypocritical warning: "If the cause fails, we shall both be covered with prosecutions." Stanton answered: "If the cause fails, I do not wish to live."

By these and other means, including the most rigid economy of nonwar costs, Morton managed to finance his dictatorship. He ignored Indiana's Treasurer except when he thought he had a way to siphon money out of the legal State till. There was one such instance in the matter of payment of interest on Indiana State bonds. There was some precedent that this could be legally done without specific legislative appropriation. But the Attorney General of Indiana, a Democrat, ruled in the negative, a test suit was brought, and the Indiana Supreme Court, controlled by the Democratic majority, upheld the ruling. Morton finally found both ways and means by which to pay the bondholders the interest on their bonds.

In this career of financial legerdemain, Morton set up what he called his Bureau of Finance. It made no use of the offices of the State Treasurer, but was established in the Governor's own official quarters. It had a small staff, devoted to the dictator, and it paid out some $457,000 without any legal authority at all.

To a large extent, these tactics were reflected in every feature of Morton's administration of his office during the two years. He was a despot about enrollment. He gloried in the fact that his methods had brought in 150,000 recruits, which almost completed Indiana's quota. He worked with Carrington almost daily, until it was hard to know which man thought what. Often the two together would journey to Washington to put some particular problem up to Stanton, or Holt, or even Lafayette C. Baker. And generally they were able to get what they wanted.

The Copperhead fifth column hated Morton about as much as it is possible to hate a man. At the height of the plotting for the Northwest Conspiracy, one of the objectives was to seize the Governor as a captive and a hostage. If he were to resist, his assailants would not hesitate to dispatch him. But this plot did not get much further than the paper stage. Despite an 1866 stroke of partial paralysis, Morton remained a dictator in everything he did until his death eleven years later.

James Ford Rhodes termed Morton "the ablest and most energetic of the Governors of the Western States." He could well have added that he was the most determined and successful dictator of the war.

FERNANDO A. WOOD

*Representative, Mayor of New York, Copperhead, and one of the
proprietors of the "New York Daily News"*

LINCOLN'S EFFORTS TO PRESERVE THE UNION RIDICULED

Apparently Lincoln and Jeff Davis want to tear the States apart, and only McClelland, the Democratic Candidate in 1864, desires to preserve the Union

A cartoon published by Currier and Ives in New York in 1864

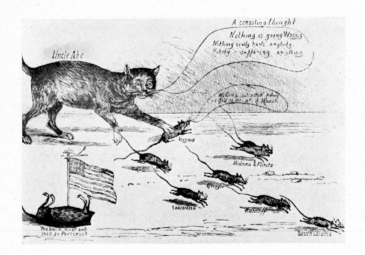

A RICHMOND VIEW OF LINCOLN

"Uncle Abe" is assuring his victims that it doesn't hurt

Chapter 11

1864: THE CRITICAL YEAR

OF all the Civil War years, 1864 would have the largest hand in shaping the American future. Not only did this prove true in the field of arms, but also in the arenas of public opinion and political control. It was the year of the national election, which became a referendum upon Abraham Lincoln's conduct of the war. The President's uncanny skill in measuring the public mood, together with some blunders by and mischances to his enemies and best of all, Sherman's capture of Atlanta, made him the people's choice for a second term.

But as the year dawned, this outcome was shrouded in doubt, and thoughtful observers could be sure of one thing only—that the political struggle would be waged upon several fronts.

In the instance of Lincoln himself, many powerful leaders within his own party wanted to send him back to Springfield. No President since Andrew Jackson had been elected to a second term, and re-election was no longer a part of the political tradition. The party feeling about Lincoln's own record in the White House was quite mixed; a number of strong leaders, and not all of them on the Radical left, felt that he had done badly. Murat Halstead, editor of the *Cincinnati Commercial*, wrote Senator John Sherman of Ohio in 1863: "If Lincoln was not a damned fool, we could get along yet. He is an awful, woeful ass." This represented the view of many conservative Republicans.

The Radicals were so embittered that late in the summer of 1863 they began their intrigues to procure another man as the Republican candidate for the Presidency. By the beginning of the new year, the field was full of hopeful and expectant aspirants. Among these were "Beast" Butler, General John C. Frémont, and Secretary Salmon P. Chase.

For a little while, they fed themselves on the hope that Lincoln would be so conscious of his own limitations, mistakes, and infirmities that he would eliminate himself from consideration. But during the fall the President determined to make the struggle for renomination. In his own way he was a proud man, thoroughly conscious of his particular individual abilities. While he did possess to an unusual degree the quality of intellectual humility—that almost indispensable catalytic agent of true greatness—in his case it was an awareness of and humbleness to the developing truth rather than any disposition to kneel to mean inferiors. Now he felt that the only way the war could be won and the Union be restored would be for him to be accorded a second term. Then his Administration could move forward on the path he had already marked out ahead.

With 1864, great questions loomed for answer; great dangers must be offset, and all the while the President must live and act dangerously. It was as though he had to find his way through fog along a mountain path, and although the mists made it impossible for him to see the pitfalls ahead, nonetheless he must step forward boldly, and abide the consequences.

Almost as important to him as his own renomination was the attitude which the Democratic party would eventually take in the national campaign. That great organization, so long the majority party in North and South alike, had been torn by feuds of rival leaders, and still had not determined whether it would make peace its paramount consideration, or would put Union at the head of its platform, and in the person of its nominee.

Three elements contended for its control. There was an important group of War Democrats who wished the Lincoln Administration to be succeeded by one led by War Democrats, so that the war could be more competently directed, better fought, and more quickly and surely won. Against them were ranged the more extreme Peace Democrats, whose desire for the restoration of the Union had never been more than perfunctory, and who now were steeped in treason. Between these, and with the decisive vote to determine the party control, were the members of the loyal opposition, the Seymour section, which wanted the war won in a constitutional way, but made victory paramount.

There were many important questions, such as the fast-growing organized fifth column in the States west of the Appalachians. This region, Lincoln's own, showed signs of a great swelling tide of sullen, embittered Copperheads, who were employing the faded phrases of the author of the Declaration of Independence as their battle cry in an attempted revolution in the Northwest. Their chosen leader, Vallandigham, remained physically in his home of exile in Windsor, right across the river from Detroit. But he never hesitated a minute in his efforts to arouse the Peace Democrats of the Ohio Valley States to challenge, even with arms, the policies of the Lincoln Administration.

Time and again this Whig in the White House proclaimed himself a Jeffersonian. Lincoln was fond of quoting axioms of the Sage of Monticello about liberty, education, the inherent rights of the common man. Lincoln knew, as Jefferson himself had known, that while philosophies live and endure and have eternal force, it is the philosophies themselves which live rather than the particular formulas for their application to each special case. He saw how Jefferson's precepts could be quoted for heinous purposes, and he feared that this would be done in the approaching canvass. Would the Copperheads write the platform and pick the nominee? Or would the spirit of Andrew Jackson and Stephen A. Douglas commit them to victory at whatever cost?

Then there was another, in the White House on the James, to whom the year portended the maintenance of Confederate independence or the completion of disaster and the doom of a "democracy" which had States' Rights for its shibboleth and slavery for its cornerstone. For the Dixie revolutionists, 1863 had been critically disastrous. Vicksburg had fallen; Bragg's unexploited hammer-blow at Chickamauga had been succeeded by panic and rout at Missionary Ridge. Lee had lost at Gettysburg, and was again at bay on Virginia soil. No more was there hope of foreign recognition, or of a British or French fleet come to lift the blockade.

By this time, the leading politicians of the South, the principal generals of the Confederate Army, and President Davis himself realized that their only hope was to drag out the war so long that the people of the North would get tired of the fight, and negotiate a peace. The only chance to do this was through the victory of the Northern Democrats in the November election. A little before Christmas, 1863, the city of Charleston, South Carolina, was in danger of capture by an amphibian Federal attack. The Confederate President went there to counsel his lieutenants. After advising them that if the danger could not be met, they should burn the city, he directed that in this event the troops should fall back into Georgia. There they should keep up the war "until Mr. Lincoln's time was out, and then they might compromise."

Of all these problems which confronted Lincoln, that of his renomination had the quickest issue. General Butler had failed to make the particular Radical connections which he must have to challenge the President effectively in the coming national convention. Not that anyone doubted the complete Radicalism of the Massachusetts worthy, but the extremist leaders had already divided their attachment between the erratic General Frémont and Secretary Chase. So to the amazement and disgust of the ambitious Butler, they ignored his aspirations.

With Chase, it was a very different story. Halstead wrote him in 1863, about Lincoln: "Can't you take him by the throat and knock his head against a wall until he is brought to his senses on the war business? I do not speak wantonly when I say there are persons who feel that it was [*sic*] doing God's service to kill him, if it were not feared that Hamlin is a bigger fool than he is." Such letters were numerous in Chase's mail, and they did not upset him in the least, for he made no bones about his own contempt for the chief he served. He told friends month after month that Lincoln's lack of efficiency in the formation of policy and in administrative application made him sick at heart. The President had no capacity to organize or to execute —victory could not be had with a leader so deficient in these vital qualities.

Chase's friends among the Radicals began a quiet canvass for the support of delegates as soon as November, 1863. They thought the enterprise was flourishing, and early in the new year they committed it to an unofficial campaign chairman,

Senator Samuel C. Pomeroy of Kansas. He was Radical enough, and amply energetic. By the end of January he had circulated a "Confidential Circular" which told the merits of his aspirant. But he very incautiously said in it that Abraham Lincoln would be defeated if he were the nominee; that even if he were able to be re-elected, he ought not to be President again. An Administration paper got hold of the letter and printed it. The Chase boom collapsed almost at once. The final blow was delivered at the meeting of the Republican members of the Ohio Legislature, who met in a formal caucus and nominated Lincoln as their choice—and that of the party—in the home State of Salmon P. Chase.

This unhappy blunder took the wind out of the extremists' sails. Chase had been their main hope, and he might have been a formidable contender against his chief in the national convention. But his hold upon the Republican rank and file was obviously superficial, or this blunder would not have forced his withdrawal.

In desperation, the agitation fringe of the party then turned to Frémont. That General was feverishly active from February on. Early that month, he accepted a Radical invitation to visit Louisville, ostensibly to make a Washington's Birthday address. Actually he wanted to line up support there for his presidential candidacy. About that time, one of Secretary Stanton's Kentucky contacts forwarded him a telegram from a Lincoln backer:

"General Frémont will be in the city on the 22nd of February, and will do his utmost to get the German papers to support him. They can be bought up unless some arrangement can be made. Can't you go to Washington and see what arrangement can be made?" The result was that Frémont did not get the

German papers. Probably their loyalty to Lincoln had been "arranged."

In March, to show their determined purpose, the Abolitionists, extreme antislavery advocates, the soft-money people, and believers in most of the other isms of the day determined to hold a convention of their own, earlier than and independent of the official party gathering.

The methods of choosing delegates, and the furnishing of credentials, were quite informal. They met in Cleveland, Ohio, the last of May, exulted over a letter from Wendell Phillips which stated his preference for the Pathfinder over the President, and proceeded to nominate Frémont. The latter hastened to accept. In his speech he denounced the Administration as "politically, militarily and financially a failure." The President got what relish he could out of a dispatch from Cleveland which put the total convention attendance at some four hundred. This gave Lincoln the excuse to read to a friend the Bible verse which pictured the gathering of the malcontents in the Cave of Adullam: "And everyone that was in distress, and everyone that was in debt, and everyone that was discontented, gathered themselves under him, and he became a captain over them; and there with him about four hundred men."

The President's own plans had matured some time before this. He thought it best not to be renominated by a *Republican* National Convention—he proposed and the machinery was set up to style it the National Union Convention. Nominated by a body so constituted, Lincoln would divest himself somewhat of the odor of a partisan political candidacy. He could say, and with much truth, that he represented not the minority Republican party, which had named him in 1860, but all men in America who made the Union of the nation, through the winning of the war, their cardinal hope and purpose.

This convention was to be called to meet in Baltimore on June 7. In the weeks before its scheduled date, the usual maneuverings of placemen and politicians occurred, and it was obvious to all that the President would obtain a unanimous vote, or practically so, from the delegates. He himself had an important problem. To give the real flavor of the union of the parties, he needed someone other than Hannibal Hamlin to be his running mate. He wanted a War Democrat. The joint candidacy of War Republican and War Democrat would make the National Union title ring true.

As a result, he sent emissaries who sounded out Andrew Johnson, the Tennessee Senator whom Lincoln had asked to go to his State as Military Governor two years earlier. The sturdy plebeian had made a conspicuous success of his service there, and was respected by the Radicals as well as by Lincoln's own group. By indirection, the word was passed, and Johnson became the candidate for the Vice-Presidency. Lincoln had to let the Wade-Chandler group get what satisfaction they could out of some of the language in the platform. So he yielded to a plank which almost said in so many words that Postmaster General Blair must walk the plank. A little later, this was arranged, as a part of the deal with the Frémont crowd, in order to get rid of the General's candidacy.

But this elimination was not arranged until several weeks after the adjournment of the gathering at Baltimore. The Radicals left the scene of the convention angry both at Lincoln's victory and at what they called the "snap nomination." By this last, they meant the "National Union" form of the gathering, which they took as a slur upon Republicanism in general and Radicalism in particular.

[*214*]

For the next two months, leaders of this cabal busied themselves in plotting the selection of a candidate to take Frémont's place and whip Lincoln. As so often is the case with angry leaders on a fringe, the Radicals endeavored to make a trade with a corresponding group in the rival camp. This led to a postponement of the Democratic National Convention, which had been summoned to gather in Chicago on the Fourth of July, until the last week in August.

Governor John A. Andrew of Massachusetts, who was as firmly fixed upon the extreme left as were Stevens, Wade, and Chandler, opened negotiations with Governor Seymour of New York, to find out if some basis of agreement could not be worked out between the Radicals and the Democrats for a common course and a single candidate.

The Massachusetts Governor wrote Seymour for the latter's counsel, and proposed that the two meet in New York City for a confidential talk on the best way to "conquer a peace." Andrew also had become excited over the efforts which the Reverend Colonel James F. Jaquess, who had gone to Richmond to see Davis; Horace Greeley, who had gone to Niagara Falls to see the Confederate Commissioners; and others were making for direct negotiation of a peace.

Instead of the meeting in New York, Seymour went to Boston on August 19 and spent the day with Andrew. Nothing came of their conference, there was no meeting of the minds on a candidate, and Andrew wrote a friend: "I hardly know what to make of Governor Seymour; he seemed very sincere. I think he is carried away by his own subtlety."

The delay in the Democratic gathering merely prolonged the intraparty tug of war. This had begun in 1863, with Vallandigham's banishment and candidacy from exile for the Ohio governorship. After his defeat by Brough, the chosen leader of the Democracy of the Ohio Valley States seemed to suffer no loss of esteem with the party faithful. But he himself made a clear choice between the two purposes he had stressed since Sumter—peace and Union. Now there was no longer question that he thought peace at any price much the more important of the two.

This also came to be the insistent purpose of the new secret society which had replaced the ineffective Knights of the Golden Circle. Supreme Grand Commander Wright gave increasing emphasis to the Military Department of the new Order of American Knights. There were almost daily drills of the military members in some sections, notably Indiana, southern Illinois, and northern Missouri, but this branch of the work continued subsidiary to the political purpose until the spring of 1864.

By that time, as we will detail in the next chapter, Wright had been found wanting in capacity to command, a new society had been set up to replace O.A.K., and Vallandigham had assumed its formal official leadership. The new Order of the Sons of Liberty increased the stress upon organized troops of treason. Its division between civil and military departments soon produced an active difference of views among the trans-Appalachian Copperheads and Butternuts.

From March on, General Bowles, head of the Copperheads' Military Department in Indiana, expressed contempt for the political prognostications of the leading Democrats of the Ohio Valley States. These believed, in the first place, that they could control the Chicago National Convention—write the platform and name the candidate. Likewise they insisted that a man of peace could be elected to take Lincoln's place at the head of the Government, and negotiate a peace. Bowles thought this utter rubbish. He did not believe that the extreme peace men could even control the Chicago caucus, and he felt quite certain that they could not elect a President. For one thing, he suspected there would be too many soldiers at the polling places, and too many Radicals influencing the counting of the ballots, for the Democrats to win, even if they actually amassed more votes than the Republicans. Then again, though the votes were fairly counted and reported, he believed the pressure would be such that many antiwar men would stay away from the polls.

It must be remembered that the elections of the 60's were conducted on an open and not a secret basis. Neither "Australian ballots" nor the present voting machine existed then. The voter in America during the nineteenth century had to go to the polling place and announce to the judges and watchers of the election the name of the candidate of his choice. In many places, this was done by word of mouth. In others, he selected from the printed ballots offered him that of his particular preference. But in all cases he could not vote without his views being known. And in many instances, an official at the polling place would crumple up his ballot and throw it away unrecorded. All of these facts gave point to the fears of General Bowles.

This point of view became increasingly controlling among the Sons of Liberty through the Ohio Valley. But the leaders of the chief State organizations fought hard against it. Grand Commander H. H. Dodd of Indiana co-operated actively with Vallandigham in getting a good slate of delegates from the State to go to Chicago. The Illinois situation was handled with equal skill. Missouri did not do so well, because Wright had left there, the Federal authorities had arrested many of the local leaders, and there was general disorganization in the

upper command. The hierarchy of the new Kentucky structure had its delegation appropriately picked for peace.

The Ohio Democracy presented a different picture. The outcome of the State election there in 1863 had left the War Democrats conscious of their power. In addition, neither the Knights
of the Golden Circle nor the Order of American Knights had
made the headway in Ohio that they had in the other Ohio
Valley States. As a result, it was not easy for peace-at-any-price
men to win unopposed choices to the delegation to be sent to
Chicago. Vallandigham had to take a desperate measure to
make sure of his own choice as one of the delegates.

The district convention which would determine his fate was
in session at Hamilton, Ohio, on June 15. At an unexpected
moment, the exile made his way through the crowd and
mounted the platform. In some way he had evaded the watch
at the border and smuggled his way across, and had journeyed
direct to the scene of the meeting. The convention crowd
greeted him with enthusiasm; he made a stirring speech and
was named a delegate that same day. The Ohio slate as a whole
was fairly strong for the peace program, but several stout War
Democrats were on it.

The Democrats were not the only group scheduled to gather
in Chicago at the beginning of July. The Order of the Sons of
Liberty had planned a meeting there, to take place just before
the party convention. Vallandigham and his principal advisers
felt this highly necessary, so that those of their members who
happened to be delegates could be prepared to take charge of
the proceedings at the party conclave. The summons for the
meeting of the Supreme Grand Council of the fifth columnists
was for July 1. The postponement of the convention itself until
late in August was not announced until so close to the original
date that many of the members of the council went on to Chi-

cago anyway. While there, they conferred with Confederate agents who had come down from Canada for that purpose. Then they returned to their respective States with many new plans, which embraced revolt as well as politics.

During the ensuing seven weeks of waiting time, before the national convention should assemble, Democrats the country over debated two critical problems: what issue the party should make paramount, and what great figure should be its candidate for the presidency. The first of the problems reduced itself to simple terms—the Democrats could write Peace at the head of the platform, or they could make Union the most important plank. They could not do both.

The field of candidates was limited. The most conspicuous of the possible choices was George Brinton McClellan, still a major general but without any assignment to duty since November, 1862, when the President had put Burnside in his place. Since then, the quondam "Little Napoleon" had been living in New Jersey, nursing his wounded vanity and mourning his lost prestige. But he remained a War Democrat— throughout the war his consistent wish was for the old Union and Constitution.

It had not been hard for the personal entourage which remained with him to present him as a martyr of partisan politics, an example of a military genius who had been thrown to the Radical wolves. Many of the War Democrats took up his cause with relish. Horatio Seymour was not among these, for he had a distrust of the General, growing out of the latter's high-handed course in Maryland in the fall of 1861.

The leaders of the New York Democracy had been looking for a better candidate for some months. In addition to the Governor, the two most important Democratic chieftains in the

Empire State were August Belmont, the sagacious financier from Frankfort on the Main, who had succeeded Dean Richmond as chairman of the Democratic National Committee; and Samuel J. Tilden, then entering the great period of his career as astute lawyer, organizing politician, and conservative statesman. These four men had been chosen by the New York State Democratic Convention, meeting at Albany on February 23, as delegates at large from the State. The whole delegation had been put under the unit rule, and these men were virtually empowered to cast its vote.

Seymour himself was importuned to become a candidate for the nomination. The idea must have attracted him, because he felt then and until his death that Lincoln had "used him badly" both in regard to emancipation and, particularly, in the controversy over the draft. The New York Governor was attracted by the prospect of being the man to challenge Lincoln, and to present to the people of the Loyal States the meaning of the record of unconstitutional conduct for which he held that the President had been responsible.

His efforts that summer to fix legal responsibility on General Dix for the suppression of the *World* and the *Journal of Commerce* illustrate the keenness of Seymour's feelings. The case itself was as mistaken a step as had been Burnside's action the year before in regard to the *Chicago Times*. In May, 1864, an embittered, perhaps crazed newspaperman concocted a pretended proclamation by President Lincoln. The *World* took it at face value and published it on May 18, 1864. The bogus proclamation called upon the people to consider the next Sunday a day of fasting and prayer. In addition, it called for a new draft of 400,000 men. The *Journal of Commerce* copied it the next day.

Stanton was furious over the blunder, charged that the papers were deliberately inciting treason and insurrection, and demanded of Lincoln that they be suppressed at once. The War Secretary prepared an Executive Order, directing the commanding general of the Military Department of the East to stop their publication. The President and the Secretary of State signed it, and Major General John A. Dix "reluctantly executed" it. Soldiers occupied the two printing establishments for three days. As was Lincoln's wont when he yielded to the urgings of excited subordinates, he accepted full responsibility for the action. But by the end of that time, it was obvious that the *World* had been the victim of a hoax. The troops were withdrawn, and the papers began to publish again.

Governor Seymour was outraged at this summary suspension. He asked the district attorney to submit the matter to the Grand Jury, then took process to cause General Dix's arrest and trial for kidnapping and inciting to riot. The trial began August 7. Dix justified his execution of the order from Washington upon the authority conferred on him by the Indemnity Act of March 3, 1863. The prosecutors assailed this congressional statute as unconstitutional. The State Court upheld this view, and ordered General Dix held "subject to the action of the Grand Jury of the City and County of New York." That body took no action.

But for all his official vigor, Seymour must have had some inner distrust within himself, or some overgrown sense of humility, because he would not authorize the preliminary affirmative steps necessary to get enough delegation commitments to head McClellan off.

Seymour's speculations, and those of Belmont and Tilden, dwelt upon two other possibilities. One was Justice Samuel Nelson, since the 40's a member of the Supreme Court of the

United States. The other was James Guthrie of Kentucky, Secretary of the Treasury in the Pierce Administration, and now the president of the Louisville & Nashville Railroad.

Nelson had made a good judge. His most conspicuous court service had been in the Dred Scott case, in which he wrote the most sensible and reasonable of the opinions which, taken together, had declared the Negro in this moot case still a slave. Nelson was at his best in the field of commercial law, in which he had specialized in the New York State judiciary before his elevation to the Supreme Court. His personality was pleasant, but except among the lawyers he had no great public hold. In addition, he had reached the alloted span of three score years and ten.

Guthrie had more appeal. His conduct of the Treasury had been a conspicuous offset to the generally low tone of administration under Franklin Pierce. The Kentuckian had determined to clean up certain Treasury abuses, to reform tax and customs collection frauds and stealings, and to instill a better fiscal conduct. In this he had been admirably successful. In 1857, he returned to Louisville, completed the railroad from the Ohio to the Cumberland, and got it working efficiently. When war came, he converted this railroad line into an extraordinary transportation system for the Union armies. As the Democrats gathered at Chicago, the Louisville & Nashville was indispensable to the supply of Sherman's army, then confronting Hood before Atlanta.

But Guthrie also was a man of seventy. In addition, he had procured his own selection as a delegate from Kentucky. He was to head the Resolutions Committee. At the time this was deemed a handicap, on the theory that the aspirant for a nomination should never be present personally, and should not take part in the vulgar quest of preferment.

[*222*]

The convention gathered in the Amphitheatre in Chicago at noon on Monday, August 29. It was called to order by August Belmont, as chairman of the Democratic National Committee. After a brief address, in which Belmont read the call, he turned the chair over to former Governor William Bigler of Pennsylvania, who had been chosen as temporary chairman. At that stage, the roll of States was called, that each might propose its members for the important committees—Resolutions, Credentials, Permanent Organization, Notification of the Candidates, and so on. These nominees for committee assignments were then appointed, and withdrew from the main body of delegates, to deliberate their assignments and prepare reports to be brought back to the convention floor. After a few perfervid speeches, the convention then recessed until Tuesday morning, when it expected the reports.

Horatio Seymour was proposed by the Committee on Permanent Organization as the convention's permanent chairman. It was an expected tribute. As the New York State delegation traveled West, Seymour had met with continuous ovations, especially in Detroit, where "crowds, cheers, speeches and salvos of fire-arms greeted him." The convention action was but another attestation of this general party esteem.

The Governor of New York was given an ovation as he went to the chair. This was his opportunity. Such was the storm of cheers and the wild huzzas that if only he had given the word, he could have been the nominee—and, what was more important, he could have written the platform and saved the party from one of the blackest marks ever put upon its record. But he took no step, sent no word, gave no sign of willingness.

In his opening address Seymour said that he hoped the Democrats, during the session, would take such action as to permit the Republican party to "die here where it was born."

[*223*]

He was the one man who had a chance to force this middle course, but he did not do it, for a fatal flair for oratory ran away with him.

The Lincoln Administration, he warned, could not "now save this Union, if it would." But the Democrats must do so, and they would. "Mr. Lincoln values many things above the Union; we put it first of all. He thinks a proclamation worth more than peace; we think the blood of our people more precious than the edicts of the President."

Seymour talked against time, and the delegates waited impatiently for matters of real importance to come before them. The Committee on Resolutions was slow in bringing back the platform that it intended to urge the party to adopt for the campaign. This was because Clement L. Vallandigham had captured the drafting subcommittee of the main body, and was choking a peace platform down its throat.

The action of this extraordinary figure at Chicago was in keeping with what Abraham Lincoln had hoped, in the middle of June, when he was confronted with the fact that the leading Copperhead had forced his way back into the United States. This had faced the President with the necessity for an almost instant decision. Did Vallandigham's violation of the sentence of the Burnside Military Commission of May, 1863, as modified by Lincoln's own order of May 19, indicate a contempt of authority so great that the failure to arrest him would have an evil effect upon the people? The President believed that if this were not the case, the exile's return probably would ensure the disruption of the Democrats in their Chicago convention. Lincoln knew that Vallandigham would be a firebrand.

The President had not been completely surprised by Vallandigham's sudden appearance at Hamilton, Ohio. A little before the event, the man had sought permission to end his

[*224*]

banishment, and had sent Fernando Wood to the White House to sound out the attitude there. For several months Wood and Vallandigham had been conspiring together to push the Democratic party into an all-out peace-at-any-price program. Wood was now Congressman as well as co-owner of the seditious *New York Daily News.* He called on the President, and his argument was ingenious.

Were Vallandigham back in the Loyal States, Wood argued, the Democrats might do the same thing in their Chicago meeting that they had done in Baltimore, following Charleston, in 1860—split the party and have two candidates for the Presidency. This would be all to Lincoln's advantage, because "these War Democrats are scoundrelly hypocrites; they want to oppose you and favor the war at once, which is nonsense. There are but two sides in this fight—yours and mine, war and peace. You will succeed while the war lasts, I expect; but we shall succeed when the war is over. I intend to keep my record clear for the future."

Lincoln's official biographers declare that Vallandigham's "dramatic reappearance came unexpectedly upon Mr. Lincoln, as his arrest had come." In view of the Wood feeler, and likewise of reports General Carrington forwarded from Indianapolis early in June saying that the heads of the Sons of Liberty in Indiana and Kentucky were expecting the exile back almost any day, the President's surprise over the return would seem somewhat strange. In the event, he did not telegraph an order for the Copperhead's immediate arrest.

On June 20, he drafted a joint letter to Governor Brough of Ohio and General Samuel P. Heintzelman, Burnside's successor in department command, instructing them: "Consult together freely, watch Vallandigham and others closely, and upon discovering any palpable injury or imminent danger to the military proceeding from him, them, or any of them, arrest all implicated; otherwise do not arrest without further order. Meanwhile report the signs to me from time to time."

After he had written this, the President changed his mind and did not send the letter. He took no public notice whatever of Vallandigham's return. The latter spoke over Ohio, denounced the Chief Executive, threw a copy of General Order No. 38 on the platform, and spat upon it, as he had done before. Still the soldiers left him alone—the Supreme Grand Commander of the Copperhead fifth column would have no new martyrdom at this master politician's hands.

And now, on the evening of the second day of the convention, Lincoln's intuition was proved correct.

As soon as the members of the Committee on Resolutions assembled, the peace men tried to elect Vallandigham as their chairman. Only Tilden's quick work prevented this from being done. He proposed Guthrie, who won by a vote of 13 to 11. The latter then named John B. Weller of California as chairman of the drafting subcommittee. This began its sessions early Monday evening.

The critical struggle, both within the drafting group and in the full committee, was the paragraph about peace. Vallandigham dominated the group; his fanatic zeal, his extraordinary force, and his almost hypnotic personality made him a hard man to counter in an argument before a small group. The leader of the Union men was Tilden, but he was a man for an office and not for a fight. There was a curious subtlety, indirection, circumlocution, in him which did not permit him to join in a free-for-all.

The platform which came before the convention at four o'clock that Tuesday afternoon had the merit of brevity. It contained only six planks, each expressed in a single paragraph. The second of these read:

"*Resolved,* That this Convention does explicitly declare, as the sense of the American people, that after four years of failure to restore the Union by the experiment of war, during which, under the pretense of a military necessity, or war power higher than the Constitution, the Constitution itself has been disregarded in every part, and public liberty and private right alike trodden down, and the material prosperity of the country essentially impaired . . . justice, humanity, liberty, and the public welfare demand that immediate efforts be made for a cessation of hostilities, with a view to an ultimate convention of the States, or other peaceable means, to the end that, at the earliest practicable moment, peace may be restored on the basis of the Federal Union of the States."

This brought the issue of peace at any price right before the Democrats. It had been fought bitterly in the Resolutions Committee. Everyone expected that there would be an even more determined battle on the floor. The fatal section had been adopted in committee by a very slender margin. But there was no fight.

For some strange reason, Samuel J. Tilden did not challenge the Ohio incendiary. Confronted with such a situation, some men seated in the presiding officer's chair would have installed a substitute and taken the floor themselves to lead the fight. But Seymour did not do so.

The delegates were wild with excitement. They shrieked approval of the platform, and when no one stood up to oppose them, they proceeded to adopt it, almost in a shorter time than the telling, by a viva-voce vote.

The rest was anticlimax. When the excitement died down, the convention proceeded to choose its candidates. The call of

States soon brought McClellan into the picture, together with a sharp attack upon him. An irate Maryland delegate protested the General's arrest of the legislature of that State in 1861, and sneered that "as a military man, he has been defeated everywhere." An Ohio man joined with the plea to the convention, "I beg of you to give us another candidate." This brought many cries of "Seymour of New York!"

But when Seymour's State was reached on the roll, the head of the delegation reported that "regretfully passing by her favorite son, who disclaims the candidacy," the Empire State cast its entire 33 votes for General McClellan.

This meant two things: to begin with, Seymour had not been able to swing his delegation to Justice Nelson. It took only a bare majority, only 17 votes, to do this. But Nelson's popularity was so little in comparison with that of the famous General that Seymour could not keep the State from going to the latter —only Tilden could have done so, and he declined. In the second place, it meant that McClellan would win the nomination on the first ballot. Unless New York had given him its voting strength this would not have occurred. The likelihood was that he would have triumphed on a later voting, but now the result was inevitable.

The Ohio delegation withdrew to caucus upon the action it should take. While it was out, Seymour made a little talk in which he said: "I cannot refrain from saying in behalf of General McClellan what in my heart I feel to be true, that when he is elected to the Presidential office, he will reflect with fidelity, boldness and zeal, the sentiments of patriotism and love of liberty and law, which animate the hearts of those who are here now assembled."

In a few minutes the Ohio delegation returned. Vallandigham cast its ballot for McClellan and moved that the choice be made unanimous. For running mate, the assemblage named Vallandigham's friend George H. Pendleton of Ohio. Thus the Democratic National Convention nominated a General who put Union first of all and instructed him to run on a Copperhead platform.

Needless to say, the new nominee was in great distress over the action he should take in regard to the platform. Apparently he did not seriously consider rejecting the nomination for the White House. But he had been put into an extraordinary dilemma as to making a campaign. Seymour appreciated his distress. The Governor had been made chairman of the committee of the convention which would formally and officially notify McClellan of his selection by the party. There were unofficial discussions in advance of the announcement of the General's acceptance of the commitment. A path out had been found.

The letter of notification was drawn up at the St. Nicholas Hotel in New York City, September 8, and dispatched to the General at Orange, New Jersey. The latter's acceptance bore the same date. In it, the candidate availed himself of a device he had employed two years before in the fighting field— he planned a change of base. His letter said:

"The Union must be preserved at all hazards. I could not look in the face of my gallant comrades of the Army and the Navy, who have survived so many battles, and tell them that their labors, and the sacrifice of so many of our slain and wounded brethren, had been in vain; that we had abandoned that Union for which we have so often periled our lives. . . .

"The re-establishment of the Union in all its integrity is, and must continue to be, the indispensable condition in any settlement. . . . The Union is the one condition of peace— we ask no more."

[*229*]

Other matters than Vallandigham's peace plank contributed to McClellan's unease of soul as he confronted the campaign. The convention had adjourned on August 31. The delegates were confident of victory until the President made public a telegram from General Willam T. Sherman, in far-off Georgia. On September 2, his pickets had entered an Atlanta the Confederates had given up. His message was terse and exultant: "Atlanta is ours—and fairly won."

These were happy words for the White House. The Democrats had pronounced the war a failure. But, as Seward so aptly put it, the word from Georgia "knocked the planks out of the Chicago platform." The combination of Vallandigham's platform and Sherman's victory assured Abraham Lincoln's re-election.

The change from despair to confidence was as sudden as it was complete. For much of the spring and summer, the President had felt the future hopeless, so far as his second term was concerned. Grant was making his slow way toward Richmond. Such casualty lists as that of Cold Harbor staggered the people at home. On August 23—just six days before the Democratic National Convention date—Lincoln felt especially depressed. He said later: "At this period we had no adversary and seemed to have no friends."

That day he wrote a memorandum, folded and sealed it, so no one could see it, and had each member of the Cabinet put his name on the back. Then he put it in a private drawer, under lock and key. It read:

"This morning, as for some days past, it seems exceedingly probable that this Administration will not be re-elected. Then it will be my duty to so co-operate with the President-elect as to save the Union between the election and the inauguration;

as he will have secured his election on such ground that he cannot possibly save it afterward."

This paper stayed in safekeeping until after the election. Then the President brought it out, opened it, and read it to his Cabinet. He recalled to the members the gloomy condition of affairs in August, and said that he had then "solemnly resolved" to pursue the course indicated by his memorandum: "I resolved, in case of the election of General McClellan . . . that I would see him and talk matters over with him. I would say, 'General, the election has demonstrated that you are stronger, have more influence with the American people than I. Now let us together, you with your influence and I with all the executive power of the Government, try to save the country. You raise as many troops as you possibly can for this final trial, and I will devote all my energies to assisting and finishing the war.'"

The cynical Seward remarked that the General would have responded to this by saying, "Yes, yes," but would not have done a thing about it. Abraham Lincoln's answer was: "At least I should have done my duty and have stood clear before my own conscience."

After the capture of Atlanta, Lincoln had little fear of the outcome of the canvass. He did not leave Washington to make any political speeches; he thought it seemly for him to remain where he could attend to the messages coming over the military telegraph at the War Department. Likewise he now had plenty of others to take the stump in his behalf, and with real enthusiasm. He visited City Point, where General Grant had established his headquarters on the south bank of the James not far below Richmond; there the Commander in Chief had close contact with the siege of Petersburg, and Grant's insistent pressure on Lee's thinning lines.

In September, after Sherman's triumph, the reluctant Radicals were forced to conclude that Frémont's continuation in the race could have no major effect on the result, but would do damage to their own future influence with the people. Therefore they welcomed negotiations to pull the Pathfinder out of the contest. As a preliminary condition, as has been noted, Montgomery Blair's scalp was thrown to them as a sop. Then Frémont withdrew.

One other event of significance occurred during the fall. Chase had petulantly offered his resignation from the Treasury, the end of June, and to his amazement the President had not sought to persuade him to stay on, but had accepted it. Three months later, however, the aged Chief Justice, Roger Brooke Taney, was gathered to his fathers, and Chase was nominated to succeed him. This act of gracious magnanimity marked the greatness of the President. It should be said that the new Chief Justice became an ornament to the bench, and that his service thereon, and particularly during the 1868 trial of Andrew Johnson before the Senate on the impeachment by the House, represented the high point of his public career.

No sooner had Chase donned his judicial robes than his former Cabinet colleagues became suspicious that he would not prove the stalwart Administration defender on the Supreme Court that they had hoped he would. In February, 1865, in connection with a habeas corpus case for which a writ of certiorari had been asked, Attorney General James Speed expressed definite apprehensions that the Chief Justice would "fail the Administration." Lincoln was astonished, but Gideon Welles made note in his daybook of the intimation that "the Chief Justice intends to make himself felt by the Administration. . . . I shall not be surprised, for he is ambitious and intriguing."

In the event, this was an unfounded view. The case referred to probably was the later famous Milligan case, upon which the decision was not handed down until the spring of 1866, under circumstances hereafter to be related. And while Chase joined the other Justices in unanimity of conclusion in regard to the illegality of the trial of the petitioner by a Military Commission, he dissented from the majority opinion that Congress had no power to authorize the commission to act.

The truth of the matter is that the apprehensions of the President's constitutional advisers proceeded out of the doubts which had surrounded the whole matter of the powers of the Government of the United States under the Constitution, even though it had exercised these to enable it to survive. It would be well to review the chief fields of controversy. So far as concerned the citizens of the Loyal States, these embraced particularly the power to suspend the habeas corpus privilege; the imposition of military rule in States which were not in the actual theater of war, and the arbitrary arrests in them; the establishment of martial law, and the employment of military commissions to try civil prisoners; the enactment of indemnity acts, to hold officers of the Government, civil and military alike, scatheless from prosecution for damages for illegal acts performed by them under authority; and the enforcement of the draft.

The first sharp conflict between the President and the judiciary came in the Merriman case. The circumstances, which arose in the early summer of 1861, have already been alluded to. This was a typical instance of direct difference between military and judicial authorities. Chief Justice Taney received the application for a writ of habeas corpus while on circuit duty in Baltimore. The prisoner, then in Fort McHenry, had been lieutenant of a drill company of Confederate sympathizers. The writ which was issued was returned by the commander of the military department, with the respectful explanation that the President had, by proclamation, suspended the writ, and that he had been instructed to hold in secure confinement all persons implicated in treasonable practices. This meant that he must decline to produce prisoners upon writs, whatever the issuing authority. The President was the target of the ensuing opinion which Taney filed with the clerk of the court at Baltimore, in which he termed the refusal a type of usurpation; he insisted that those suspected of treason should be dealt with by the judicial process. If not, "the people of the United States are no longer living under a government of laws; but every citizen holds life, liberty and property at the will and pleasure of the army officer in whose military district he may happen to be found."

The Chief Justice addressed himself directly to the President. His opinion declared that it would "remain for that high officer, in fulfillment of his Constitutional obligation to 'take care that the laws be faithfully executed,' to determine what measures he will take to cause the civil process of the United States to be respected and enforced."

The President's response to this, in its final form, has already been given. In his original draft, he made direct reply to Taney, saying, among other things, that, at the time he authorized commanding generals to suspend the writ, he had requested the officers to use this authority sparingly. He added that:

"Of course I gave some consideration to the questions of power and propriety before I acted in this matter. The whole of the laws which I was sworn to execute were being resisted

[*234*]

. . . in nearly one-third of the States. Must I have allowed them to finally fail of execution? Are all the laws but one to go unexecuted, and the Government itself go to pieces, lest that one be violated?"

Irrespective of the legal rebuke of the language of the Chief Justice, it was a fact that, when the high distress of the times were considered, the power was used with a considerable restraint. The records have been carefully searched, and they do reveal a number of instances in which civilians were carelessly imprisoned by blundersome or officious subordinate officers. There were many frivolous arrests. But most of the men who were thrown into Old Capitol Prison in Washington, or in any of the other prisons for civil offenders, were arrested and confined with good reason. Either they had been agents of the Confederate Government, or had been spies, furnishers of supplies to the enemy, inciters of desertion, committers of sabotage, or in other ways directly helpful to the enemy. Their confinement was a necessary precaution. Additionally, in most instances they were well treated, and often could secure release upon taking a general oath, with specific obligations.

One of the legal complexities of the suspension of the writ was concerned with the specific identity of the arm of the Government constitutionally empowered to do this. Lincoln acted on the assumption that he had the power. Many of the Union members of the Congress, including several Radical leaders, insisted that it was the legislature, and not the Executive, which could do so. Finally, when the Congress passed an act to suspend, it very carefully employed an ambiguous phrase which failed to indicate the seat of power. It was a deliberate lack of clarity, indicating a compromise between the opposing views of Administration supporters.

Abraham Lincoln had an extraordinarily broad view of the

extent of his authority as President in time of war. He believed that the Constitution restrained the Congress much more than it did the President in time of war; he never hesitated to invoke the doctrine of implied powers, or to use the plenary authority of the joined position of Commander in Chief. It would hardly be too much to say that he acted as though the totality of his implicit powers embraced any act necessary to preserve the Union.

The result was an extralegal rule, the success of which eventually gave it the stamp of the approval of the court of last resort—the consent of the people. It is significant that the Supreme Court took no effective step *during the war* to halt the extraconstitutional policies and actions. Only after the country had returned to peace did the court proclaim that the Constitution controlled the Government in peace and war alike.

There were many conflicts between Federal officers and State courts. In a great many instances the Indemnity Act of March 3, 1863, had to be applied to safeguard agents of the Government from personal civil damages for carrying out orders. This became conspicuously necessary in Border States such as Kentucky, in 1865-66, when returned Confederates tried to make the Union officers pay the price. There was bad blood on both sides throughout Reconstruction. But the Supreme Court avoided important rulings on the terms of this act during the war.

It must be said further, in reviewing the Lincoln policy, that the ordinary civil-court practice was not attuned to the effective control of the war emergency. The courts, Federal as well as State, took a passive rather than an active attitude in treating cases of disloyalty. The elaborate mechanism of Grand Jury, court of the first instance, exceptions to talesmen, cross-examination, judicial charges, appeals, and so on was too cumbersome, and full of pitfalls. The restraint on treason was not effective. Perhaps this was because the chief danger from a traitor is what he *plots* to do—this must be foiled. But a court never sits unless there is a case before it—which means after and not before the fact.

To his harsh policy, Abraham Lincoln brought the saving grace of a humane spirit and an understanding heart. Had he been a fierce, stern prophet, the policy might well have been intolerable in fact as well as extraconstitutional in form. But this man of the people, in all humility, exerted power only when he felt he must.

The Democrats did not let the campaign lack for fireworks. General McClellan's course was dignified enough, and ineffective. George H. Pendleton sought to arouse the Ohio Valley States, and attracted large and enthusiastic crowds. There was no question as to the frantic efforts of the fifth columnists of that region to hold back the Lincoln tide. Such leaders of the political side of the Sons of Liberty as were out of prison, or not facing trial for treason before Military Commissions, made desperate plans to get Copperheads and Butternuts to the polls, or to keep Union men away. The collapse of the Northwest Conspiracy had frightened them at the same time that it made them angrier than ever.

One instance of the bitterness of the anti-Lincoln feeling among the extreme Peace Democrats was furnished by Cyrus McCormick of Illinois. He had gone abroad in 1862, ostensibly to promote the reaper. In April, 1864, in a letter to the editor of the *Chicago Times,* his former paper, he urged: *"Stop the war,* declare an armistice. Call a convention and consider *terms of peace. . . .* May the Democratic party not falter at this stupendous crisis! . . . Another Republican President elected and the country—*the Union is lost."*

He returned a short while later and became a candidate for Congress, upon which the Radical *Chicago Tribune* remarked: "Mr. McCormick has not an instinct that is not in sympathy with the rebellion." Soon after Lincoln's re-election, the rich reaper-manufacturer could not see the impending Confederate fall, and published a letter that negotiations must be opened with the Southern Government. The "last chance" was to negotiate a peace, either on the basis of the Union with the slave States back, their "peculiar institution" safe; or on that of Confederate independence but no slavery in the Loyal States. On December 7, he wrote President Lincoln asking permission to go to Richmond to negotiate with Davis to this end.

Lincoln's own lieutenants were full of wiles. They were determined to beat Seymour in New York State, and went quite close to the borderline of unscrupulousness to do so. The Governor had reluctantly let himself be drafted for another gubernatorial candidacy, and it was obvious that he was in dire danger. The New York soldier vote was one of the resources he expected to use at the ballot box. The Commissioners appointed by the State of New York, and instructed to convey ballots to the soldiers from that State, were arrested by Stanton's order. Practically no New York Democratic soldiers had the chance to vote for their party's nominee. General John A. Dix, who opposed Seymour, won by a margin of but 8,000 votes. The Governor believed that but for Stanton's political chicanery he would have been re-elected.

Doubtless there were other instances of this sort of War Office interference. But it had no importance in the outcome except in such individual State situations as that of New York. The results of the September States pointed the path. Those that balloted in October made the trend unmistakably plain. By November it was a landslide.

General McClellan carried but three States of the Union: New Jersey, Delaware, and Kentucky. Lincoln won in all the rest, and in most of them by quite handsome majorities. He had 212 electoral votes, while McClellan obtained only 21. The people agreed with the Man from Springfield that "it is a bad thing to swap horses while crossing the river." And even more, they joined him in the determination to save the Union, at bayonet point.

Chapter 12

THE ANATOMY OF TREASON

THE year 1864 was marked in the Loyal States by the rapid rise and fearful fall of organized treason. Soon after the New Year, the chief society of subversion adopted a new name, and made detailed plots for armed revolt and Northwest secession. In the early summer, these plans threw General Carrington's secret service into a dither of apprehension. Thanks, however, to counterspy work as lucky as it was clever, the Federal authorities foiled the plots, seized the chief conspirators, and brought the secret orders to an inglorious end.

The leaders of the fifth column were chief contrivers of their own undoing. From the outset they were cursed with a blind faith in the fidelity and the discretion of the men admitted to their inner councils. And for all their talk of desperate deeds, they rarely stood up and fought, but ran at the first clap of thunder.

It was in 1862 that the Knights of the Golden Circle had reached their peak. The next spring and summer, their decline was swift, and the Order of American Knights was brought forward to replace them as the focus for the disaffected. Thus the antiwar forces revived, and became embarrassingly dangerous to the Administration, particularly through their encouragement of desertion and of resistance to the draft.

But in the late fall, a few conspicuous Government moves dislocated the O.A.K.

With 1864, the leaders of subversion made a fresh attempt—and the most dangerous one made during the war period. When the Supreme Council of the Order of American Knights had met in Chicago, in September, 1863, it had adjourned to meet again on Washington's Birthday, 1864, this time in New York. During the interval, the O.A.K. suffered heavy blows. By December it was in retreat, particularly in Missouri.

Phineas C. Wright, the Supreme Grand Commander of the order, living in St. Louis, concentrated on the Missouri problem, and O.A.K. locals mushroomed all over the northern part of the State. The Federal Provost Marshals, however, soon insinuated spies or found informers in the new castles, lodges, or temples. The reports on their meetings and plots were full, and some were fairly accurate. A great trap was prepared for the conspirators, and kept ready to be sprung.

But Phineas Wright seems to have been an incurable romanticist even in matters other than those of rhetorical efflorescence in the rituals of initiation. Either he did not see or did not apprehend the danger hanging over the order. While he felt that the conspiracy was swelling its ranks and achieving discipline, he thought that one of the greatest unfilled needs was a metropolitan newspaper organ to carry fifth-column propaganda over the Loyal States.

The record does not disclose whether or not he negotiated with Storey in Chicago for the use of the *Chicago Times* for this purpose. This paper was promoting the Copperhead cause even more vigorously than it had just before General Burnside closed it down temporarily in June of the preceding year. Perhaps Wright concluded that the Chicago sheet was so assailed for treason that it would be more a liability than an aid. In any event, it was to New York that he turned for an unofficial organ for the Order of the American Knights. He began negotiating with the owners of the *New York Daily News,* to get on its staff as principal editor. Wright expected little difficulty in making this connection—and for the best of reasons, since Fernando Wood and his brother Benjamin were its proprietors.

Fernando Wood was one of the most extraordinary figures, and had one of the strangest careers, of almost anyone of that day and generation. Years later, John Bigelow, the author and statesman, who knew him well, saw Wood's portrait in the corridor of the City Hall. He gazed at it a little while, at the deep-blue eyes and the patrician features as symmetrical as though Praxiteles had chiseled them. Then he remarked: "He was the handsomest man I ever saw, and the most corrupt man that ever sat in the Mayor's chair."

Born in Philadelphia in 1812, of old Quaker stock, young Wood went to New York in the middle 30's, and in 1836 opened a water-front grogshop. With his first year's profits he bought three small ships. In 1849, he used one of these to go to California, where he struck it rich, and came back East a millionaire. Then he entered Manhattan politics. The Society of St. Tammany was then divided into two factions, both of which proclaimed opposition to the Know-Nothings and the other antiforeign groups. Wood professed agreement, but was reported to have taken the Know-Nothings' oath secretly. After his return from California, he formally retired from business, and entered politics. He was beaten in his first campaign for mayor, but in 1853 he won the office, and in 1855 he won again. This second administration has been portrayed as a high point in municipal corruption up to that time. In 1857 he was defeated, and this led him to organize a new society in opposition to the time-honored Tammany. He called it Mozart Hall, and with its backing in 1859 won a third term in the mayor's chair.

To help in his political career, in 1860 Wood and his brother Benjamin bought the *New York Daily News*. Benjamin, indeed, became the paper's publisher, and continued in direct charge until his death in 1900. In the late 50's both Fernando and his brother, a member of Congress, were the owners of lotteries which had been chartered by Southern States. The Woods were bound to the South by other bonds, and openly championed the slavery cause in the *Daily News*. The paper's staff had a generous sprinkling of Southern sympathizers as rabid in their views as were the most pronounced Abolitionists at the other extreme. Editors from the South seldom visited the metropolis without calling at the *Daily News* office.

When secession started in December, 1860, Mayor Wood made a formal proposal to the Municipal Legislature that New York City secede from the Union and institute her own independent government. With the fall of Sumter, the *New York Daily News* attacked the Lincoln policy so vigorously that the Federal Grand Jury returned a presentment to the court against it (as well as other suspicious papers), the charge being that its printed utterances were "calculated to aid and comfort the enemy." The Grand Jury sought the instructions of the court as to whether, in addition to deserving the condemnation and abhorrence of all loyal men, the conduct of this paper was not also subject to indictment. The court thought not, but the Postmaster General at Washington was informed, and for a while prohibited the transmission of the paper through the mails. This ban was removed a little later, but the Woods' paper never failed to attack Lincoln's conduct of the war.

Wright had no trouble in becoming a principal editor. On

January 18, 1864, the Supreme Grand Commander of the Order of American Knights took over the editorial control. That same day he broadcast a circular letter to leading members of the order throughout the Loyal States. It read:

"New York Daily News
"Office 19, City Hall Square
"New York, January 18, 1864
"Dear Sir:

"I have this day connected myself with the Editorial Department of the 'New York News.' You will remember that the News has, from the first, advocated the principles inculcated by Jefferson & his illustrious compeers, and has fearlessly & openly denounced the usurpations of power which have wrested from the citizen his cherished rights, and thrown down the last barrier between him & irresponsible Despotism.

"The News will be *our especial organ,* & will be a medium of the interchange of sentiments & opinions of the friends of peace touching the momentous concerns involved in the existing crisis.

"I entreat your kind offices & influence in extending the circulation of the News throughout the entire field of our labour.

"Yours sincerely,
"(Signed) P. C. WRIGHT"

By the time of Wright's shift to New York, several of the most important leaders of the order had already lost faith in the efficacy of his tactics. The January 18 circular crystallized this dissatisfaction. Certain among them began to look for a change in the top command. When the Washington's Birthday date for reassembly of the Supreme Council neared,

[*244*]

two of the most important members, James A. Barrett of Missouri and Amos Green of Illinois journeyed to New York by way of Windsor, Ontario, where they had had extended prayerful communion with Clement L. Vallandigham.

Up to this time, the Ohio exile seems to have been careful to sidestep actual initiation into either the Knights of the Golden Circle or the Order of the American Knights. He steered clear even of the vestibule degree, so he was enabled to deny membership and at the same time to express sympathy for the public purposes of the secret societies. Now, however, the visitors solicited him not only to join but to accept election at the approaching New York meeting as the Supreme Grand Commander of the order.

Vallandigham gave the bid careful consideration, then agreed to accept. But he insisted on certain changes. The order must have a new name; the ritual must be rewritten—the schoolboy mummery Wright had delighted in must be dropped; and a new clause must be added to the oath, pledging the initiate to the Kentucky-Virginia resolutions of 1798.

The Supreme Council assembled in New York February 22. A good representation was on hand, among them H. H. Dodd of Indiana; Doctor Massey of Ohio; James A. McMaster of New York; Amos Green of Illinois, and James A. Barrett of Missouri, along with Supreme Grand Commander Wright. For a month the latter had been turning the *New York Daily News* into a thoroughgoing fifth-column sheet. The meeting was elated at the word from Windsor, and promptly elected Vallandigham to Wright's post.

The delegates agreed readily to the changes the new head had suggested. A number of them felt that the conception of "American Knights" was antidemocratic. For a new name, they selected Order of the Sons of Liberty. This name, freighted with the memory of the patriots of New York City in the years she was under British bayonets during the American Revolution, was expected to give new zeal to the defenders of human freedom.

Dr. Massey headed a committee which brought in a new constitution and bylaws. These pruned a few of the ritual's verbal flowers, dropped one of O.A.K.'s five degrees, and adopted new signs and grips. Under its new setup, the subversive society created a Supreme Council for over-all control. The head officer was the Supreme Commander, and each State had a State Grand Commander, subject to a State Grand Council. The county was commanded by a Grand Seignior.

The ritual called for four degrees: the vestibule, the first degree, the degree of the first conclave, and the degree of the second conclave.

Most of the examination, instruction, and responses of the ceremony were couched in the well-known vocabulary of Jefferson's epoch. Most of the thousands who joined the order never got beyond the vestibule. In getting into this outer door, they were given no "secrets" and put under no "oaths" calculated to make them regard the order as anything more than a Democratic club. The oath of the vestibule was innocent enough except for one section, in which the neophyte must declare:

"I do further promise that I will, at all times, if need be, take up arms in the cause of the oppressed—*in my country first of all*—against any Monarch, Prince, Potentate, Power or Government usurper, which may be found in arms, and waging war against a people or peoples, who are endeavoring to establish, or have inaugurated, a Government for themselves of their own free choice, in accordance with, and founded upon, *the eternal principles of Truth,* which I . . . now in this presence do swear to maintain inviolate, and defend with my life. This I do promise, without reservation or evasion of mind; without regard to the invading or coercive power, whether it shall arise within or come from without!"

Having been admitted to the vestibule, if he wished to go further the neophyte would be brought next within the Inner Temple for the first degree. In this ceremony, he listened to a long and labored exposition of strict constructionist doctrine, the essence of which was that "the Federal Government can exercise only delegated powers; hence if those who shall have been chosen to administer that Government shall assume to exercise power or authority not delegated, they shall be regarded and dealt with as usurpers. . . . It is the inherent right and imperative duty of the people to resist such officials, and if need be, expel them by force of arms. Such resistance is not revolution, but is solely the assertion of right."

Step by step the obligations became more precise and more treasonable. The third degree, called that of the first conclave, contained Vallandigham's personal contribution to the ritual: the epitome of the Kentucky-Virginia Resolves of 1798. The new chief quoted Jefferson for his purpose, and was pleased with the Monticello mask for revolt. The final degree did not increase the charges upon the candidate; he merely pledged to defend the principles of the Sons of Liberty as already outlined.

These completed the normal or ordinary degrees, those put in print. There were others, carried only in memory, the degrees of the Grand Council of each State and those of the Supreme Council over the whole order. The texts of these sublimations of the ritual of revolution exist only in report. Spies said they were infamous in their treason; those charged with conspiracy gave them quite an innocent, angelic garb.

The new order, however, continued the password of the American Knights: "Calhoun" spelled backward in the three syllables "Nu-oh-lac." This, along with the initials S.L., and the sentence "Give me liberty or give me death," were the passwords to the vestibule.

The most important departure, however, was the elaborate provision for a Military Department of the new order. Theretofore the secret groups had sought to drill their members, and to arm and munition them. But the same leaders who handled the ritual and the political efforts had had charge of the military phases. Now this was changed, and there was a separation between the control of the two branches. This grew out of the divided view of the chiefs over the proper path to the success they sought.

One group insisted that victory would be won at the ballot box: Therefore the order must concentrate on the presidential campaign, to elect a new President who would negotiate peace with the Confederacy. Vallandigham himself was a conspicuous example of this attitude. It could succeed only if the Democrats would nominate a peace man for the Presidency. Doubtless the Ohio leader's willingness to take the headship of the order arose in large part from his desire to use its members in getting control of the party's national convention, to write a peace platform and name a peace candidate—to do which, the War Democrats must be routed, which could be done only after a sharp intraparty fight.

The political-minded leaders had ranged against them a number of firebrands who thought these hopes quite foolish, and preferred an actual armed revolt. The outcome was that the order was split into the two sections; the actual operating structure within each State was left to the leaders there. The Military Department, however, was strictly secret.

Indiana afforded a good illustration of the new technique. There the political head was Dodd of Indianapolis. Together with his council, he established an elaborate apparatus of county parent temples, each with many community castles within them. In all these, the new ceremonials were carefully installed, and the political pot was watched day and night. So the Sons of Liberty held political conclaves all over the State, and made great plans to carry the election.

The Military Department was a different story. Its commanding general, our old friend Dr. Bowles of French Lick Springs, had supreme command of all military matters. His rank was major general and his word was law. He divided Indiana into four Military Districts, each under a major general reporting direct to Bowles. Each district was subdivided into divisions, roughly one to each congressional district, and each was supposed to raise and train a division of troops for the Sons of Liberty. Arms and ammunition would be procured, the men would drill, learn the manual of arms, march discipline, and so on, and be ready to fight to defend their constitutional rights. Members of this branch need not attend the oratorical conclaves, for which Bowles had a thoroughgoing contempt. And from the outset, plans were made to attack the prison camps, release the Confederates, arm and equip them, and redress the balance for the failing Confederacy by a Northwest secession.

Some other States had a different table of organization. Illinois divided the State on a congressional district basis, with a brigadier general over each. Missouri declined to shift from O.A.K. to Sons of Liberty. Kentucky set up a new structure, with no dual branches.

The central fact of the whole matter, however, was the new drive against the effective prosecution of the war. As soon as the leaders of the new Sons of Liberty got home from the New York meeting, the fires began to burn.

So much for the anatomy of secession's fifth column in the North at the beginning of this critical year of the war. Now it is needful to examine the counterespionage of the Lincoln Administration. By 1864, its pattern was close to final form. The chief command was in Washington, with Stanton the top man. He was under enormous pressures in the ordinary administrative concerns of a wartime Secretary of War. In addition, he could not keep himself from constant dabbling with Radical politics; intrigues with the Joint Committee on the Conduct of the War; favoring pets with promotions, and punishing enemies by freezing them in low rank or poor assignments. A veritable bundle of nerves and irritations, his energy kept him at it day and night. The operations of the Secret Service and its campaign organizations fascinated him; he insisted on personally dispensing the Secretary's secret fund, and was never too busy to consider this hidden world of stealth, double-dealing, corruption, and betrayal.

Equally Radical, equally unscrupulous, and more self-possessed, Joseph Holt had a leading hand in the Federal spy work. His title of Judge Advocate General, his position as chief of the Bureau of Military Justice—a title tipped with unconscious irony when attached to his name—put him right at the center of the web. Holt had courage, boldness, and imagination, and for him the end generally justified the means.

Provost Marshal General Fry had importance in this picture, though not as much as his position justified. Fry had knowledge without wisdom. He had a habit of excusing his mistakes rather than learning from them. This was illustrated by the complaints of draft procedures, uncorrected even after the

New York riots, and gave the measure of the man. His logic was good, his purpose patriotic, his stature small.

His subordinates through the country, however, became one of the most effective secret-service groups the Administration had. This grew out of the nature of the case. These men on the spot had run into trouble from early 1862. At first it was the Copperhead campaign for desertions. When the draft machinery got into motion, resistance to it, as we have seen, was immediate and often violent.

Much of the desertion was spontaneous, the homesick boy yielding to the impulse of the moment. Much of the draft-dodging and resistance to the draft was similarly individual action. It was clear, however, that in both a large part of the trouble had been induced and organized by the Copperheads. The Provost Marshals knew this; they had to identify the sources, discover the conspiracies, and take measures in advance to foil the plots and seize the plotters. This led them to insinuate spies into the meetings of the conspirators, buy informers, and otherwise keep up with the developing dangers. Holt and Fry supported these activities, and Stanton doled out his secret funds.

Lafayette C. Baker continued to exhibit pompous zeal. The official head of the United States Secret Service had shriveled in importance. He still held forth at Washington, filled Old Capitol Prison with his prizes, and made great show of ubiquitous activity. And he was Target Number One for pretty rebel spies in skirts.

But Washington was not the setting for the great spy stories of 1864. These developed in the Ohio Valley States.

It did not take the Federal agents long to ferret out the fact Vallandigham had moved from dissent to treason, and had become the actual leader of a conspiracy for a revolt. They got several inside stories of the New York meeting and the secret conferences preceding and following it. On March 25, an Illinois informer named David Trumbull made affidavit that the exile had determined that he would return to Ohio at an agreed time, and that should the Union authorities arrest him, the Sons of Liberty would rise at once. The informer alleged that Vallandigham claimed that at least 380,000 men would flock to the revolutionary standard, and that arms for them would be purchased by money coming from New York and Canadian sources. Trumbull reported also that the new editor of the *New York Daily News* "is the agent of the South in the whole matter. Longstreet's forces are expected to raid across the Ohio in the spring." The Confederates had already advanced $50,000 in gold to Vallandigham, according to Trumbull's report.

In any event, no sooner had the delegates to the Supreme Council got back from the New York meeting than they set feverishly to work shifting the old organization over to its new title, ritual, and setup. They used a simple transfer technique. O.A.K. members needed no new initiation; the old State officers carried over; county temples received instructions about the new ritual. In Indiana it was done through circulars, in Illinois by traveling agents or "Grand Missionaries."

States' Rights bobbed up in Missouri. Now that the O.A.K. founder had moved to New York, the heads of the order took charge of affairs in that State. Charles L. Hunt, the Grand Commander, and his aides resented the changes made at the New York meeting and refused to put them into the Missouri lodges. The result was that the new name was never adopted there. The old order co-operated actively, however, in the program of action now under way west of the mountains.

The Missouri organization spread rapidly over central and northern Missouri; nearly every St. Louis ward set up a castle; Hannibal, Palmyra, Renick, St. Joseph, and other cities in the north of the State organized large temples, and a belt of counties in the center fell in line. Arms and ammunition were bought in St. Louis and shipped to the outside lodges. Estimates of the total membership began at 10,000 and ran as high as 60,000.

Illinois, however, promptly accepted the change in orders. From the time the O.A.K. had started there, in June, 1863, it had been much more political than was the case in Missouri. The Illinois American Knights opposed the Lincoln Administration politically, but were reluctant to plot armed resistance.

True enough, many lodges drilled, and carried arms; but most of them believed these military acts would merely enable them to safeguard their rights at the ballot box against the Loyal Legion or other enemies. Their quick growth was in central Illinois, and in "Egypt" Federal spies reported a membership of 80,000, about eight times larger than it really was. The O.A.K. exposures and trials in Missouri and Indiana in the summer of 1863 quieted the activities of the order in Illinois. Several leaders withdrew. Those who held on welcomed the change of name, and they started a vigorous drive for new lodges and new members. They built up an effective organization in Chicago, with headquarters in the McCormick Building, and the *Times* for their organ. By August they claimed 5,000 members in that city, and about 15,000 more out in the State.

But from the start of the new secret conspiracy, their membership contained many betrayers. Late in April, one of the employees of the *Chicago Times* tried to find a proper channel by which he could betray the looming Northwest Conspiracy

[*253*]

to the Federal Government. This was J. L. Rock, one of the editors, who wrote a letter to Schuyler Colfax, Radical Congressman from Indiana, signing the fictitious and difficult-to-identify name of Sam Jones. He informed Colfax that "a matter of vital importance to this Government" had come up, disclosed the talk of the conspiracy, and then added:

"What I want to know is, what course the authorities will pursue and what protection will they render the person who will give them names, number of men, number of arms in hand, number of arms in deposit, where deposited, and the place of the meetings of the general encampments, etc. I mean in short to lay the whole organization in this State, Indiana, and Ohio fully open to the friends of suppression." The would-be informer asked if he could come personally to Washington as an informer and be protected, or would he be arrested?

Colfax thought Carrington had enough spies of his own and knew enough of the story not to bother with the double traitor on the *Times,* and did not answer. After the collapse of the November conspiracy, Rock, alias Jones, wrote a frantic letter to a Washington friend, asking help to escape arrest for his part in the Camp Douglas plot. In this he cited his anonymous letter of April 29.

The Ohio Copperheads responded much more slowly. To be sure, that State was the home of the new Supreme Grand Commander, and Vallandigham's official biographer (his brother) declared that lodges sprang up in nearly every Ohio county. Holt at Washington, in a report written with an eye to the election, claimed that there were 80,000 Ohio members. This was thunder in the index. There is no evidence that more than a few thousand ever joined.

Indiana was a very different story. Just before the gathering in New York, forty Indiana counties were organized and half

"D"

New York Daily News
Office 19 City Hall Square
New York January 18. 1864

Dear Sir,

I have this day connected myself with the Editorial Department of the "New York News." You will remember that the News has, from the first advocated the principles inculcated by Jefferson & his illustrious compeers, and has fearlessly & openly denounced the usurpations of power which have wrested from the citizen his cherished rights and thrown down the last barrier between him & irresponsible despotism.

The News will be our especial Organ & will be a medium for the interchange of sentiments & opinions of the friends of peace touching the momentous concerns involved in the existing crisis.

I entreat your kind offices & influence in extending the circulation of the News, throughout the entire field of our labour.

Yours Sincerely,
P. C. Slight

FROM ONE COPPERHEAD TO ANOTHER

HENRY BEEBEE CARRINGTON

Adjutant General of Indiana and bitter foe of Copperheads

that number more were in process. The shift-over was prompt
and effective. In June, the Grand Secretary reported a membership of 15,000, a fifth more than it had four months earlier.

These new moves were straightway reported to Washington,
generally magnified in the telling. The Missouri picture
seemed so ominous that a new Provost Marshal was sent out
there. This was Colonel John P. Sanderson, who immediately
started an investigation. Soon his secret agents insinuated
themselves into the castles in St. Louis and out in the State,
sending in copious and often quite fanciful reports. Sanderson
seems to have taken these at face value, for a little later he
reported to General Rosecrans, the commander of the Department of the Missouri, that nearly every county was corroded
with treason.

Rosecrans' Provost Marshal also sent his spies into Illinois,
Indiana, Ohio, and Kentucky, and their reports led him to
term the Order of the Sons of Liberty "most dangerous to the
public peace and welfare of the Government."

General Carrington, commander of the District of Indiana,
likewise had hints that dirty work was afoot, particularly in
Kentucky. One of his spies reported on a trip through the
southern part of that State, where Confederate guerrillas had
captured him and kept him two days. Their leader said it was
the Confederate intention "to put into the border counties of
Indiana, 2,500 to 3,000 men, under the pretense of hunting
work as refugees; and if they could not control the election
in one way, they would do it in another way, as all of them
would be arrested." A main purpose would be, if possible, to
"bring about a collision between the Civil and the Military
authority" in Indiana. Likewise, "the time was not far off
when the men of the Northwest would withdraw from the New

[255]

England States, and a greater rebellion than that now on hand would be the result."

On April 1, Carrington outlined to his Department Commander the general picture of what the fifth columnists had planned to do. He boasted that "a thorough system of espionage gave me possession of their entire machinery, resulting in the arrest, conviction and punishment through United States Courts of 150 persons, thus demoralizing and for the time being disbanding the organization." The Indiana leaders of the order claimed 100,000 members. An informer among them said that already they had received from New York and elsewhere 6,000 muskets, 60,000 revolvers, and other military arms.

The purposes of the conspirators, according to Carrington's piecing together of reports from spies, were:

1. To prevent a four-year succession of the war party.
2. To force a recognition of the Southern Confederacy's freedom, after which it would be bound to the North by an offensive and defensive league in respect to foreign Powers.
3. To resist all military process and to prevent the reelection of the present Government by fraud at the ballot box, and if necessary by force.

Carrington determined to be forehanded in meeting these menaces. To do this, he needed some new secret agents in Kentucky. Some of those already there were suspected by the order and might disappear any day. Therefore he wrote Captain S. E. Jones, the Provost Marshal in charge of Kentucky, and ordered him to pick a trusty man to put inside the order in that State. In addition, he suggested that the best mode of approach was the indirect one. Let Jones's man first get close to Dr. Bowles, the commander of the Military Department of the Sons of Liberty in Indiana.

The Captain received these instructions on May 5, and picked his man at once. This was one of his own clerks, who was mustered out of the army that same day and started his secret-service job. By the end of the month, this agent was at the very heart of the Kentucky Council. By late August, he had dealt the death blow to the Order of the Sons of Liberty.

Chapter 13

STIDGER, THE SPY COMPLETE

CARRINGTON'S new secret agent needs identification. His name was Felix Grundy Stidger, his age a little under thirty, his birthplace Bardstown, Kentucky. After boyhood there, he had farmed a few years, then had gone with his family to Mattoon in southern Illinois. There he clerked a while in a dry-goods store, then took up the carpenter's trade, and worked at it until the war. Stidger was of good presence, had a wide acquaintance over rural Kentucky, and was fond of both money and intrigue.

In the fall of 1861, young Stidger drifted back to Kentucky, soon enlisting in an infantry regiment. For several months he was with Buell's army, serving as a soldier clerk in the Adjutant General's office of the Fourteenth Corps. Then he was invalided back to the rear, and on recovery was attached to the headquarters of the District of Kentucky. Here he clerked for Captain Jones.

His work with the Provost Marshal had familiarized him with the general background of the secret orders in the State. On May 5, Jones received Carrington's appeal for help about Dr. Bowles and the Indiana-Kentucky plot, and sold Stidger on the job. That night the latter absorbed more background. He agreed to report by letter rather than in person. He also got a little money for expenses, and the next day was on his way.

The rest of the story of his spying is largely autobiographical, for most of its detail comes either from the reports Stidger penned to his superiors, or the testimony he gave in the Indiana treason trials. The reader should keep in mind the subjective nature of this first-person evidence and estimate its reliability with this in view.

It should be remarked that the officers to whom he reported —Captain Jones; then a new post commander, Lieutenant Colonel Thomas Fairleigh, also in Louisville; and General Carrington in Indianapolis—seem to have regarded the first few letters with some skepticism, deeming their revelations the result of either romantic writing or blind luck. And it must be admitted that, in general, secret-service chiefs have good reason to look on spy reports as low-grade ore. But the red-ink endorsements the officers made, from Report No. 1 to the end, indicated that they turned from doubt to belief that he had plumbed treason to the depths.

At the outset, Stidger signed his own name to the letters, and sent them to his superior by ordinary post. But he soon saw his personal danger; he began disguising his hand and signing "J. J. Eustis," a fictitious name, and sending the reports to secret letter boxes.

The letters themselves make exciting reading, particularly in the manuscript. Stidger's story has been in print for three-quarters of a century, but there is something about the actual letter and its handwriting, interlineations, and mistakes of haste that stimulates the mind's re-creation of the living scene, and gives flesh and blood to the wraiths of history.

A War Department record, on deposit at the National Archives in Washington, the Stidger reports are done up in a small bundle tied with faded tape. But the letters have not faded, nor has the story they tell.

Stidger's first task was to get into the good graces of Dr. Bowles, the military commander of the order in Indiana. His Report No. 1 to Captain Jones, written May 13, told how he had done the job. Leaving Louisville May 6, he had taken train to Salem, Indiana, then to Paoli, where he met a friendly chap who helped him no end. This was a Mr. Horace Heffren, who boasted of the neighborhood's anti-war feeling. He said he had been a lieutenant colonel of an Indiana regiment for nineteen months, but had resigned after the Emancipation Proclamation; now he was a high figure in O.S.L. Heffren, who mistook Stidger for an expected commissioner or courier from the South, said Indiana would furnish 10,000 armed men if needed. Then he sent Stidger on to French Lick Springs.

The spy, who saw General Bowles the next Sunday, reported that it could be seen at a glance that Bowles was a plotter. "He has one of the worst countenances I near ever saw a man have, he cannot look anyone in the face one minute." He had cunning and nerve, but not courage.

The next day Stidger called again. Bowles asked if he knew of the Democratic organization being formed in Kentucky. Stidger said he had taken the vestibule degree, but Bowles did not put the usual identifying tests. Rather, he seemed satisfied, and revealed his hidden plans.

As military head, Bowles was anxious to make Kentucky the battle ground. He spoke of the "perfect understanding with the Confederate forces" of the order and said that it would work in conjunction with them. He estimated they could gather 60,000 soldiers of the order in Indiana, the chief difficulty being getting arms for them. As commanding general, he received reports each week from all over Indiana of the condition of the military branch of the order. He described operating details; for example, most of their correspondence was sent by private courier. If any must go by post, there was a cipher which could be used, a figure resembling the Greek letter theta, which told the initiate to understand the item in question in precisely the reverse of its surface meaning.

Then Bowles revealed a major division among the leaders. The politicians wanted them to wait for the election before taking any armed action. The war leaders had no faith in the ballot box and wanted to show the standard of revolt as soon as possible. The Indiana State Council would meet in two weeks; he invited his new friend to sit in on its sessions.

Stidger's Letter No. 2 told of his second trip to Indiana, beginning May 24. He saw Heffren again, who said Indiana's organization was about complete; they could call out up to 80,000 men. Bowles was not at French Lick, didn't get there until the twenty-eighth. When the Doctor did arrive, Stidger found him in a bad frame of mind.

The military chief sounded off that he was "very much opposed to these anti-Administration conventions to send delegates to the Chicago [Democratic National] Convention; he says that Mr. Lincoln is bound to be elected; and is opposed to wasting time in that way; but desires the completion of the organization and coöperation with the South, and for the work to begin.

"He informs me that they have two regular lines of communication with the South, but did not tell me where they are located. They, as yet, have no regular communication with Ohio, but some of the leaders for Indiana, Illinois, Missouri and Kentucky, in conference at Indianapolis last week, ap-

[*261*]

pointed a Commissioner to start for Ohio yesterday and open up communication with that State."

The major generals at this meeting, Bowles went on, had changed the military program. Bennett of Missouri now pledged 30,000 men and Illinois could be looked to for 50,000, both of these contingents for use west of the Mississippi River, where they would be a left wing for Price's army.

And there was new word from Richmond: "Davis agrees to send Buckner, or Breckinridge, or even Longstreet, if they ask, into Kentucky. . . . They are very anxious about the organization in Kentucky, and Bowles says that if they get ready, he thinks that the work will commence in sixty days."

Bowles wanted Stidger to come along to a further session at Indianapolis. He did not ask in vain. Among the things the leaders discussed there was the problem of arms and equipment for the planned rising. They talked of a recent essay at the sabotage of a river steamboat at Louisville, in which Greek fire had been used. It had been made of phosphorus and brimstone and wasn't good enough. So Bowles had got a Dutch chemist to perfect it. The new stuff was demonstrated at Indianapolis, and seemed just what the Doctor ordered. "It is a liquid," Stidger reported, "and can be carried in a vial." The Confederates had proposed that they would pay the order 10 per cent of the value of all United States Government property destroyed by these or other means of sabotage. They would use Northern newspaper estimates of damage as their measuring rod for payment. .

Then, and in the immediate issue even more important, Bowles instructed Stidger to make the acquaintance of Judge Joshua F. Bullitt, the head of the Kentucky Council of the order, as soon as possible.

Stidger made quick use of this new opening. Returning to

Louisville, he scraped acquaintance with Judge Bullitt, and then really took the vestibule degree. The Judge liked him. He needed a handy man for office work in connection with organizing the State, and tried out the young man Bowles had sent. Stidger worked hard, got the paperwork done, seemed discreet and decent. Nearly every day he was given new and more confidential tasks.

During this introductory period, the secret agent called clandestinely on Jones to warn him of a Confederate spy then in Louisville, one Curran, but soon sent a note urging that the arrest not be made in that city: "But send a man that may make his acquaintance, and be able to identify him where he stops, and then have him arrested, in that way taking off all blame or suspicion of the authorities or anyone about the city. Someone may have seen me visit you, though I think not."

To this, Stidger added that Bullitt had remarked to him that evening that "he was willing to spend the last damned dollar he had in this organization, for he hoped to soon be able to steal a good living from the damned sons of bitches, meaning the Union party."

The next day there was an important development, of which Stidger wrote Jones in tones of mingled joy and fear:

"Captain, I am to be Secretary of the Grand Council of this State. You shall know everything, but I ask of you to let as few as possible, or no one, know where you get your information. So have no one arrested on my reports, if you can avoid it. Set other men on the track of the men whose names I give you, and let them give the evidence, if time will admit of it. Assassination awaits me on the least suspicion.

"I do not feel safe in even any longer reporting to you through the Post Office. I know of no one here I can trust to go to you regularly for me. I would suggest that you select some reliable man that I could find at any time to send to you. . . . My only safety now is in entire secrecy." And he left the letter unsigned.

Nor was this an idle fear. His report continued: "In caucus it is decided that we cannot organize a Grand Council for the State until Mr. Coffin is killed. He is a detective for General Carrington. I go tomorrow to Dr. Bowles to have the work carried into execution, of hunting him up and having him killed. I go from there to Indianapolis to H. H. Dodd on the same business. Can you not try and get word to Mr. Coffin in some way? . . . To hear the way those men talk about murdering Coffin is sufficient to make me guarded."

Other matters of consequence came up at the meeting. B. B. Piper of Springfield, Illinois, the Grand Missionary of the order and a member of its Supreme Council, had been present. He revealed that Vallandigham had made up his mind to return to the United States, come what may, between June 20 and the end of the month. Robert Holloway, then in Springfield, was acting for the Supreme Commander until his exile ended. In regard to the over-all program of the order, "everything is now awaiting the organization in Kentucky. . . . They want to get ready for action while the Federal forces are out of Kentucky, at the front. . . . They consider Kentucky now fully ripe." In Piper's view, "the force will be in the field before August 1." They planned soon to start a man to Richmond, to confer with Jefferson Davis.

Stidger felt it most important that the Kentucky schemes be thwarted. "Pardon the suggestion," he wrote, "but you must delay the organization in this State as much as possible, and in time I will get you the names of all the officers and leaders in this State and elsewhere as much as possible, and before the time of their rising they must be arrested, and by that it may be delayed or broken up. . . . I will receive any note left at J. Winter & Co., corner Third & Market before 7 p.m."

He left soon thereafter for Indiana, taking with him a note Judge Bullitt had written, addressed to H. H. Dodd. "My friend, Mr. F. G. Stidger," it recited, "goes to Indianapolis on business in which I think it probable that you can aid him. He is entirely reliable and any aid you can give him will confer a favor on your friend, J. F. Bullitt."

Stidger's report on the Indiana trip was dated June 17. He had left Louisville four days earlier, had met Bowles at the Palmer House in Indianapolis. The Doctor asked him some questions about Kentucky, and if the leaders there had any expectation of a visit from General Morgan. Then he related the contents of the letter received from his friend Dickerson, just back in Baltimore from a trip to Richmond. Morgan was not in Kentucky, had not been there recently, "he is in Virginia, and there was only a small force in Kentucky to get horses to mount the dismounted part of Morgan's command, destroy railroads, etc."

Then Bowles got hold of J. J. Bingham, the proprietor of the *Indiana Sentinel*. Stidger told them both of the Kentucky Council's determination about Coffin. The Indiana man "claimed to have uncontradicted evidence of his business. Bingham says that General Carrington told Mr. Dodd himself that Coffin was in Government employment. . . . Their decided conclusion was that he should be made away with."

The Grand Council of Indiana met that same morning, but discussed subjects of a little more general nature. Most Excellent Grand Commander Dodd said they had gathered to pass on "setting up what the politics was, if they would have any at all; to discuss the subject of education and not patronize any teachers of other than Democratic principles." Resolutions to this end were unanimously carried. Then again, "to consider the propriety of at once forming a military organization, and as to the time of action, if it was not near at hand."

Delegates from over the State reported the names of the officers of their county organizations, and the probable strength. Representatives were there from twenty-seven counties; thirty more were organized, and another seven partially so. Only thirty-five were unorganized, but all of these had old units of the Knights of the Golden Circle. The reports were very imperfect. The Committee on Military Organization "reported in favor of an immediate military organizing and arming and equipping." They would pay for this by putting a tax on the members. Bowles said he had a man who would furnish the arms.

After the meeting Stidger learned something that alarmed him. The Indiana Council "have men employed as spies. They do not belong to their order, so they have no chance of working both ways." He added a little chitchat about methods: "The book they use for their cipher in Indiana is the address of the M.E.G.C. [Most Excellent Grand Commander] February 16 and 17, who was Mr. Dodd. The present M.E.G.C., Ristine, Auditor of the State, is also a member of the Order, and nearly all the men in his employ. . . . In dispatches or correspondence, 'Aunt Lucy' is the Confederacy." The State organization was $700 in debt. And Dr. Gatling, the inventor of the famous gun, was a member of the order. Nothing that came to Stidger's ears was omitted from his reports.

The council had its mind fixed on Chicago, to some extent because the Democratic National Convention was scheduled for July 4, and because the Supreme Council of the Order, as we have noted, had been called to meet in the same city July 1. The Indiana Council elected delegates to the conclave.

Then it discussed the Coffin matter, and agreed he should be put out of the way. Heffren volunteered to find the spy, pick a quarrel with him, and shoot him down.

The meeting broke up June 15, but Stidger stayed over until the next morning, ostensibly to make better rail connections. Actually he had arranged for a personal interview with General Carrington, his chief, which took place that night. While the spy did not describe it in his report to Jones, the General wrote his own superior about it. This was Major General Heintzelman, who had moved Department headquarters from Cincinnati to Columbus, and was handling things much more smoothly than his predecessor, General Burnside, had done.

Carrington related that Stidger, whom he did not name but identified as one of the high officials of the order in Kentucky, "left this city this morning with the cipher, seal and private books required for use there. He is charged with its dissemination, but being in my confidence, had one of his own agents, who was sent to Henderson, arrested. He came here with an order to 'have put out of the way' (assassinated) Detective Coffin, who was found out through his Kentucky friends. . . . Judge Bullitt furnished money for the trip."

Incidentally, Carrington used this report as an excuse to renew his plea for more money for his counterespionage setup. He had been operating almost on a pauper's oath, but felt that $10,000, or even $5,000, spent in this work would be of great utility.

Heintzelman sent his letter on to General Halleck, who turned it over to Secretary Stanton, and four months later the latter grudgingly sent Carrington's successor $5,000 from his secret fund.

Soon his associates in the order were to get quite suspicious about this Grand Secretary whom Bullitt had attested "entirely reliable." In his report of June 21, before disclosing the events of another Indiana trip—these were now to be almost weekly until the military closed in on the conspirators—he made this statement:

"Some suspicion has been cast upon me here by someone, but I was gallantly defended by Judge Bullitt. I have at present thrown it [the suspicion] off on the indiscretion of Dr. Bowles . . . but I am compelled to still insist on Mr. Coffin being sent to some other place to operate."

The Radical Republicans in Indiana, in the heat of the State political campaign, were demanding propaganda, attacks on the Copperheads, and every other sort of verbal ammunition with which to slaughter their hated rivals. Both Governor Morton, who used vilification as a prime weapon in his campaigns, and General Carrington were anxious to employ some of the Stidger disclosures in the party press. Without Stidger's knowledge, Carrington supplied the *Indiana Journal,* the Radical organ, with a highly doctored version, which caused a sensation, and some scurrying for cover by the men accused. It gave Stidger concern too, for he wrote he did not think the paper "ought to be furnished any more information in regard to this Order and Vallandigham, but let it go ahead with what it has, and comment all it can."

Every time Stidger visited Indianapolis, he saw Carrington on the side. Already the two had cooked up the general plans for a final pounce. The spy wrote his chief June 23, that "when I saw you in Indianapolis you mentioned something about your taking possession of the building where the books of the Council are kept. If such a step is not absolutely necessary before the first of September, the propriety of putting it off until about that time is plain." This was because the last quarterly reports of the county temples had been made as of

May 1. The next would be asked for the first of August. Stidger himself would get behind the job of forcing the county scribes to send in the lists. Through delaying the date of seizure, the net could catch nearly all.

Chiefs of the order in Indiana had wanted Stidger to go up to the Supreme Council meeting in Chicago, but he thought the tasks in Kentucky so important that he had better not attempt it.

A few days later he asked Captain Jones to make out an order of arrest for one Captain Bocking. This grew out of a recent experiment with Greek fire, which the captain-chemist had about perfected for the military chiefs of the order. It burned well, and Bocking "uses it in an explosive shell, or in what he terms hand grenades. He also makes a machine running something like a clock, which can be set to strike off a cap or any explosive at any length of time. . . . Those hand grenades are to be about three inches across and weigh about two and three quarter pounds. They are used in close quarters, and thrown by hand. This is the article mentioned at Indianapolis for self-protection against the enemy."

Dr. Bowles had been at the experiment, and had been much taken by the inventor's new device. The Confederate spy Curran had been there too, and he was leaving the next day with samples, to carry them through the lines to the Southern ordnance experts, for their possible manufacture. So Stidger wanted Curran nabbed along with Bocking, and "Bowles too, if you wish." But no action was taken then.

The tension increased, until Stidger thought the crisis was right at hand. Kentucky's Grand Council met on June 27, with Grand Missionary Piper present again. Stidger discovered that Piper had come there with secret and confidential orders for Bullitt from Vallandigham, and would give them to no one else. Bullitt was away, so Carrington's spy was on tenter-hooks at his inability to get all the facts. The best he was able to do was to worm out of the unsuspecting Piper the name of a Chicago lawyer, D. W. Mitchell, who was general disbursing agent for Vallandigham, and could be addressed at Box 2925 at Chicago. But he felt sure that "they are preparing for action."

There were delays and upsets, and on July 11 Stidger reported that Piper now put the date at either August 3 or August 15. Likewise he had extracted the fact that Dr. Bowles would be ordered to take his Indiana men across Illinois, to attack the prison at Rock Island, free the Confederates, seize the arms and munitions, and otherwise join in the general revolt. There was a hint, too, that Captain Tom Hines and other Confederate plotters in Canada were about ready to launch another attack on Johnson's Island. The general atmosphere was as tense as could be. "The leaders are so anxious that I would not be surprised at hostilities commencing in this State before the third of August."

With July, Stidger got a new subchief in Louisville—Lieutenant Colonel Thomas Fairleigh, who had become post commander. On the third of the month he sent Farleigh "an imperfect list" of the members of the order in the State, and announced his purpose to call upon each separate temple in Kentucky to report to him "by name all the prominent members of the county, also the number and kind of arms and amount of ammunition of every form."

The next day Stidger was at Bardstown, held an initiation ceremony there, and collected the initiation fees for his expenses. It appears that he was not getting money from Uncle Sam these days, but that Bullitt had promised him $40 a month for his work as Grand Secretary, together with any initiation

TWO ANTI-COPPERHEAD CARTOONS

Showing that Loyal cartoonists knew how to strike back

THE COPPERHEAD PARTY.—IN FAVOR OF A VIGOROUS PROSECUTION OF PEACE

The caption reads: THE COPPERHEAD PARTY—in favor of
A VIGOROUS PROSECUTION OF PEACE

HEADS OF THE DEMOCRACY.

*This time Messrs. Currier and Ives contributed a pro-Administration
print (1864)*

LIEUTENANT
COLONEL HENRY F.
BURNETT

*He presided at the treason
trials in Indianapolis*

MAJOR GENERAL
SAMUEL P.
HEINTZELMAN

*Commander of the Mili-
tary Department of the
Ohio*

fees he might pick up. Nor did he prove reluctant in taking them.

On his return to Louisville, he ran into Piper once more, who had just come in from Springfield with further orders from Vallandigham. The date of the rising was still confidential, and perhaps unfixed. But at a meeting the previous week the Illinois Grand Council had adopted resolutions that if Kentucky rose, the Illinois group would see to it that no bands of the Loyal Legion of that State would cross the river to help suppress the insurrection. Likewise Captain Hines of the Confederate Army had joined Vallandigham's personal staff and was in Canada awaiting orders.

Another State Council was summoned for Louisville, July 16, but so few members attended that the formal meeting was called off. Bullitt, just back from Indianapolis, related that the purpose of his visit had been to put the point-blank question to the Indiana leaders: If any Kentucky leaders were arrested, would the Indiana branch of the order try to rescue them?

The answer returned was that such a thing was impossible. So Bullitt "has no hope for any assistance from anywhere but Jeff Davis for Kentucky. He thinks Illinois may help Missouri. He goes to Chicago to attend a meeting on July 20, and when he returns he proposes conferring with the South, and setting a day for action for Kentucky on her own hook. Vallandigham will not attend in Chicago. He is afraid. The time of uprising appears to have been set by Barrett, on the enthusiasm of Illinois. It now appears to amount to nothing."

The uncertainty of the date for the uprising continued one of Stidger's deep concerns. Soon it had been pushed still further off, to August 17. He possessed his soul with what patience he could, and nearly every day sent a further list of members of the order, and new people to arrest.

But on July 28 we find him striking still another note in his official correspondence. He wanted money, and he wanted it from the Government of the United States.

It may be said, parenthetically, that there seems something insidiously debasing about the business of being a spy. Such men play a two-faced game of false representation and connivance. They employ the general principle that the end to be served—the service of their country—is so important and so fine that they are justified in almost any sort of conduct to carry out their task. Yet there is something inevitably corrupting and cankering attached to evil, whether the evil lie in the means or in the ends. Character can seldom stand up against these unseen assailants. Perhaps this is why many spies come to betray both masters. Moreover, the profession seems to have the almost inevitable accompaniment of the money itch.

Something further needs to be said about the breed of spy and counterspy. Almost never do these men become great heroes in the public mind, either during the war itself or in the pages of history thereafter—but this does not mean that they are free from hazard to their liberty and their lives. The work is such that almost at any moment the spy may be suspected, or detected and rushed to a firing squad. The danger, indeed, differs from that of combat on the battlefield only in that, like the sword of Damocles, it hangs forever over the secret agent's head. The fear is not of the bayonet, or the bullet, or the chance of capture by raid. It is that of sudden suspicion, secret betrayal, or chance blunder—any one of a number of things might mean an end of all things.

And yet, despite all this desperate danger, most spies are looked on as interesting but somewhat shabby scoundrels. This must stem out of another basic characteristic of the craft—the way it is steeped in double-dealing, misrepresentation, and deceit. There can be little doubt that the physical courage of spies is at least the equal to that of the soldier on the battle-field.

At the same time, it deserves remark that Stidger was not done away with, and that there were a great many spies who were just as lucky as Stidger was, and did not have to meet the firing squad.

At any event, Spy Stidger wrote his Louisville chief on July 28 that he had been robbed. This loss had not taken place since he had become a spy, but had occurred in March, while he was still in soldier uniform. Then he had been held up by bandits—he would have them Confederate guerrillas, for that put a better face on the story—and robbed of "$260 in money, two watches, one of which I had paid $140 for and the other $30." He was too poor to sustain such a loss at the hands of the enemies of the country, and insisted that his claim be investigated and a way found to repay him. A few days later he wrote again upon the same subject, with an even more vigorous appeal: "I need every cent that I will be able to command."

Soon thereafter Stidger went to Indianapolis, and had an extended conference with the new Commanding General of the District of Indiana, Major General Alvin P. Hovey, and Carrington, and Fairleigh. They went over the whole Kentucky and Indiana conspiracy pattern, and made detailed plans for the raids, arrests, searches, and seizures to be carried out. Stidger gave an amplitude of detail: where to find this document, that cache of arms or ammunition, and so on. The probable hiding-places of the suspects were disclosed and written down.

Then the next morning he addressed a letter jointly to all three men. It seemed that he had neglected to inform them about a personal problem. Therefore:

"I deem it my duty to give you timely notice that I shall have to give up my present employment on the first of September, if my services can be at all dispensed with.

"On or about that time, I form an alliance with one whose happiness I deem it my duty to do all in my power to protect." The lady of his affection knew about his work as secret agent, and she liked neither the danger nor the small pay.

"You will please determine," he continued, "how I am to be enabled to quit without suspicion. I cannot be arrested and remain in prison any length of time. If arrested in Louisville, say the last of next week, and sent here" (he was still in Indianapolis), "I want to go to Illinois for a week or two about that time."

This arrangement for the ease of heart having been discussed, he turned once more to preparation for the raid, advising Colonel Fairleigh "that in the seizure of articles at Dr. Kalfus's office I have a six-inch Colt pistol. General Carrington will find all my papers, books, et cetera, in the fourth story of Dodd's Building." But he returned to the matter of heart—and money—a day or so later, when he described the danger of the testimony he would be called on to give before the Military Commission. It would endanger his life, and probably would arouse such enduring enmities that he could not make a good living in Kentucky or Illinois. Nevertheless, he would be willing to testify to everything "if I am furnished with a sufficiency to live hereafter in protection!"

Now, at long last, things came to a head. The Supreme Council of the Order of the Sons of Liberty had met in Chicago, and Judge Bullitt had attended the session. Plans were made, specific tasks assigned to the order in each State, funds provided, and the date set. It looked as if it would be more than a revolt—almost a revolution.

The Kentucky Grand Commander came back by Indianapolis, and Stidger met him there. Before they took train for Louisville, the Grand Secretary suspected that his chief had become a most dangerous man. As soon as they talked together on the train, he knew that this was right, that Bullitt "had all the information in regard to the plan of operations, time of action," and so forth. Stidger made up his mind that the Grand Commander must be arrested as soon as he got off the train at Louisville; otherwise he might see some trustworthy lieutenant there and disclose the details to him. Bullitt likewise had on his person several checks on Canadian banks, for large sums of money. These had been given him in Chicago, with instructions to convert them into cash before leaving for home. Bullitt had failed to do this. The character of the checks indicated that Confederate secret funds in Canada had been their source.

As soon as they reached Louisville, Stidger's apprehensions were at an end. Fairleigh had had some word of the probable time of Bullitt's arrival and had a squad of soldiers on hand at the Ferry Station on the Indiana side, to take Bullitt off the train. They very conveniently failed to see Grand Secretary Stidger. And true enough, when they searched the captive, the checks were discovered on him.

Stidger was doubly fortunate. When the other members of the Kentucky Grand Council found that Bullitt had not confided the details of the plan to him before arrest, they promptly sent him back to Indianapolis to procure them from Dodd. The Indiana Grand Commander, whom he saw August 3, had been depressed by the newspaper dispatch about Bullitt's arrest, but dutifully outlined the plan of operation in detail, and enjoined Stidger that no part of it could be put on paper. The secret agent suggested an attempted rescue. Dodd said that this matter would have to be taken up with Dr. Bowles—as the commander of the military branch the latter would have to decide.

The plan for the uprising was that secret-society meetings would be dropped and mass meetings would take their place. These would be turned into musters of men ready for the uprising, which would come on August 17.

On that day, armed bands were to descend on Chicago, Springfield, and Indianapolis. Camps Douglas and Chase were to be seized, along with Rock Island; the prisoners released; the arsenals occupied and the arms and ammunition therein used to equip the released Confederates. Then the various forces would march on Louisville, capture it, and throw Kentucky into the Confederate camp.

Bowles talked to Stidger on August 4. He complained bitterly that Dodd had changed the program agreed on at Chicago, and insisted that the new scheme was quite hopeless. Actually, the program adopted at the Supreme Council had been that they would "await the coöperation of the Confederate force" to be sent into Kentucky. Through his man Dickerson of Baltimore, Bowles had already asked Davis to dispatch it forthwith. Bowles did not seem much upset or deterred by the arrests already made; on the contrary, he thought that the members of the order must act, leave the country, or go to prison.

One question both Dodd and Bowles asked Stidger: Did Bullitt have checks on him, or money? Both thought the Kentuckian most stupid not to have cashed the checks. Dodd denounced this carelessness, which put real give-away evidence on the prisoner's very person.

Stidger then returned to Louisville, conveyed his Indiana information to the members of the Kentucky Council, and found that at last they looked upon him as a traitor and a spy. He lost no time in letting Colonel Fairleigh know the great personal danger in which he stood. The Federal commander acted quickly. In a few days there was a tidal wave of arrests. Stidger went to jail with the really guilty men.

Soon he was shifted from the military prison at Louisville to that at the Indiana capital. After a few hours there, he was smuggled out of his cell, and made his way to Mattoon. There he stayed with his family and his sweetheart for some weeks.

During his absence, the new district commander, General Hovey, appointed a Military Commission and set the stage for the trial of the Indiana leaders of the revolt that had not come off. It met the first time on September 22. After the preliminaries of the reading of the charges and specifications against the men accused of high treason, the first witness was called into the courtroom.

Then the leaders of the Sons of Liberty saw, for the first time, the trusted Grand Secretary of the Council for the order in Kentucky to be none other than former carpenter, former corporal Felix G. Stidger—the spy complete.

Chapter 14

THE NORTHWEST CONSPIRACY

THE arrests of the conspirators in Kentucky and Indiana, which Stidger had made possible, were accompanied by others in Ohio, Illinois, and Missouri. These together marked the failure of a widespread plot through the region west of the Appalachians. This has borne the name of the Northwest Conspiracy.

In none of the States was the work of the Federal secret agents more daring or more nearly complete than that which Stidger and others performed for General Carrington. But it was not so desperate as were the plots of the Confederates and the Copperheads. Yet these had some chance to succeed in their attempts to raise a revolution in the Northwest and form a new Confederacy there.

When Abraham Lincoln issued his definitive Emancipation Proclamation on New Year's Day, 1863, the Confederate authorities realized that now there could be no negotiated peace with the Lincoln Administration. Jefferson Davis and the Government at Richmond knew that so long as the man from Springfield stayed in the White House, he would focus the energy of the Loyal States upon the military conquest of the Southern rebellion. After Vicksburg and Gettysburg, and even more after Bragg's rout at Missionary Ridge, the Confederate command sought some new way to redress the balance of the battlefield.

In particular, they grasped at the expedient that it might be possible to create a new military front by action in the Northwest. Arguments for a new secession were advanced repeatedly through 1863 and the following year. Chief among them were these:

From a standpoint of blood relation and common economic interest, the South and the West should stick together. Both sections were predominantly agricultural—and both had for years been drained by the Northeast, which had exploited them as colonial economies.

In the next place, the Mississippi River was the common carrier for the produce and commerce of both regions. It was unthinkable that the West should depend upon a great watercourse the mouth of which was in the hands of an inimical government.

Then finally, the artificial alliance of the Northwest with the Eastern States, and particularly with New England, was unequal in the benefits to the partners—its harm to the West was great, and would increase.

Southern papers editorialized on these themes throughout the war. The Confederate President made several speeches proclaiming their force. Abraham Lincoln received evidence that arguments of this nature were persuasive to a type of people in the Ohio Valley States who were of more substance and strength than the disaffected fringe which theretofore had constituted the chief source of recruitment for the fifth column. It was this development, as much as the spread of the castles of the Knights of the Golden Circle, which had caused him to remark to Senator Charles Sumner of Massachusetts in

January, 1863, that he feared "the fire in the rear more than any military chances."

But the Confederates found this disaffection static rather than dynamic. Through 1863, they sought desperately to find some way to energize it. Vallandigham's vicissitudes in Ohio, the rebellious course of the Copperhead majority in the Indiana Legislature, and other evidences led Davis to experiment with a cavalry raid across the Ohio. When the glamorous John Morgan swept out of Tennessee, through Kentucky, and into the Indiana and Ohio region, he expected that sympathetic groups would rise immediately to join his forces and support the Confederate cause. But from the start, things went wrong with this exploit, as we have seen. And never again during the war did a Confederate column cross into the Ohio Valley States.

That Fall the Confederates attempted another raid—this time from Canada rather than Tennessee. For some months the Richmond Government had pressed its agents in British North America to organize an expedition to capture the Federal military prison on Johnson's Island, in Lake Erie, immediately off Sandusky, Ohio. In September, a party of thirty-six officers was sent from Wilmington on the blockade runner *Robert E. Lee.* Colonel W. B. Bate, later a Senator from Tennessee, was their leader. Most of the enlisted men came overland.

The Confederate officers studied the situation closely, and at length worked out a scheme, the immediate objective of which was to break into the military prison on Johnson's Island, to release and carry to Canadian soil the 3,500 Southern soldiers there. As they developed the plans, a further purpose stemmed out of them; should the strength available

[*280*]

after the prison exploit be great enough, they would descend upon Buffalo and attack that city.

Through the summer and early fall they worked on the details. It was essential to seize enough lake steamers to carry the released soldiers back to Canadian soil. The conspirators noticed that one of the most important of the lake carriers was the American Daily Line, which had a fleet of propeller ships regularly plying through the Welland Canal, between Ogdensburg, New York, and Chicago. It was arranged that the disguised Confederates should go aboard these ships singly or in small numbers at the different stopping-places where the ships touched. By the time they reached Lake Erie, there would be enough on board each vessel to seize and control it.

Thereupon the ships would rush for Johnson's Island, surprise the guards, break open the prison, and fill the ships with the Southerners. Were they strong enough, Buffalo would be attacked and burned. Otherwise the released men would be landed on Canadian soil, and would make their way back to the Confederacy by blockade-runners from Halifax.

The plotters established a contact inside the palisades at Johnson's Island, and the prisoners were organized to cooperate. A considerable group of Confederates gathered at or near Windsor, and in Quebec, Montreal, and Toronto. The chiefs were about to set the date for the desperate coup.

Among the leaders of the enterprise was an officer who had served bravely with troops, but had not received the reward of either promotion or pay to which he felt that this sacrifice had entitled him. He came to Canada for the exploit, but nursed his grudge, and determined to satisfy it. Late in October he journeyed to Montreal, and undertook to make contact with D. Thurston, a detective Seward had stationed in

Canada as a consular agent to help the secret-service work there.

On November 1, this disgruntled conspirator sent Thurston a note in pencil, proposing a conference, and signed with the assumed name of William S. Fousha. The detective disregarded it, and a second note. The next warned Thurston that "in ten days you will regret" this failure to listen.

When the two got together, a few days later, "Fousha" made Thurston pledge never to reveal his informant's identity—a promise which the secret agent kept scrupulously, before and after the event. Then the Southern officer told his story and said: "I am ready to give you certain information, provided your Government is ready to pay me for the same." He could reveal "the names of all the leading parties" to the plot.

At length tentative arrangements were made. "Fousha" then told of the Confederate agent on Johnson's Island; the captain of a blockade-runner traveling through Canada in disguise; the $200,000 fund at the disposal of the plotters; the way they planned to seize the lake steamers; and the imminence of the attempt.

Thurston rushed to Quebec with the disclosures. These so impressed the consul general there that he called upon Lord Monck, the Governor General of Canada, immediately. The Queen's representative checked up, became fearful of the danger of this raid from British soil, and telegraphed Lord Lyons, the British Minister in Washington, to communicate news of the plot to Secretary Seward.

Late in the evening of November 11, 1863, the British envoy wrote, in his own hand, to the Secretary of State:

"Persons hostile to the United States who have sought an asylum in Canada appear to be engaged in a serious and mischievous plot. Indeed, if the information which has reached the Governor General be correct, they have a project for invading the United States and attacking and destroying the city of Buffalo.

"They propose to get possession of some of the steamboats on Lake Erie, to surprise Johnson's Island and set free the prisoners of war who are confined there, and to proceed with them to attack Buffalo. The Governor General suggests that steamboats should be watched, and he appears to have some suspicions connected with Ogdensburg.

"He has taken all the precautions in his power, has ordered a sharp lookout to be kept on the Welland Canal, and directed that any steamboat giving cause for suspicion by the number or character of her passengers on board shall be arrested."

The Washington authorities acted instantly. Stanton sent telegrams of warning to the governors of Pennsylvania, New York, Ohio, Indiana, Illinois, and Michigan. He ordered troop reinforcements to Johnson's Island, Buffalo, Erie, Pennsylvania, and Detroit. The plot was exposed in the press on both sides of the border, and the conspirators did not carry through their plans.

Brigadier General Jacob D. Cox, commanding at Sandusky, was a soldier of splendid courage and rich battlefield experience. He soon had the Johnson's Island situation well in hand. On November 13, he telegraphed the Secretary of War that "the artillery has arrived. . . . I think I can answer for the safety of everything, in any emergency." Two days later, he relayed a dispatch from Detroit, to the effect that "the rebels who left Windsor to join the raid are returning, saying that the plans are frustrated for the present."

The Confederate leaders and sympathizers in Canada put the best face they could on this failure. On November 13, the Montreal *Evening Telegraph,* which was charged with being owned or controlled by Secession gold, claimed that the "deliberate cruelty" of the Federal authorities to Confederate captives had forced the effort: It had been wrong to take men accustomed to the mild climate of the Southern States, and put them in a prison in the cold and rigorous climate of the Far North! Because of this, the editorial continued, the Confederate authorities had planned the expedition.

Seward sent Preston King, a Republican politician of the Ogdensburg region, later to be a United States Senator, to Canada to confer with the Governor General, and to clean up the plot. King reported on November 21 that "Mr. Thurston feels bound by his promise not to expose in any way his informer." Therefore King, Consul General Giddings, and Thurston jointly wrote the unnamed Confederate: "The United States Government will pay him fairly for any information that may prove valuable to the United States Government." Whether or not "Fousha" ever received his betrayal money does not appear.

The winter of 1863-64 made it an imperative necessity for the Confederacy to find another plan for the Northwest. It was true that there was little activity in the field. Sherman was at Ringgold, Georgia, strengthening his army for the attack on Dalton and the Atlanta campaign. Grant had been commissioned Lieutenant General and put in command of all the armies. He had established his headquarters close to the Rapidan, in northern Virginia, and was preparing the Army of the Potomac for a hammer blow against Lee's ill-fed veterans. The quiet was deceptive—Confederate statesmen as well as soldiers knew that it was the lull before the storm.

Consequently, in April, 1864, President Davis determined upon another effort to raise a revolt in the Northwest. He concluded that it would have to be directed from Canada, rather than from the South, and that a really competent group of men would have to be sent there to undertake the task. The result was that he appointed three accredited Commissioners, and ordered them to proceed to British North America as soon as possible. He gave them a number of subordinates, secret agents, and organizers of revolt.

The principal Commissioner was Jacob Thompson of Mississippi, a conservative politician and public servant who was both sagacious and untiring. Joined with him was Clement C. Clay of Alabama, a brilliant figure in the United States Senate in the 50's, a man with skill in debate and intrigue. The third, James P. Holcombe, was an administrator.

The Commissioners and their party sailed from Wilmington, North Carolina, on a swift blockade-runner. A number of Confederate army and navy officers accompanied them, to plan and lead expeditions to capture Federal military prisons and release the Confederate soldiers there. In addition, the authorities loaded the vessel with a rich cargo of cotton and tobacco. This was to be sold in Canada, and the proceeds used to finance the Confederate agents and their plots. The goods sold for $910,000, and this sum was needed before the year was done.

Another group of officers and men made their way through the Loyal States and joined the party in Canada late in May. The most conspicuous of these was Captain Hines, the Morgan raider. In the escape from the prison at Columbus, the Kentuckian had established a reputation for instant decision, cool daring, and desperate courage. After his return within the Confederate lines, the Richmond Government gave him a special detail. He was to make his way to Canada, from which point he would organize the escape of Confederate prisoners from the Federal military bastilles. At the same time he would incite the Northern fifth columnists to raise the standard of revolt.

When the Confederate leaders got together and discussed the first steps to take, they agreed that they must see Vallandigham at once. Hines had the opening interview, on June 9. Thompson met the exile two days later. A Chicago representative of the O.S.L. joined them later. The result was a complete meeting of the minds of the Confederates and the Supreme Grand Commander of the Sons of Liberty.

They reached an agreement both for political action and for co-operation in attempts at revolution. In the first-named field, the Democratic leader would exert every resource at his command to commit the party, at its national convention the next month, to a peace platform and a peace candidate. This was a purpose Vallandigham had had for many months. He had already made the preliminary moves to go back to Ohio, in defiance of the Lincoln-Burnside sentence, so that he could work out the necessary arrangements for the fight upon the convention floor.

The second branch was much more ambitious. The Copperhead leader undertook to work with the Confederates in the effort to take the Northwest out of the Union. To do this, several specific projects must be got under way. The Military Departments of the various State Councils of the Sons of Liberty must be put on the alert, the arms and ammunition for the "troops" secured, and careful plans made for a simultaneous rising of the malcontents throughout the Ohio Valley States. In addition, such military prisons as Camp Morton at Indianapolis, Columbus and Johnson's Island off Sandusky—both in Ohio—Camp Douglas at Chicago, and the prison and arsenal at Rock Island, Illinois, must be captured by O.S.L. bands.

As soon as these prisons had been broken open, the released

Confederates were to be armed, munitioned, and equipped. Then they could join in the battle to separate the Northwest from the Union. Perhaps the number would be sufficient for a strong party to be dispatched into Kentucky, to capture Louisville, bring the State into the Confederate fold—and then retake Tennessee.

Vallandigham had boasted to the Confederates, during the conferences which preceded his departure, that the Sons of Liberty were almost ready for an uprising. He promised that they were "ready to defend the principles at any cost." They had some arms already, and more had been ordered from New York. In many States, the Military Departments had drilled the men well. Furthermore, the membership was large. The head of the order put it at about 300,000, of whom Illinois was supposed to have 85,000, Indiana 50,000, Ohio 40,000, and Kentucky a substantial number.

So that Commissioner Thompson could have a better understanding of the society, Vallandigham and others of its officers who had come from Chicago to the conference initiated him into membership. The ritual and the oath impressed him well. The Confederates arranged for a direct distribution of funds for the use of the county and township O.S.L. troops, so that these could be better armed and mobilized. The Chicago representative insisted that he himself had "two regiments organized, armed, and eager for an uprising."

Thompson, Vallandigham, and Hines continued their discussions. They had word from the responsible leaders in Indiana, Illinois, Missouri, and Ohio about what these thought they could do, and how much time they would need before taking action. As a result, July 20 was selected as the date for the simultaneous revolt in all these States.

The chief Confederate agent was elated. Vallandigham and

the visitors from the States had convinced him that the Sons of Liberty meant business. The money was turned over and the word sent out. But Holcombe did not think the revolution would materialize. He acknowledged that the evidence indicated clearly that the Ohio Valley region was "fermenting with the passions out of which revolutions have been created." But there had not been sufficient incubation. It would take more time, and much more careful, detailed, efficient work.

These things done, there was no longer any question that Vallandigham must return to the United States without more delay. Even before the conferences started, he had made tentative plans to this end. The Grand Missionary of the Order, B. B. Piper of Springfield, Illinois, had proceeded from State to State to tell each Grand Commander that the chief would return almost any day. Kentucky, Indiana, Illinois, were in a state of excited expectation. Finally, on June 14 Vallandigham dashed across the border and took a train to Hamilton, Ohio.

During his address at the Democratic District Convention at Hamilton on June 15, the firebrand for peace was asked about his rumored connection with the fifth-column group. He referred to the Knights of the Golden Circle only to deny in the most explicit terms that he knew of any disloyalty in that organization, or that there was "any other secret society, treasonable or disloyal in character," which had among its purposes the resistance in arms to the governmental authorities, either State or Federal.

So far as he knew, Vallandigham continued, no such society of treason had existed in the past years of the war, and he was absolutely certain that none existed at the time that he spoke!

This did not mean that there were not large and powerful organizations of men throughout the Northwestern States which had banded together to help the Democratic party. There was need of these, because of the loyal Union League. This he termed a "dangerous, secret, oath-bound combination," which would do almost anything for the Lincoln Administration. But Vallandigham himself was acquainted with only one great conspiracy, the Democratic party, which intended to overthrow the unconstitutional politics of the Lincoln Administration by defeating him at the polls in the fall elections.

Therefore he warned the men who then sat in the seats of the mighty that there was a "vast multitude bound together to defend, by whatever means the exigencies of the time demanded, their natural and Constitutional rights as freemen."

One of the hopes of the head of the band of treason was that there would be some new Burnside to arrest him, and march him off to prison again. Vallandigham believed that were this done, the Sons of Liberty would take it as a signal for instant revolution. But, as we have seen, he was disappointed in this expectation. Heintzelman was a shrewder man than his predecessor. He took no step, sent no squad of soldiers, left Vallandigham completely alone. To fill the cup of disappointment to the brim, Lincoln said publicly no single word about the homecoming of the incendiary Copperhead.

Jacob Thompson continued sanguine that the uprising would occur on the scheduled July date. He wrote Judah P. Benjamin, the Confederate Secretary of State, that "the rank and file in the Northwest are weary of the war, and eager to accept, from any source, relief from the existing conditions." He believed that any event in which an open, public blow was struck would be a lighted match to a waiting powder train.

Throughout the latter part of June and the first week of July, the leading conspirators worked like mad to get things

[*289*]

in shape for the explosion. The effort to take practical steps to translate words into action proved a little too much for their powers. This was not strange, for in the main these men were wordy revolutionists. Some of them did not know anything at all about how to get things done. The agitator type often exhibits this lack of essential qualities for an uprising. Debating societies are not always good schools for successful treason.

It did not take Vallandigham, General Bowles, Grand Missionary Piper, and others of the leaders any tremendous length of time to find this out.

The conspirators knew already that they could expect little help from Missouri. Reference has already been made to the thorough investigation Colonel Sanderson, Provost Marshal for that State, had made of the secession societies there. By May, he was ready to take action. Soldiers arrested twenty-four of the leaders in St. Louis, and three times that number in the northern part of the State. The imprisonment of Charles L. Hunt, the State's able Grand Commander, ended the activities of the lodges for some time to come.

Elsewhere the officer personnel of the order had not been importantly disturbed. General Carrington at Indianapolis; Colonel Sweet, Commander of Camp Douglas at Chicago, and a few others had made a few arrests. Carrington had already sent his spy, S. P. Coffin, "a thoroughly reliable man," to Canada "to talk to the rebel traitors." Coffin's reports from there backed up Stidger's disclosures at home. The main trap remained baited but unsprung.

It was not fear so much as incompetence which caused the cancellation of the twentieth of July as the date for the uprising, for the unpreparedness of the lodges was appalling. So the Supreme Grand Commander informed the Confederate

Commissioners of this change of plan. At the same time, he sent high-placed aides around with the word of the postponement.

Instead of beginning a revolution on July 20, that was the day the Supreme Grand Council met in Chicago to make a new estimate of the situation. The Grand Councils of four States were well represented. Bowles, Dodd, Wilson, and Walker were there from Indiana. Bullitt and Williams represented Kentucky. Barrett brought the bad tidings from Missouri. Illinois had Charles Walsh, the head of the Military Department of the order for that State; Piper, Holloway, and Swen.

Captain Majors, a Confederate paymaster, represented the Commissioners in Canada. He had some cash with him, and large drafts on Canadian banks. He came with authority to spend several hundred thousand dollars on the revolution.

All the delegates reported reasons why they were unable to act, and they agreed unanimously that an uprising on July 20 would have been disastrous. They selected August 16 as a day sufficiently far away for the completion of their arrangements.

Captain Majors then reimbursed the delegates for the expenses they had incurred in coming to the meeting. Likewise he turned over a large sum to a leader in each State, to be spent in financing the equipment and gathering of the local military groups. A committee was selected to go to Canada, to confer with the Confederate Commissioners about the immediate program.

This meeting took place in St. Catharine's two days later. The fifth-column leaders insisted that the Confederate Army must co-operate if the rising was to have any chance to succeed. As leader of the Military Department, General Bowles declared that unless Confederate armies moved into Kentucky and Missouri in such strength that they could keep the Federal forces busy, there would be no use in any attempt by the Sons of Liberty. Thompson pointed out that Southern troops had already entered the two Border States, and that they would be strengthened.

The Copperhead committee then argued that the public must be prepared for the revolt. This called for a great many public meetings over the Ohio Valley States. This seemed sensible, and the conferees determined to change the secret meetings of the lodges and State Councils into public mass meetings. Thompson said the Confederates would put up the money to finance these gatherings of public protest.

The Richmond delegates also agreed to the proposal that August 16 be made the day for the uprising. In the operations order, St. Louis was added to Louisville as a rendezvous for triumphant columns of Confederates and Copperheads marching to relieve the beleaguered South. The other elements of the plan for July 20 were substantially unchanged. The O.S.L. columns would seize upon the various military prisons and arsenals. They would take over railroads and telegraph lines. The disaffected on their line of march south would join them, the present State governments would be broken up and new provisional State governments established in their places.

The conspirators believed that these disasters would disrupt the whole Federal plan of campaign. Grant must relax his pressure against Petersburg. Sherman would have to cease his feinting and fighting on the Atlanta road, and rush his troops north of the Ohio. During this much-needed breathing spell, the Confederates would stanch their wounds, renew their arms and supplies, and be in a position to win peace with independence.

[*292*]

The committee came back from Canada assured of the fullest Confederate support for the plot in its new form. Some of them were confident of success, but others, like Bowles, were not sanguine. The Indiana "General" doubted the effectiveness of the Confederate columns, because of recent Kentucky experiences. Nathan Bedford Forrest had driven deep into that State—but not to hold it. He had taken occasion to "disband" one of his regiments whose troopers came from the region. These were to carry their arms with them to their homes, and be prepared to aid the expected Copperhead revolt. When this had not come off, many of the men drifted back to their old command. Now there was promise of another incursion by Forrest, and the disbanding of another regiment of Kentuckians. Bowles, however, put little faith in it. He wanted a powerful invasion, not a subsidiary raid, and he doubted if the hard-pressed Confederates could spare the force for this.

But there was one thing which the committeemen brought back in quantity. Thompson and his paymaster furnished them with ample funds. This was in the form of bills of exchange drawn on Canadian banks. The fifth-column leaders were urged by the Commissioners, Captain Majors, and others to turn these into cash in Chicago, and to carry the currency on south with them—Canadian checks were endorsed with treason, but cash had no odor.

Some of the conspirators followed this sage instruction. General Bowles, Grand Commander Dodd, and Dr. Walker of Indiana turned their checks for almost $200,000 into greenbacks before reaching home. The Ohio, Illinois, and Missouri leaders followed the same course, and were not taken into custody.

A part of Indiana's funds went to an arms merchant in New York City, for more boxes of "hardware," but the rest was used in organization work among the county lodges and in preparation for the great revolt. Runners sped to the local leaders to give them the details of the new coup.

Judge Bullitt of Louisville, as we have seen, ignored the precaution. The Canadian checks were in his wallet when Stidger, his Grand Secretary and betrayer, rode with him on the last leg of the return trip. Federal soldiers arrested the Grand Commander at the ferry at Louisville, and the incriminating bills of exchange on Canada constituted irrefutable evidence. The arrest of twenty-four other Kentucky leaders pretty well ended the danger of revolt in that State.

Nor were there many further developments of consequence in Missouri. The men who had met at St. Catharine's may have regarded St. Louis as a fine rendezvous for the mythical brigades of the revolution, but the conspirators on the spot found it a most unhealthy spot. Madame Velasquez, the Confederate spy who had sirened a pass out of Lafe Baker, visited the Missouri metropolis in the summer, but found little good news to report. The June arrests had disorganized the order throughout Missouri.

Sanderson began a general cleanup in August. His agents seized more Copperheads in the St. Louis precincts. But in the north of the State they operated on the guerrillas as well as the conspirators. They tried to break up the Quantrell, Thrailkill, and Thornton bands or "brigades." County jails were crowded with these prisoners. Union detectives shared their cells and reported their intimate confidences. Military trials followed shortly, with sentences of death.

No such distresses attended the efforts in Illinois. The Chicago picture was promising, chiefly because Charles Walsh, the head of the military branch in that city, was vigorous and had many followers. He lived within a few hundred feet of the

[*294*]

main gate to Camp Douglas, and his home was a secret rendezvous and storehouse for the attempt on the prison. The situation in "Egypt" was even more ominous. The word had passed; the men drilled nearly every night, and talked and acted as if they meant business.

The Illinois leaders set to work upon the "educational" meetings, and held three large ones. That at Peoria, in the south, succeeded in evoking intense enthusiasm—but for peace, not uprising. One was held at Springfield, Lincoln's own city, with disappointing results. That at Chicago was a flat failure.

The Indiana experience was the most unsatisfactory of those in the Ohio Valley States. Bowles had come back angry and disillusioned, and saw no chance to go ahead if the Confederates failed to invade with a real army, which they could not do. Dodd tried to go ahead anyway, on the basis of only local strength.

The Grand Commander talked to J. J. Bingham, who was on the O.S.L. State Council, but only because P. C. Wright had overpersuaded him the year before. Bingham placed his Democracy before his newspaper, and he put both far ahead of the Copperhead plans. In addition to editing the *Indiana State Sentinel*, that year he was chairman of the Democratic State Committee, and was working day and night for the ticket.

When Dodd asked the editor-politician to announce a great Democratic mass meeting for Indianapolis on August 16, and told him why, Bingham was aghast. He saw instantly the visionary folly of the projected uprising. He saw even more clearly the way this would deliver a body blow to every political hope the Democrats might have in Indiana that year.

Bingham acted at once to head off this insane scheme. He called together a group of the leading Democrats of the State, and told them what Dodd wanted to do. Congressman Michael

Kerr of New Albany, a lodge member, related that the rumors
of revolt were frightening the farmers into almost giving away
their crops before harvest. Other reports were equally ominous. The whole group agreed that Dodd and his fellow conspirators must give up their madness. Dodd was called in,
confronted with the demand, and called off the plans for the
scheduled Indiana revolt on August 16.

The Federal authorities kept a close watch on the tergiversa-
tions of the chief conspirators. Some of the Confederate leaders
in Canada held daily meetings with Copperhead lieutenants
in Toronto, and it was not long before the Federal consul
there had a spy inside. Soon he reported to Seward: "A deep-
laid plan was made to sever Illinois and Indiana from the
Union, and that the recent troubles in Illinois had their origin
in this plan. They boast that the States had been sounded and
were ripe, and that through those States, the South will have
peace on their own terms." Early in August, rumors of impending raids came almost every hour.

About the same time, Baker informed Stanton that one of
his spies in Canada had found a schooner on Lake Erie, the
Montreal, armed with two 24-pounders, commanded by a Confederate Navy lieutenant and with a crew of fourteen men
who had been prisoners. Soon word came of another ship, the
Saratoga, with four 18-pounders in her battery. These boats
were to aid a new attack on Johnson's Island.

General Heintzelman at Columbus became alarmed over
the possibilities of revolt. It was not that he had any illusions
about the leadership of the heads of the fifth column in his
department. But the rank and file might be of sterner stuff.
In any event, his own forces were weak, and he did not have
the margin of safety he needed to feel secure.

On August 9, the commander of the Department of the Ohio telegraphed General Halleck at Washington that he expected the disturbances to develop mostly in Indiana and Illinois, but that he had no troops to quell disorders, and the prison guards were too few. "The outbreak will be formidable," he went on. "We had better arrest the leaders quickly. Morton agrees." He wanted to send the arrested men East, under strong guard, "to thwart the temptation to attempt rescue."

Three days later he wired Governor Yates of Illinois to advise him of a spy report of secret drills at Galena, and inquired whether the leaders had not better be arrested. He sent a new regiment to Rock Island and another to Chicago.

That same day Carrington had a message from Heintzelman that he had posted cavalry at Evansville, Indiana, to check any rebel attempt to cross from Kentucky. In addition to the troops sent to Rock Island and Chicago, he had dispatched regiments to Indianapolis and Johnson's Island.

"I am confident," the message continued, "that there is a division in the ranks of the disloyal, and they are not able to make up their minds to fix the day to strike. This will give the Government time to make further preparations. The authorities in Washington will soon be satisfied that there will be the most active resistance out here, and must prepare to meet it in a determined manner. It must not for a moment succeed at any point. . . . Until we are fully prepared, we must act with great caution and secrecy."

A little later, the General telegraphed Sweet, at Camp Douglas: "One Captain Hines may be in Chicago." He should be arrested at once.

But the day of August 16 passed almost without incident. A Confederate Colonel Johnson seized a steamer on the Ohio, at Shawneetown. Carrington organized a pursuit, and Heintzelman telegraphed the item in cipher to Halleck. But this was the only event of the day fixed for the Northwest revolt. For the department commander had judged quite rightly the "division in the ranks of the disloyal." This had been so great that the chiefs of the Sons of Liberty went once more to Canada to report disorganization and delay to their Confederate allies.

The Southern Commissioners met the Northern fifth-columnists at London, Canada, on August 7. In the morning's discussion, Thompson and his associates made plain their disappointment, in terms of growing bluntness. That afternoon the O.S.L. group submitted a written justification of their failure, and mild hopes for an outbreak at a later date—this one being set for August 29, the first day of the National Democratic Convention in Chicago. They wrote:

"A movement unsupported by vigorous coöperation at Indianapolis and Springfield had better not be undertaken. We are willing to do anything which bids fair to result in good; but shrink from responsibility of a movement made in the way now proposed. . . . You underrate the condition of things in the Northwest. By patience and perseverance in the work of agitation, we are sure of a general uprising which will result in glorious success. We must look to bigger results than the mere liberation of prisoners. We should look to the grand end of adding an empire of Northwestern States."

The Confederate Commissioners had to accept the situation, and after some talk agreed to fix August 29 for the new date. But they insisted that this was the last change; there must be no more delays. Thompson, Clay, and Holcombe carefully selected the Confederate officers to lead the different fifth-column troops, and these began to filter into the appointed places.

It was a notable array of brave adventurers. Hines had command of the total task of opening the military prisons in the Northwest. Captain John B. Castleman was his second. They selected about sixty Southern officers and men then in Canada, the chief among whom were out of John Morgan's old command: Colonels George St. Leger Grenfel, once Morgan's chief of staff; Vincent Marmaduke, of Missouri; Benjamin Anderson, of Kentucky; and Captain Cantrill, of the same State.

They planned to concentrate on Chicago, for the circumstances there should be the most favorable. Another group, under Captain Charles H. Cole, was sent to Sandusky to seize Johnson's Island, release the prisoners, and march them to the Louisville rendezvous.

Federal secret agents were at London, Ontario, during the conferences, and secretly accompanied the Confederate leaders back. Coffin kept Carrington advised from Canada, while Stidger siphoned out of Dodd, Bowles, and Heffren the orders that came to them in Indiana. Furthermore, a new reporting service began to function.

Colonel Benjamin Jeffery Sweet, the commander at Camp Douglas, had set this up, to keep him advised of the details and dates of the attack being prepared against that military prison, which had about 8,000 Confederates within its enclosure. Sweet had entered the war as a Wisconsin infantry officer and gained promotion for his field service, but was wounded in the battles around Chattanooga. He was now a colonel of the Veterans Reserve Corps.

Late in June, 1864, he cast about for likely confidence men to get into the ranks of the O.S.L. conspirators and betray them. Among those he picked up was a patent-medicine vendor named J. Winslow Ayer. This worthy seized the opportunity to change from hawking his nostrums on street corners and in barrooms, and in July began a spectacular career as spy. The

Colonel also secured the detail of Thomas H. Keefe, of the United States Secret Service; early in August he sent the detective to Canada to establish a listening post there. It was Keefe who journeyed to Chicago on the same train with several of Hines's men.

Sweet, who knew that his camp was poorly guarded, kept the wires hot for reinforcements of good fighting troops. Heintzelman had already sent one regiment, and now dispatched another.

About this same time, Carrington's Provost Marshal at Terre Haute furnished some important information. The New York arms merchant had begun his shipments, and "large and heavy boxes" were passing on the railroad.

Incidentally, there was something strange about the ease with which the treasonable bands got arms and ammunition. In the spring of the year, during his organizing tour in rural Indiana, Phineas Wright had boasted that he would get all arms the Sons of Liberty needed; that "if he could not get them in New York, he could in Canada." Certainly such had proved the case.

The Provost Marshal's report was confirmed by word Governor Morton had on August 20 from a New York agent, that the Copperheads had "ordered and paid for 30,000 [sic] revolvers and forty-two boxes of ammunition." The report continued that "thirty-two boxes of the above have been forwarded to J. J. Parsons, Indianapolis, via Merchants Dispatch and marked Sunday School books."

Stidger told Carrington the exact spot the items could be found. The General dispatched a company to search Grand Commander Dodd's private office. The soldiers found the boxes, which contained about 400 navy revolvers and 135,000 rounds of ammunition. At the same time they seized a supply of Sons of Liberty rituals, a list of the members of the order in Indianapolis, and Dodd's private files of correspondence. It was in this mass of treasonable letters that they discovered the letter of P. C. Wright announcing his editorship of the *New York Daily News.*

This exposure delighted Morton, because it came at just the right time for effective use in the State election campaign. He called a public meeting for the night of August 22, "to consider the present aspect of political affairs in the State." It was strictly a Republican meeting, and its resolutions viewed the conspiracy with alarm, and denounced the whole Democratic party as the ally of the bands of treason. The Governor made a dramatic speech, in which he claimed the arms seized were but a drop in the bucket in comparison to the quantity brought into Indiana in the previous eighteen months.

He went on to link the Democratic State ticket to the conspiracy, because "five men upon it are members of the Sons of Liberty—one half of the whole ticket. This secret order is but the nucleus; it does not embrace all the traitors, nor indeed the principal ones . . . the men who expect to reap the fruit of this revolution."

Morton pressed the same theme at Republican rallies throughout the State, the Radical press worked it overtime, and it made large inroads into the conservative ranks. The Democratic candidates found it necessary to publish their denial of membership in the Sons of Liberty, or knowledge of any conspiracy. There is no doubt that the exposure damaged the plot's chance for success throughout the Ohio Valley States.

On August 23, Jacob Thompson wrote Mason and Slidell, chief Confederate diplomats abroad, that "everything justifies the belief that success will ultimately attend the undertaking." But some of his associates in Canada had lost all hope.

The approach of the opening date of the postponed Democratic National Convention brought huge throngs to Chicago. A day or so in advance, Hines and the other Confederate officers reached the city, and sought to appear and conduct themselves as though they were merely interested citizens coming to observe the political show. Other Southern soldiers came, in civilian clothes, through Indiana and Illinois. Many of the delegates to the convention were members of the secret order. Nor had their coming been unheralded. On August 27, the *Chicago Tribune* had sneered about the gathering "for the last time, under the soiled banner of Democracy, to put in nomination the last Democratic presidential candidate." It claimed that Chicago was "full to overflowing already with the gathering clans of Copperheads, Butternuts, O.A.K.'s, Sons of Liberty, original peace men, gentlemen from Canada, Fort Lafayette graduates, and border rebels under military parole." The Sons of Liberty established headquarters in the Richmond House. The sign "Missouri Delegation" was over the door to their suite.

The night before the convention opened its sessions, the Confederate leaders assembled the various Grand Commanders and other officers of the Sons of Liberty, to find out exactly how things stood. Hines and his subordinates reported that they had done everything they had agreed to do. The prisoners inside Camp Douglas were organized to attack their guards from within the instant they should hear the sound of the attack by the Sons of Liberty troops without the gates. The Confederate leaders then asked the Copperheads for specific information in regard to the strength of the armed forces they had ready for the morrow's battle.

The answers filled them with disgust. Vallandigham, Bowles, Dodd, Walsh, Piper, and the other O.S.L. committee-

men and conferees in the meetings in Canada had failed to
do almost everything that they had promised. The county and
township lodges had not been notified, the members who had
happened to come to Chicago had done so, with few exceptions,
individually and without any organization or gathering-place.
Nor was any among them ready to take the initiative in bringing order out of chaos.

While the meeting was in session, two further pieces of disturbing news were brought in. One was that Vallandigham
had no chance to take over the Democratic National Convention and nominate a peace candidate. He might be able
through some fluke of convention emotion, to get a peace
plank in the platform, but this was problematical. General
McClellan was likely to be the nominee. Were Seymour, the
New York Governor, selected instead, the candidate would be
for Union before he was for peace. Neither man would give
any countenance at all to the idea of a new Northwest secession.

The second communication was equally ominous. The
guard at Camp Douglas had been suddenly strengthened with
several regiments of seasoned fighting men. No longer would
it fall an easy prize to a surprise attack.

A near-panic swept the Sons of Liberty. A wave of disgust
went over the Confederates. These last now had to admit to
themselves the bitter fact that the Copperheads were no potential soldiers. They had neither the courage nor the organization to make a fight. Instead of wearing on the lapels of their
coats the accustomed copper Liberty heads, they should wear
white feathers.

Captain Hines was desperate. Was there anything that could
be salvaged from this wreck of all their hopes? At dawn the
next morning he gathered the Grand Commanders, to propose
that they furnish the Confederates with five hundred de-

pendable men. Hines and Castleman would take them, seize a passenger train due to leave for Rock Island at 9:00 that morning, cut the telegraph wires, capture the Rock Island arsenal, and release the Confederate prisoners there. Even this smacked too much of real danger for the champions of revolution. They preferred oratory in the secret sessions of the lodges. The Confederate money had been useful. But Confederate courage had no currency among the Copperheads.

That very day, Hines and his associates shook the dust of Chicago from their feet. The Northwest Conspiracy had failed, owing to no fault of the Confederates but because of the cowardice of the parlor, hotel-lobby, and barroom fifth-columnists. Camp Douglas was not attacked, Camp Morton remained undisturbed, and this chapter of attempted treason had been closed.

Chapter 15

THE INDIANA TREASON TRIALS
AND EX PARTE MILLIGAN

THE debacle at Chicago brought great relief to the Federal authorities throughout the Northwest. For it furnished them with proof positive of two important results which they had hoped would prove true, but had feared might be otherwise. One was that the Democratic party had had no intention of supporting Vallandigham's Order of the Sons of Liberty in any treasonable conspiracy, that by and large it was not sympathetic with the extreme Copperheads, and that while it wanted peace, it would not join any movement for peace through defeat. McClellan's choice, and his prompt repudiation of the Vallandigham plank in the platform, made this assurance doubly sure.

Then again, and from the standpoint of possible immediate danger, the events of August 29 had exposed the pitiful ineffectiveness of the fifth column in the States of the Northwest. Morton, Carrington, Sanderson, Sweet, and others had believed the menace of the insurrection more mythical than real. Heintzelman had felt sure of it. But all had been fearful that they might have let their wishes shape their views. Now they knew that the flood of information that had come to them about it had been right. Their army of detectives, secret agents, spies, and betrayers had furnished the evidence of the lack of

[*305*]

leadership, futile disorganization, and ineffectiveness of plan
of the conspiracy. Under such circumstances, not even daring
Confederate leadership could give it any vestige of backbone.
Conceived in weakness and in sin, it was bound to fail.

The inglorious end of the Northwest Conspiracy had three
immediate sequels. The Copperheads themselves now knew
their own futility. The wrappings of rhetoric had been torn
from them, and they looked at their own nakedness and could
see how shrunken and misshapen they were. Now they knew
that the Democratic party would have no truck with them, that
the Confederates in Canada and in the South regarded them
with sorrowful contempt, and that their day was done.

It was true that on September 2 one effort was made to break
into a military prison. But this was Confederate and not Copperhead in origin and execution. Captain Charles H. Cole, to
whom had been assigned the task of seizing Johnson's Island,
refused to abandon this enterprise without an effort. He had
several score of trusted men, who had come from the South or
from Canada, carefully posted to seize key points. The attempt
at the island was repulsed, Cole himself was captured when he
sought to seize the gunboat *Michigan*. But a lieutenant managed to get hold of a small passenger steamer, and some of the
party made their way to safety in a Canadian port.

The Grand Commanders of the Ohio Valley States returned
from the convention in a state of great alarm. H. H. Dodd,
the Indiana leader, insisted, in a formal address to the people
of Indianapolis, that the charges which had been made against
the Sons of Liberty were without foundation. A little later
one of his aides published a pamphlet, supposedly for a mythical "Committee of Thirteen," which alleged the charges were
"absolutely and wickedly false." This admitted that there had
been some talk of a Northwestern Confederacy, said that it

was "not an impossibility, but its establishment would be the effect rather than the object of an uprising of the people: an event which the continuance of the acts of tyranny of the party in power will certainly produce."

These efforts to exculpate themselves for their part in the plot that failed had little effect. Nor did Dodd help matters much when he undertook, either deliberately or stupidly or both, to implicate the Democratic party in the conspirators' design. His words were that "the immediate purposes of the Sons of Liberty and the Democratic Party were identical." It was a statement which was used by the Republican campaigners throughout the Northwest with telling effect.

None did so with greater relish than Governor Morton. As has been seen, a week before the Chicago gathering he had charged publicly just such an alliance of the Indiana State Democratic ticket and the treasonable conspirators. After Dodd's admission, the Governor returned to the charge, the Union papers printed many columns of double-leaded editorials denouncing it, and the air was full of vitriol. Throughout the Northwest the advocates of the President made capital out of the Copperheads. It was among the most important factors in the large majorities Lincoln received in the States that had swung away from his policies two years before.

The third immediate aftermath of the Copperhead collapse was the arrest, imprisonment, and then the trial of many of the leaders who had conspired with the Confederates, taken their money, and then failed to carry out their part of the treasonable bargain. These military actions served a double purpose. The arrest of the leaders fed further fuel to the flames of the political campaign. They afforded the occasion and the excuse for a formal public report which Judge Advocate General Joseph Holt, head of the Bureau of Military Justice, is-

[*307*]

sued on October 8. This paraded the story of the secret societies, the conspiracies, the Confederate agency in plans for its execution, and the implication of the whole Democratic party from beginning to end. A thoroughly partisan electioneering device, it was couched in impeccable military form. It appeared in the papers just before the elections in the October States.

Combined with this political purpose was the desire to punish the men who had participated in these plots. It is impossible to tell today whether or not those who put the conspirators on trial expected to do more than to make public record of the actual circumstances which proved the responsibility and the guilt of the accused. Certainly the actual details of the plotted treason needed to be put on record and made public. Doubtless many of those who were behind the trials likewise hoped that these would result in many executions at the hands of firing squads.

The leading Kentucky plotters had been arrested in July, under circumstances which have already been described. Not many of the chiefs elsewhere were taken into custody until after the collapse at Chicago. But on September 7, Grand Commander Dodd was seized, and new arrests occurred until October 10. General Bowles was among those arrested, as were his three subordinate major generals, Andrew Humphreys, Lambdin P. Milligan, and Stephen Horsey. Of the heads of the political branch of the order, Horace Heffren, the Deputy Grand Commander, Stidger's first contact in the State when he began his work for Carrington in May, was seized and jailed, and so was Grand Secretary William H. Harrison. Editor J. J. Bingham of the *Indiana State Sentinel* was of the number apprehended—doubtless the fact that he was chairman of the Democratic State Committee did not decrease the relish with which the Indiana authorities put him under confinement.

[*308*]

There were a number of others in that State, and Dr. Barrett was brought over from Missouri to be tried at the same time.

Carrington's Indiana career came to an end with these arrests. In addition to having crushed the Copperhead fifth column, he had recruited 100,000 Indiana men for the Federal army and had handled the draft in that State. His temporary rank of brigadier general lapsed with his departure from the office of commander of the district. A colonel once more, after the trials he joined the Army of the Cumberland, and was with Thomas in the Nashville campaign. After the surrender, he served in the Indian wars, was a constant platform figure at meetings of the Grand Army, and was almost ninety at the time of his death.

Major General Alvin P. Hovey, who took over the command of the District of Indiana, was a native of that State. During the 50's he had been a Douglas Democrat, an attachment which led to his appointment as United States District Attorney for northern Indiana. It also caused President Buchanan to remove him in 1857, at the height of the Le-Compton controversy. The next year Hovey ran for Congress on the Republican ticket, but was defeated.

His army career was creditable; in 1864 he was brevetted major general and sent to Indiana to raise 10,000 new recruits. In addition, he was given the district command.

Hovey took over from Carrington in August, just after Stidger had discovered the chief secrets of the conspirators, and the trap was about ready to be sprung on them. The new district commander inspected the plans, changed them a little, and ordered them carried out.

The Military Commission to try Dodd was appointed in a

Special Order issued September 17. It assembled five days later and got to work.

Like General John T. Wilder, of Chickamauga fame, most of the members of the commission had come from hard service with Rosecrans, Thomas, or Sherman, and had few qualms about being tough with traitors back of the lines. Major H. L. Burnett, who was appointed Judge Advocate, had been preparing his case with the utmost care. The authorities at Washington deemed it so important politically that Stanton overcame his covetous grasp of his secret fund and sent Hovey $5,000 for expenses. "This sum," according to the Adjutant General, "is found to be as large, in the present state of the Treasury, as can be devoted to that purpose."

At the same time, and at Stanton's direction, he added a rather bitter complaint against the continued calls for more troops to hold the Copperheads in check. He informed the new district commander that "it has been the unfortunate experience of the Department that officers exercising your command are all the while calling for troops, or inventing excuses for not raising them, or keeping them back from the field."

Hovey made careful preparation for the trial. He secured the services of a famous court reporter, Benn Pitman—brother of the famous inventor of a new system of shorthand—to report the proceedings word by word. Pitman brought with him three assistants, and they took in turn the questions, evidence, and cross-examinations. The original transcriptions of these shorthand notes, now in the records of the Judge Advocate General and deposited at the National Archives in Washington, make a bulky mass. But from reading them, and noting their corrections, interlineations, and erasures, the historian can re-create the picture of the courtroom drama a little more vividly than from the cold type of the printed version.

The commission itself met in Indianapolis on September 22, the fifth day following its appointment. No sooner had the order been read, and other initial procedures completed, than H. H. Dodd was arraigned. His counsel immediately challenged the right of the commission to put him on trial. The reasons advanced were the same that Vallandigham had urged in his own behalf in May, 1863, when on trial before General Burnside's Military Commission in Cincinnati: The civil courts were open, the State was not under martial law, and both conditions must exist before a military commission could legally exercise any jurisdiction over civilians.

Judge Advocate Burnett claimed, as Captain Cutts had done in Cincinnati, that martial law had been declared by the President two years before. He argued that the proclamation of September 25, 1862, put all those who aided and abetted the insurrection under the authority of martial law. The commission solemnly withdrew to confer on the judicial issue presented, then returned and overruled the objections of the defense. A five-day recess was then permitted for the Grand Commander to get up his case.

Burnett then pressed five charges, with many specifications, against Dodd. These were conspiracy against the Government of the United States; affording aid and comfort to the rebels against the authority of the United States; inciting insurrection; disloyal practices; and violations of the laws of war. The substance of all these was that the prisoner's part in the Order of American Knights and the Sons of Liberty made him guilty of the charges, because these secret societies had as their purpose "the overthrow of the Government; holding communication with the enemy; conspiring to seize munitions of war

[*311*]

stored in the arsenals and to free the rebel prisoners in the North, and attempting to establish a Northwestern Confederacy."

Dodd pleaded not guilty to all the charges and specifications. Then the commission ordered the prosecution to summon its first witness.

The soldier bailiff brought Felix G. Stidger into the room; he took the witness stand and was duly sworn. Dodd gazed at him with amazement and fright. The Judge Advocate proceeded to develop Stidger's secret inside story, with the main details of which the reader is already familiar. Objection after objection was made by defense counsel to questions asked by the prosecutor, upon the ground that they were leading in form, or were irrelevant. In each instance these were brushed aside as of no consequence.

The Grand Secretary of the Kentucky Grand Council of the Sons of Liberty told not only of his deception of the leaders there, but also the many and direct relations he had had with Dodd, Heffren, Bowles, Horsey, Harrison, and the other Indiana men under arrest. He detailed with particular emphasis the meeting in Indianapolis the previous June, at which he had presented the Kentucky insistence that Detective Coffin be "eliminated," and the accused deliberated how best to do this. Before he was through, Stidger had disclosed as evidence practically everything that the Kentucky and Indiana leaders had told him, before or after the event.

Among the interesting questions addressed to Stidger on the witness stand were a number by the counsel for defense, on cross-examination. They asked who had paid him for his service as Grand Secretary. Had he received and used the money Judge Bullitt had paid him as salary for his services? Where were his loyalty and his duty to his employer? This did not faze the witness, who admitted that he had taken the Copperhead money with no qualms at all. Pitman did not write up the notes of some of this examination, and put in the printed record the statement that "a lengthy cross-examination here took place, but no additional facts were elucidated." The printed record elides the text of the defense cross-examinations in many cases, but the stenographic transcript contained them, and they do not greatly alter the general weight of evidence indicating the clear guilt of the accused. But at the time of original publication, in 1864, the Government desired the official record to present practically no offset of even minor details which would help the conspirators.

After Stidger, there was a parade of witnesses to corroborate the occurrence of events concerning which the Spy Complete had been able to relate only the fact that the incident involved had been related to him or mentioned in his hearing. The New York arms merchant described his sale of revolvers and ammunition, its shipment as Sunday-school books, and so on. An Illinois Copperhead told the story of the O.S.L. organization in that State, its military troops, and the plans for revolt. An Indiana informer gave similar testimony, and included the plan to attempt to seize Governor Morton, and to kill him should he resist.

When the court opened October 7, a startling announcement was made. Judge Advocate Burnett said that during the night prisoner Dodd had escaped from the room in which he had been confined. This was on the third floor of the Post Office; he had swung under the window and descended by means of a rope. Little activity was displayed to apprehend him. He made his way, and in a most leisurely manner, to security on Canadian soil.

The Republicans made a great to-do over this. The escape

occurred just four days before Indiana's State election, and therefore furnished excellent ammunition for the final fusillade of the battle for the ballots. Carrington, who had not yet left for his new field assignment, issued an excited statement through the Radical organ, the *Indianapolis Journal*.

"The exposure of the Sons of Liberty has been made," he declared, "every word is true. Harrison H. Dodd, Grand Commander of Indiana, has been on trial. Proof was overwhelming. Night before last he escaped from the third-story window by a rope. . . . Innocent men do not do so. The act confesses the guilt. . . .

"I am no politician. I know from two years' labor what this secret order means. Citizens, every day shows that you are upon the threshold of revolution. You can rebuke this treason. The traitors intend to bring war to your homes. Meet them at the ballot box while Grant and Sherman meet them in the field."

The best that the Democrats could do to offset this was to make the charge that Governor Morton had arranged with the prisoner for the latter to escape—had done so in order to "get up a show of conspiracy against the Government, to be exposed upon the eve of the election, and afford a fund of political claptrap to assist the Republicans in carrying the State." The only person who had been confined in the room with Dodd had been Bingham, the editor of the Democratic organ. Now that paper hinted Morton's complicity, and the *Cincinnati Enquirer* quite legitimately seemed surprised that the well-known figure of Democratic politics could have made his way out of the city at a time when it was so full of secret agents who knew him.

Burnett asked for an adjournment, which was granted. When the commission reconvened a few days later, he asked the members to take the findings and pronounce sentence.

Dodd's lawyers protested that the evidence was almost altogether hearsay, and again challenged the jurisdiction of martial law. The Judge Advocate countered that "no argument of the counsel, or finely drawn sophistries can change the perilous and treasonable nature of the circumstances testified to." He claimed that it had been proved "that there exists in this State an organization numbering from fifty to eighty thousand men, military in character, and about two-thirds armed, ready at any time to be called out to obey the orders of their superiors, regardless of the law and authority of the United States."

The Military Commission considered the evidence; it did not take the members long to find Dodd guilty upon each charge and specification, and to sentence him to be hanged by the neck until dead. The Commanding General later approved the sentence, as did Judge Advocate General Holt, at Washington. But the culprit was in Canada.

The commission met again on October 21. Then charges identical with those leveled at Dodd were laid against Bowles, Humphreys, Heffren, Milligan, and Horsey. In these new trials Stidger once more was the principal witness for the Government. Much of his story was confirmed by the evidence of others. Some of it was denied, particularly the things he told about Horace Heffren. The latter, after several weeks' imprisonment, decided to turn state's evidence, and told quite an extended story on the stand. In it he denied any memory of ever having met or talked to Stidger. In the testimony, the denial reads convincingly. Judge Advocate Burnett had to handle Heffren almost as an adverse witness to induce him to change his story to correspond with Stidger's. But Heffren remained unpersuaded, on the witness stand at least, that he had ever met Carrington's spy.

This second chapter of the trials developed still further surprises. Among the witnesses who appeared for the Government right at the beginning to give state's evidence were J. J. Bingham, Dr. James B. Wilson, and William H. Harrison. A little later Horace Heffren joined them; his apostasy to treason furnished the greatest single surprise of this performance.

The four men together, released to make them willing witnesses for the prosecution, testified from personal knowledge of the actual facts of which Stidger's statements had been secondhand, or hearsay. As Grand Secretary, Harrison identified and authenticated the documents seized in Dodd's office, and admitted his employment at a salary of $800 a year by the Grand Council. He also told of his destruction of the records immediately after Carrington had exposed the conspiracy.

Editor Bingham's role was to describe Dodd's demand for a Democratic mass meeting for August 16, his own alarm, and then the meeting of the Democratic leaders of the State to force this to be dropped. He told of his own initial reluctance to have anything to do with this secret-order scheme, beginning with the time that P. C. Wright had solicited him to become an O.A.K. in the spring of 1863.

Bingham had then declined, but the *Sentinel* had got into financial difficulties, and Dodd came to see him, urged him to join the order, and agreed to help the paper financially if Bingham would make it an organ for the Democratic society. The editor reluctantly undertook to do this, and in November, 1863, was initiated in a hall leased by the Democratic Club of Indiana. He soon found out that "Mr. Dodd is a gentleman very fond of excitement." In February, 1864, he was amazed to discover that Dodd was fond of treason too. From that time on he had had nothing to do with the order, which he thought a "humbug."

Dr. Wilson had been with Dodd and Bowles at the Chicago meeting on July 20, at which they had conferred with the Confederate paymaster, Captain Majors, and had taken the enemy funds. He testified to the events of this meeting, and the succeeding one on August 29, at which Vallandigham had told the council that McClellan's nomination should be accepted.

Heffren portrayed the pattern of relation of the civil and military departments, and told a great deal about the work General Bowles had undertaken. This was conclusive data both on the scheme of organization and on the later plot for revolution.

These witnesses in chief were succeeded by a great many small fry from over Indiana. These testified to hazy recollections of what Wright had said in a lodge organization meeting in a rural loft, what Dr. Bowles had told some drillmaster, and so on. Much of it was hearsay, the stories did not match, and their discrepancies of detail permitted defense counsel to attack both the credibility of the witnesses and the accuracy and relevance of what they said. The whole case was before the commission on November 25. It then adjourned until December 6, to enable the opposing counsel to prepare their final arguments.

These were separate, both in respect to the prisoners, who had different lawyers, and in relation to the matters at issue. J. W. Gordon, on behalf of Bowles and Humphreys, challenged jurisdiction, with elaborate citation of English and American precedent. Martin Ray denied that membership in the Sons of Liberty in itself constituted participation in a conspiracy. He would not deny that there had been a military department, nor "that a few desperate men of that branch in and out of the State sought to precipitate the order into a revolution."

But he did deny that his clients—and one of them was Dr. Bowles!—were implicated in it. Milligan's counsel, John R. Coffroth, defended the latter's anti-New England attitude, attacked Heffren as that "mudsill of infamy, who turned informer to purchase his own release," and in general sought to besmirch the testimony of the witnesses for the prosecution.

Judge Advocate Burnett defended the arrests and the trial by military law as having been justified by "overpowering necessity for military interference." His other arguments were much the same as those Burnside had used in his statement to the United States Circuit Court at Cincinnati eighteen months earlier.

The Military Commission did not waste much time in reaching and returning its decision and its sentence. It found each of the four remaining accused guilty of every charge. It sentenced Milligan, Bowles, and Horsey to be hanged, "at such time and place as the Commanding Officer of the District shall designate." Humphreys got off more lightly, with a sentence of confinement at hard labor for the duration of the war.

General Carrington wrote Stanton a letter on December 13, 1864, just a week after the verdict of the commission on the four traitors. In it the General urged that Stidger be paid, beginning May 5, for six months' work at the rate of $100 a month. This expenditure was justified by "the value of his work, and the risk incurred." The reader has the right to hope that Stanton sent him the $600. This is the last entry in the available official files about the spy whose work caused these convictions.

There was, however, a famous epilogue to the case itself. This fell in a period subsequent to that with which this volume has concerned itself. But it is an integral part of the Indiana treason trials, and note must be made of it. The first change was in regard to Humphreys, whose sentence was soon altered to confinement within Wright and Stockton townships in Greene County, Indiana. The designation by the commanding general of time and place for the execution of the three other men was delayed, and by the time it reached the President, as Commander in Chief, for final approval, Andrew Johnson had succeeded the murdered Lincoln. He fixed May 19, 1865, as the date upon which the sentence should be carried out.

The presidential mail during Johnson's first six weeks in the White House was heavy with petitions for clemency for the doomed men, now that the Confederates had surrendered and the war was over. Some of Johnson's own intimates pressed this course of clemency. Judge David Davis of the United States Supreme Court, who was on circuit duty, wrote from Indianapolis, together with the local circuit judge, an urgent appeal for commutation to life imprisonment. The Indiana politicians almost en masse sent in petitions, many upon printed forms. Three days before the time fixed, the President commuted Horsey's sentence, and postponed the execution date for Bowles and Milligan for a fortnight.

In the meanwhile, the convicted men had resorted to the Federal courts for redress. In their petitions to the United States Circuit Court for the District of Indiana, they recited that they were not in the armed service of the United States, were not subject to trial by a Military Commission, and they asked to be "turned over to the proper civil tribune, to be proceeded against according to the law of the land, or discharged from custody altogether."

The Court then certified a disagreement between the two judges, so the cases went forward to the Supreme Court at Washington. There was no chance for it to be heard for some months. The War Department in Washington did its utmost to ensure the execution of the sentences before the Supreme Court could act. The appeals came at the very time that Stanton and Holt were setting up the Military Commission to try the Booth conspirators, and both were savage in their determination to have no mercy shown the Indiana traitors, or to those in Old Capitol Prison in Washington. Holt sent instructions to General Hovey to disregard any sort of legal process from a civil court, and to carry out the death sentences unless the Bureau of Military Justice should instruct him otherwise. Confederate prisoners from Camp Morton were put to work erecting gallows on the parade grounds.

Justice Davis remained in Indianapolis. His views of the expediency of the execution did not alter. At the same time, Governor Morton began to fear the political consequences of the odium of so stern an act after peace had come. Close to the date set for the hanging of the convicted men, the Governor called upon the Justice. The latter said frankly that he doubted gravely if the sentence of the Military Commission had any standing in law. Upon this, Morton wrote the President, and sent the Speaker of the Indiana House of Representatives to the national capital to plead for commutation.

Andrew Johnson had been reluctant to take a hand in this matter. He had not yet cut the leading-strings which had made the Republican Radicals so pleased at his succession to the Presidency that they jubilantly termed it "a Godsend to the country." Wade had said bluntly to him: "Johnson, we have faith in *you*. By the gods, there will be no trouble now in running the Government."

But at length, and with great reluctance, the new President yielded to the importunities, overrode the objections of Stanton and Pope, and commuted the execution sentence. The

War Department dispatched a telegram in cipher to Hovey at Indianapolis, ordering him to send Milligan and Bowles to the Ohio State Penitentiary. There they were to be kept at hard labor for the rest of their lives. They were promptly sent.

In March, 1866, the Supreme Court heard elaborate arguments in *Ex parte Milligan*. In its opinion, handed down on April 3, the court reprehended the type of crime of which the Indiana prisoner had been tried, in the severest terms. "If guilty of these crimes imputed to him, and his guilt had been ascertained by an established court and impartial jury," the Justices declared, "he deserves severe punishment. Open resistance to the measures deemed necessary to subdue a great rebellion, by those who enjoy the protection of Government, and have not the excuse even of prejudice of section to plead in their favor, is wicked. But that wickedness becomes an enormous crime when it assumes the form of a secret political organization armed to oppose the law, and seeks by stealthy means to introduce the enemies of the country into peaceful communities, there to light the torch of civil war, and thus overthrow the power of the United States."

Note the phrase "if . . . his guilt had been ascertained by an established court and impartial jury." This was the controlling question. The Supreme Court declared, in solemn terms, that "the Constitution of the United States is a law for rulers and people, equally in war and in peace, and covers with the shield of its protection all classes of men, at all times and under all circumstances. No doctrine involving more pernicious consequences was ever invented by the wit of man than that any of its provisions can be suspended during any of the great exigencies of Government."

So far as concerned the case before it, "martial laws cannot arise from a threatened invasion. The necessity must be actual and present; the invasion real, such as effectually closes the ports and deposes the civil administration. None of these conditions existed in Indiana at the time of the arrest and trial. . . . Therefore one of the plainest constitutional provisions was infringed when Milligan was tried by a court not ordained and established by Congress and not composed of judges appointed during good behavior."

On direction of the President, on April 10 the War Department ordered the prisoners discharged, and Milligan and Bowles returned to their homes in Indiana. Some time later, they were indicted in the Federal courts of that State. Milligan himself was arrested and forced to give bail. None of the cases, however, ever came to trial. Bowles interested himself in developing French Lick Springs into a nationally famous spa. In 1868, Milligan brought a civil suit for money damages against the individuals who had made up the Military Commission which tried and convicted him. It dragged on without hearings for three years. In 1871 the court took it up. Thomas A. Hendricks presented Milligan's case and Benjamin Harrison spoke for the defendants. The jury brought in a verdict for the Copperhead, but awarded him damages of only $5. Thereafter, Democrats hailed the suit result as a vindication, while Republicans sneered that the imprisonment of a Copperhead did little damage to anyone, including the man himself.

Chapter 16

THUS BE IT EVER

DROWNING governments, like drowning men, clutch desperately at straws. Sherman's capture of Atlanta intensified Southern fears, and necessity knows no law and no philosophy.

The humiliating failure of the attempted revolution in the Northwest, culminating in the fiasco at Chicago, had convinced the immediate Confederate leaders in Canada and across the border that absolutely no dependence could be put on these Sons of Liberty—that on any project, large or small, whatever their promises or pretensions, they would run at the first clap of thunder.

But the overwhelming nature of the need called for the immediate re-examination of the chances in the Northwest. The lack of practical hope for them to succeed had never been a deterrent to Jefferson Davis. Even then he was looking with favor upon the crackpot scheme of General John B. Hood to abandon his contest with Sherman and turn the Army of Tennessee northward, with no limit to its objectives. The time called for taking desperate chances.

Much of Davis's correspondence with his confidential agents was burned when Richmond was abandoned, or lost on the ensuing flight southward, which brought the unhappy Southerners neither oblivion nor safety. There is little available evidence to show the nature of his hints at this juncture either to his Commissioners or to military chiefs in Canada.

The Confederate President can have found little comfort in the report which shrewd, dependable Jacob Thompson forwarded about that time. It contained a plain statement of the things which had "totally demoralized the Sons of Liberty." Information he had received subsequent to the Chicago failure convinced Thompson that the disaffection of the masses in the Northwest was as strong as ever, and that they were true, brave, willing and ready for revolt. "But they have no leaders," he went on, "the vigilance of the Administration, its large detective force . . . added to the large military force stationed in those States, make organization and preparation almost impossible. A large sum of money has been expended to little profit."

Perhaps Davis pressed Thompson to take new risks. Perhaps the Commissioner had some word from another quarter, for the wise among the secession leaders knew that unless there were some stroke of luck, theirs was a lost cause.

Suppose they could no longer hope for a people's rising, a secession in Ohio, Indiana, Illinois. This did not necessarily mean that they must abandon their plans to pounce upon the military prisons. Could these be seized by simultaneous attack, they could release about 50,000 experienced Confederate soldiers, arm them from captured arsenals, and march them south. This would divert the attention of the Federal armies from Virginia and Georgia to new fronts in Missouri, Kentucky, Ohio, Indiana, and Illinois.

Captain Hines and a few aides, who lingered around Chicago, studied this smaller-scale problem, and their hopes began to mount. Furthermore, the chance was well worth taking; it could succeed. In Camp Douglas, almost 9,000 Confederates, including many desperate men of Morgan's raiders, were guarded by only about 800 bluecoats—and these were mainly invalids, ill-trained conscripts, or other shoddy fighting material. The camp, covering about sixty acres, had a light board fence twelve feet high around it.

The Confederate leader concluded that such conditions were almost made to order for a bold attack by a few hundred brave men outside, the prisoners within rising at the same time. Circumstances at Camp Morton, in Indianapolis, at Camp Chase, in Columbus, Ohio, even at the prison and arsenal at Rock Island, were little more secure. Hines made tentative plans, and Cantrill, Anderson, and other Confederate officers endorsed them. Leading Illinois officers of the Sons of Liberty were sympathetic to the new plot, and promised that they would provide the men to help capture Camp Douglas.

The plans for this last desperate gamble, maturing through October, depended for success upon the three essentials of war strategy: perfect timing, complete surprise, and mobility of movement.

The approaching presidential election day, Tuesday, November 8, they believed would be the perfect date. It was to be expected that from early morning to deep night the city's streets would be filled with canvassers, voters, election officers, and watchers; and thousands of visitors from all over the region would be milling around—a turmoil in which no one would be likely to suspect the presence of a few well-disguised Confederates, and perhaps 2,000 Confederate sympathizers from southern Illinois.

Captain Hines made the most careful study of the actual terrain right around the prison camp. Fortunately for him, as we have learned, Charles Walsh, the brigadier general of the Chicago District of the Sons of Liberty, lived just a block from

Camp Douglas. His home provided a rendezvous; and when the plotters began getting arms and ammunition, it also became the arsenal for them. A careful map was drawn, indicating, to scale, the location of the Walsh house, the main prison gate, the guardhouse where the defenders would be seized, and so on.

Then a dependable leadership was recruited. Thomas Hines himself remained in command, as he should have, for he showed more imagination, courage, and common sense than any other leader in the plot. Agents set out for "Egypt," with money to pay the way to Chicago of about 1,500 Sons of Liberty, who would make up the actual attacking force. Hines's assistants revealed the plans to the leaders inside the prison, so that at the given signal these too would rise.

On election night the conspirators would attack the camp from three sides; inside Confederates would assist, and overpower the guards. Special squads would cut the telegraph wires, to prevent Federal calls for outside aid. The plotters would break open the vaults of the banks and remove the cash. A special force would rush west to Rock Island, to seize the prison camp, release its prisoners, and take over the arsenal.

These things done, Confederate armies of sturdy, experienced soldiers, armed with the latest Federal weapons, would control northern Illinois. They would march from Chicago and Rock Island through Indiana and Illinois to a carefully chosen gathering-place on the Ohio, gaining recruits as they went along. There General Forrest and his troops would join them. Thus the Confederates would have established a new and formidable front.

It was a brilliant campaign plan. And what is more, it might have worked. The history of war records a number of conspicuously successful gambles which started with more handicaps than this one. And whatever the odds against it, it was about the last chance for the Confederacy.

The trouble was that it failed to take into account a few important factors. The leaders had been forced to assume that certain things would be true that they almost knew would be otherwise. One was that the Federal authorities on the spot would be unaware of the developing danger. A second was that the Confederate prisoners within Camp Douglas would be sufficiently loyal to the Southern cause to revolt at the given signal—or at least not to betray it in advance. Then again, that the Sons of Liberty would be on hand at the time agreed, and would fight.

In any event, Hines must act. The middle of October his little group of Confederate officers began growing, and by various means and under different guises they drifted into Chicago. George St. Leger Grenfel, the fascinating British gentleman-adventurer, had employed the stratagem of coming from Canada to the prairies west of Chicago to go bird-hunting, as British country gentlemen always like to do "in the season."

After two weeks hunting quail—in the neighborhood of the Rock Island prison and arsenal—and being satisfied with his bag, the Colonel came on to Chicago about November 1, went direct to the Richmond House, signed the register as "Colonel George St. Leger Grenfel, Great Britain," and quietly ascended to his room.

This was the story he told in a touching letter he wrote three months later, after his trial and sentence of death, trying to put the best face he could upon his Chicago sojourn. Grenfel claimed to have chosen this hostelry because in the late 50's it had been the Chicago stopping-place of His Royal Highness the Prince of Wales. In the middle 60's, however, the Richmond House had acquired another distinction—it had become a preferred meeting-place for Confederate agents and Copperheads.

Hines himself avoided the hazards of hotels; he had a room with a Doctor Edwards, on Adams Street. Colonel Marmaduke was there with him, and their plans rapidly shaped up.

Within a few days they were to discover that they were confronted by a first-rate opponent on the spot. This was mischance as well as misfortune. The usual commanders of military prisons, on both sides of the line, were men who had not made conspicuous successes at the fighting front. In war, it seems to be the usual thing to put the misfits, the martinets, the blunderbusses, on the important jobs back of the lines. But Camp Douglas was commanded by Colonel Benjamin J. Sweet, who had already been tested in late August. Thoughtful and imaginative, he foresaw that the growing Confederate distress at home would force the renewal of plans for a release of prisoners, if not for some new sort of Northwest revolt.

Early in September, Sweet revamped his secret service. He put new men to work, both within the prisoners' group inside the barricades and in the lodges of the Sons of Liberty, both in Chicago and deep downstate. Before the month was out, he had wind of the schemes afoot and laid plans to foil them. At the same time, he tried to impress his military superiors with the danger ahead and insisted on adequate reinforcements. But this plea went unheeded until almost the last day.

Another significant fact was that not every Johnny Reb within the Camp Douglas palisade continued to be a devoted Confederate partisan to the bitter end. Nor was this strange, for the South had begun conscripting early in 1862, almost a year before the Loyal States did so. The depleted gray battalions were replenished by tens of thousands of men and boys of the lower middle class, poor boys, or even "mudsills"—whence the biting phrase, current in the North as well as in the South, that it was "a rich man's war and a poor man's fight."

When such men were captured and kept in prison, the new prison life at least secured them against further hazards of the battlefield, and many lost all zeal for exchange and new chance of casualty. Stanton's letter books at Washington were filled with letters from Confederate prisoners appealing to be allowed to take the oath of allegiance to the United States. Almost always these bore the endorsement: "Not to be exchanged against his consent."

The earlier work of J. Winslow Ayer, the patent-medicine vendor, has already been mentioned. After the collapse of the late August plot, Sweet had Ayer build up new contacts among the prisoners and find some likely informers, perhaps some men who could be carried outside, to gain the confidence of Confederates like Hines.

It should be remarked, parenthetically, that Ayer's case illustrates the way spy work enlarges the greed of the spy. Many betrayers, informers, and spies never could get over the idea that they should be paid at least twice, and perennially if possible, by the Government for the work they had done, without which, obviously (to them), the war would not have been won.

Colonel Sweet knew the breed, and whenever he paid off one of his secret agents, had the latter sign a carefully prepared receipt which described the services rendered and recited that the payment was in full for all services and expenses incident thereto. In Ayer's instance, the slip he signed acknowledged the receipt of $1,400 cash, and that he had been paid "in full for services in ascertaining and reporting the nature, character and purposes of the Sons of Liberty in Chicago from the first of July, 1864, to the first of February, 1865, together with all expenses."

After the war, Ayer moved to Kalamazoo, Michigan, and began practice there. The record does not disclose the type of service he rendered his patients, but it does reveal the persistence with which he sought to raid the United States Treasury. From April, 1865, through 1885, if not later, he besieged each new Judge Advocate General, Secretary of War, Attorney General, and President, wanting to get a huge sum paid him for having "foiled the plot to burn Chicago." He demanded to be put on the Army rolls as a colonel, with back pay from 1865. The only redeeming feature of the epsiode is that his efforts were consistently repulsed.

But let us return to the stream of contemporary events. The vendor of strange nostrums managed to establish a fair contact with Hines and other Confederate leaders. Then he asked Colonel Sweet for a companion, one J. T. Shanks, a captive from Morgan's raiders. Ayer thought this turncoat could be of great aid in getting more details of the plotters' plans. Soon Shanks was smuggled out.

Apparently he got close to Captain Hines, who sent him to the Richmond House to work with Grenfel. As luck would have it, the Colonel immediately recognized him as a man he had found, in Tennessee two years before, stealing a saddle off his favorite horse. Now he put the past aside and did not voice his suspicions of Shanks's fidelity. From the plotters' standpoint this was a bad blunder, for Shanks was able to ferret out much of the detail of the Confederate scheme.

Colonel Sweet did not neglect the part the Sons of Liberty were expected to play in the unrolling drama. As in the summer, he found plenty of turncoats and informers in these oathbound ranks, men quite willing to be bought for a stated sum for each report. They told him the intimate details of Charles

Walsh's connection with the plot. The camp commander learned the spot of concealment, and almost the exact inventory, of the store of arms and ammunition accumulated in Walsh's house. He was informed of the arrangements with the Copperheads in "Egypt," and the Rock Island plans. It all looked so ominous that he persuaded "Fighting Joe" Hooker, commander of the department, to come to Chicago to confer with him about the plot.

Throughout October, the Federal authorities had planned not to spring their trap until the very day the conspirators sounded their signal. By waiting until the last moment, Sweet and his men thought they could capture almost everyone involved. But the Sunday before election day, reports reached Sweet that many hundreds of suspicious-looking people had arrived—either escaped Confederate prisoners, Confederates sent from Canada, or Sons of Liberty from southern Illinois. The closeness of the danger seems to have upset his equilibrium, for early that afternoon he telegraphed his immediate superior, Brigadier General John Cook, commanding the District of Illinois, in considerable alarm.

"The city is filling up with suspicious characters," he reported, "some of whom are known to be escaped prisoners, and others who were here from Canada during the Chicago convention plotting to release the prisoners of war at Camp Douglas." He recited the weakness and fatigue of his small force of guards, "only 800 men all told, to guard between 8,000 and 9,000 prisoners.

"I am certainly not justified," he went on, "in waiting to take risks, and mean to arrest these officers if possible, before morning. The head gone, we can manage the body." At the same time he would perfect the arrests by seizing "two or three prominent citizens who are connected with these officers, of which the proof is ample."

Early that Sunday evening Sweet acted. He sent three picked companies; one squad sped to Charles Walsh's home, the second to the Richmond House, and the other, the largest of them all, to the center of Chicago, to arrest suspicious characters and quell any tumult.

There was opposition at the Walsh home, but the soldiers broke in, found and arrested the Brigadier General of the Sons of Liberty and three Confederate captains, and took them all to prison. They had no trouble turning up the accumulated arms and ammunition—a rich haul—including 210 carbines and double-barreled shotguns, 350 pistols, nearly 4,000 rounds of ammunition, and other dangerous tools of war.

Colonel Grenfel was captured at the Richmond House and the informer Shanks was arrested too. But this did not conceal the latter's duplicity. The British soldier of fortune now had bitter knowledge that Shanks had come there for no other purpose than to betray him. The tragic epilogue to this deserves description. The Military Commission which tried the Chicago plotters sentenced him to be hanged. It was with the greatest difficulty that President Johnson was persuaded to commute this to "imprisonment for life, at hard labor, at the Dry Tortugas." For three years the unfortunate British adventurer languished in Fort Jefferson, off the Florida Coast, in great physical distress. Hundreds of appeals for pardon met no response. On March 7, 1868, Grenfel escaped, and was never heard of again. The supposition is that he died in a rowboat at sea.

Colonel Marmaduke was apprehended at Dr. Edwards's home, and Judge Morris, the Sons of Liberty treasurer, was seized at his residence. The troops sent to the center of the city made a good catch. Before midnight they had taken up about a hundred Confederate soldiers, Sons of Liberty, and bushwhackers from "Egypt" and farther south.

But the choicest prize of all had escaped their net. Captain Hines must have been clairvoyant. He was not to be found at any of his accustomed hangouts. After a few days in hiding, he made his way to Canada.

In the years to come, much praise was to be accorded such daring Confederate leaders as Captain Hines, and much sympathy to such unfortunates as George St. Leger Grenfel. But there was neither praise nor sympathy for the fifth columnists.

Nor is this strange, for it seems a constant in the history of nations that the betrayer of his country leaves no memories save those of disgust and contempt. When Benedict Arnold became a British general, his unwilling associates termed him "Mr." Arnold—any military title was too good for him. The betrayer has ever been doubly cursed. The people he seeks to ruin look upon him with indignation and outrage. The enemy for whom he works has nothing but contempt for him. And this is true, whether the enemy capital be in Richmond, Berlin or Tokio.

This sudden Sunday-evening movement utterly destroyed the Camp Douglas plot. The news of this disaster put an end to the feebler enterprises planned for Indianapolis and Columbus. By his energetic work Colonel Sweet crushed the whole conspiracy, and foiled the desperate last resort of the traitors. No longer would the organized Copperheads be an ever-present peril to the Union cause.

The immediate consequence was that Tuesday's election went quietly and without undue incident in Chicago, as it did elsewhere through the country. As had been foreshadowed, McClellan proved no more of a "Little Napoleon" at the ballot box than in the field. President Lincoln carried all but two States, a record not equaled again until 1932.

Now the war had about run its course. Not only had President Lincoln been elected for a second term, but also he had won a complete victory over the secessionists' fifth column in the Loyal States.

It had taken time, and patience, and the exercise of powers no other President has sought to wield. Yet through employing them—and perhaps only so—had this child of a Kentucky cabin, this master politician self-developed into a statesman, this backwoodsman who became a Commander in Chief extraordinary, this poet and prophet of the people, been able to keep the Union safe.

BIBLIOGRAPHY

There are three main sources for the specific fifth-column information in this volume. These are first, the official records and documents of the United States Government, in their original state, in the National Archives, in Washington, D. C., and certain other original manuscript material relating to the contending forces in the Loyal States, either in the Library of Congress, in Washington, or in State or local historical collections. The second is the elaborate official printed reports and documents. Then again there is a mass of narrative and descriptive reminiscences, biographies, histories and evaluations, both in books and periodicals.

My own exploration of this general field began in early December, 1928, when I was gathering material for a biography of Andrew Johnson. This led me to study the records of the Military Commission which tried those charged with the assassination of Abraham Lincoln. From the time that I found, under the eaves of the State Department Building, in the records of the Judge Advocate General's Office, the unheeded petition for clemency for Mrs. Surratt, I examined and sought to relate together relevant items regarding conspiracy, espionage, and secret service work in the Civil War.

The great repository of material of this nature, supposedly, is the records of the United States Secret Service, parts of which, shortly after the close of the Civil War, were excerpted by those preparing the Official Records of the War of the Rebellion. In the late 80's these materials were boxed up, and were put under seal of secrecy by the then Adjutant General of the United States Army. Since that time the packing cases containing them have never been opened and it is, therefore, impossible to pass judgment upon the richness or leanness of the material they contain.

Efforts on the part of the author to obtain permission to examine them in connection with the present volume met the courteous but firm determination of the then Adjutant General to continue to keep the records under seal of secrecy. Therefore it is impossible for me to judge whether the copyists for the official records put into the printed volumes of that series the relevant and significant material, or how appropriate were their excerpts and omissions. The only aid to judgment upon the Secret Service is the volume, *History of the United States Secret Service,* published in 1867 by General Lafayette C. Baker. It is a large book, and its contents are so vigorous and tart that one is led to doubt whether any harmful details about persons the General did not like were left unsaid. Baker's reputation for fairness and accuracy, however, is under such a cloud that the value of his own self-justifying history is none too great.

The official records of the War Department, in the National Archives at Washington, are the most useful single source of primary material now available. This is a labyrinthine mass. Unlike the admirably indexed and codified records of the State Department for that period, and also unlike the fairly well-kept Navy records, those of the War Department are both huge in volume and extraordinarily difficult to identify by subject matter or type. The Archives staff for War Department records has made herculean efforts to bring them into usable shape. Even so, the diversity and complexity of the War Department's filing methods during the Civil War result in it being largely a matter of chance or guess today whether or not the right type of record is asked for by the investigator; and whether it can be found in the expected file, or has been transferred to some location impossible to be determined.

Certain of the files were particularly rich for investigation into the fifth-column activities. Chief among them were those of the Office of the Judge Advocate General and the Bureau of Military Justice. In these, I was enabled to read the actual reports of Felix G. Stidger, the spy complete, to his various chiefs. Likewise, they contained the original handwritten transcription by Benn Pitman of the Indiana Treason Trials. These gave me much more of a sense of vicarious participation in the trials than I ever had received through reading the printed reports. It was in these files that I found the original letter of P. C. Wright, of the *New York Daily News,* announcing to his fellow conspirators that the paper had become "our especial organ."

Another rich source was the letter books of the Secretary of War. Here one quickly sensed the weird pattern of interests of Secretary Stanton, and of the problems to which he gave attention. The letter books of Henry Halleck, General of the Army, proved most pertinent and suggestive. There was much of value in the files of the Military Department of the Ohio, both under Burnside and under Heintzelman, his successor.

The records of the State Department were another useful source. Secretary Seward kept separate letter books dealing with his secret service experience, from May, 1861, until he transferred that function to the Secretary of War early in the

spring of 1862. The consular dispatches from Canada likewise were full of useful reports on Confederate plot activities
in British North America.

Of printed material, the great source is the Official Records.
Next to these in value for background and attitude, though
not for dependability, are the reports of the Joint Committee
on the Conduct of the War. Appleton's *American Annual
Cyclopaedia* for the war years is most useful. Moore's *Rebel-
lion Record,* McPherson's *Political History of the United
States during the Rebellion,* and Richardson's *Messages and
Papers of the Presidents,* were, as always, useful.

Of the other literature, that upon the battle on the home
front is much less in volume than that upon the military
aspects of the conflict, and likewise inferior in penetrating
analysis and competent generalization. Of the general treatments, that of Dr. James G. Randall of the University of Illinois affords both the best detail and the best judgment of
differential values of evidence and importance of matters
treated. Dr. T. Harry Williams' *Lincoln and the Radicals*
affords considerable new material on the fight the extreme
Left made against the President. The role of Horatio Seymour
as the leader of the Loyal opposition is given sympathetic and
adequate treatment both by Alexander J. Wall and by Stewart
Mitchell.

Perhaps the most valuable single study of the Secret Orders
in the North was that which Mayo Fesler published in 1918,
in the *Indiana Magazine of History,* under the title "Secret
Political Societies in the North During the Civil War."

Mr. Fesler did his research and shaped his thesis under the
supervision of Dr. James Franklin Jameson, a thorough
scholar, then head of the Department of History at the University of Chicago. At the request of James Ford Rhodes,

whom he had informed of the Fesler inquiry, Dr. Jameson arranged a conference between the distinguished historian, then at work on the Civil War period, and the graduate student. After an extended discussion, Mr. Rhodes declared that he agreed with the Fesler analysis "in every particular." There can be no question that it is a careful piece of work, which throws great light on the fifth columns in the Loyal States.

BIBLIOGRAPHY

Appleton's *American Annual Cyclopaedia*. New York, 1862-66.

Baker, Lafayette C. *History of the United States Secret Service*. Philadelphia, 1867.

Bates, Edward. *Diary, 1859-1866*. (Howard K. Beale, ed.) Washington, 1933.

Belmont, August. *Letters, Speeches and Addresses*. New York, 1890.

Berdahl, Clarence A. *War Powers of the Executive in the United States*. (University of Illinois Studies in the Social Sciences, Vol. IX, Nos. 1 and 2.) Urbana, Ill., 1921.

Browning, Orville H. *Diary*. (J. G. Randall, ed.) Springfield, Ill., 1925-33.

Brunner, Sidney. *The Political History of New York during the Civil War*. New York, 1919.

Bryan, Wilhelmus B. *History of the National Capital*. New York, 1914-16. 2 vols.

Buchanan, James. *The Works of James Buchanan, etc.* (John Bassett Moore, ed.) Philadelphia, 1908-11. 12 vols.

Burgess, John W. *The Civil War and the Constitution*. New York, 1901. 2 vols.

Carpenter, Francis B. *Six Months at the White House*. New York, 1866.

Carroll, Thomas F. "Freedom of Speech and of the Press during the Civil War." *Virginia Law Review.* Charlottesville, Va., 1923.

Castleman, J. B. *Active Service.* Louisville, Ky., 1917.

Chandler, Peleg W. *Memoir of Governor Andrew.* Boston, 1880.

Cole, Arthur C. "Lincoln and the American Tradition of Civil Liberty." *Journal, Illinois State Historical Society,* Springfield, Ill., 1934-1935.

———— *Era of the Civil War 1848-1870.* Springfield, Ill., 1919.

Crook, William H. *Memories of the White House.* (Henry Rood, ed.) Boston, 1911.

Dana, Charles A. *Recollections of the Civil War.* New York, 1899.

Davis, George B. *A Treatise on the Military Law of the United States.* New York, 1915.

Dicey, Edward. *Six Months in the Federal States.* London, 1863. 2 vols.

Dictionary of American Biography. (Dumas Malone, ed.) New York, 1936. 20 vols.

Ellis, John B. *Sights and Secrets of the National Capital.* New York, 1869.

Fahrney, Ralph R. *Horace Greeley and the Tribune in the Civil War.* Cedar Rapids, Ia., 1936.

Fesler, Mayo. "Secret Political Societies in the North during the Civil War." *Indiana Magazine of History,* Bloomington, Ind., 1918.

Foulke, William Dudley. *Life of Oliver P. Morton.* Indianapolis, 1899. 2 vols.

Fremantle, A. J. L. *Three Months in the Southern States: April, June, 1863.* London, 1863.

Fry, J. B. *Operations of the Army under Buell.* New York, 1884.

———— *New York and the Conscription of 1863.* New York, 1885.

Gorham, George C. *Life and Public Services of Edwin M. Stanton.* Boston, 1899. 2 vols.

Bibliography

Greenhow, Rose O. *My Imprisonment and the First Year of Abolition Rule at Washington.* London, 1863.

Harris, Wilmer C. *Public Life of Zachariah Chandler, 1851-1875.* Lansing, Mich., 1917.

Headley, John W. *Confederate Operations in Canada and New York.* New York, 1906.

Hesseltine, William Best. *Civil War Prisons.* Columbus, O., 1930.

Hines, Thomas. "Reminiscences." *The Southern Bivouac Magazine,* Louisville, Ky., 1888-89.

Hudson, Frederic. *Journalism in the United States.* New York, 1873.

Jones, J. B. *A Rebel War Clerk's Diary.* Philadelphia, 1866.

Journal, Illinois State Historical Society, XIX, XXIV.

Julian, George W. *Political Recollections.* Chicago, 1884.

Kelley, William D. *Lincoln and Stanton.* New York, 1885.

Kendall, Amos. *Letters Exposing the Mismanagement of Public Affairs by Abraham Lincoln.* Washington, 1864.

Kirkland, Edward Chase. *Peacemakers of 1864.* New York, 1927.

Livermore, Thomas L. *Numbers and Losses During the American Civil War.* Boston, 1900.

Lonn, Ella. *Desertion During the Civil War.* New York, 1928.

Lynch, Denis Tilden. *Boss Tweed.* New York, 1931.

Marshall, John A. *The American Bastile: A History of the Illegal Arrests and Imprisonment of American Citizens During the Late Civil War.* Philadelphia, 1869.

Milton, George Fort. *The Age of Hate: Andrew Johnson and the Radicals.* New York, 1930.

———. *The Eve of Conflict: Stephen A. Douglas and the Needless War.* Boston, 1934.

———. *Conflict: The American Civil War.* New York, 1941.

Mitchell, Robert Stewart. *Horatio Seymour of New York.* Cambridge, Mass., 1938.

McClure, Alexander K. *Abraham Lincoln and Men of War-times.* Philadelphia, 1892.

Bibliography

McClure, Alexander K. *Old Time Notes of Pennsylvania.* Philadelphia, 1905.

McPherson, Edward. *Political History of the United States During the Rebellion.* Washington, 1882.

Moore, Frank (ed.). *The Rebellion Record.* New York, 1862-65. 11 vols.

Morrow, Curtis H. *Politico-Military Secret Societies of the Northwest, 1860-1865.* New York, 1929.

Myers, William Starr. *A Study in Personality, General George Brinton McClellan.* New York, 1934.

Nicolay, John G., and Hay, John. *Abraham Lincoln: A History.* New York, 1890. 10 vols.

Pearson, Henry G. *Life of John A. Andrew.* Boston, 1904. 2 vols.

Perkins, Howard C. (ed.) *Northern Editorials on Secession.* New York, 1942. 2 vols.

Pierce, Edward L. *Memoir and Letters of Charles Sumner.* Boston, 1887-1893. 4 vols.

Poore, Benjamin Perley. *Perley's Reminiscences.* Philadelphia, 1886. 2 vols.

Pitman, Benn (ed.) *Trials for Treason at Indianapolis.* Cincinnati, 1865.

Randall, James Garfield. *Constitutional Problems Under Lincoln.* New York, 1926.

Republican Party, *Proceedings of the First Three National Conventions.* Minneapolis, Minn., 1893.

Richardson, James D. *Messages and Papers of the Presidents.* New York, 1917-29. 24 vols.

Riddle, Albert G. *Life of Benjamin F. Wade.* Cleveland, O., 1886.

Rowland, Dunbar (ed.) *Jefferson Davis, Constitutionalist.* Jackson, Miss., 1923. 10 vols.

Russell, W. H. *My Diary North and South.* London, 1863.

Sandburg, Carl. *Abraham Lincoln, The Prairie Years.* New York, 1926. 2 vols.

Schuckers, J. W. *Life of S. P. Chase.* New York, 1874.

Seitz, Don C. *Lincoln the Politician*. New York, 1931.

Shannon, Fred Albert. *The Organization and Administration of the Union Army, 1861-1865*. Cleveland, O., 1928. 2 vols.

Smith, Edward Conrad. *The Borderland in the Civil War*. New York, 1927.

Stidger, Felix Grundy. *Treason History of the Order of Sons of Liberty*. Chicago, 1903.

Swiggett, Howard. *The Rebel Raider; A Life of John Hunt Morgan*. Indianapolis, 1934.

Tenney, William Jewett. *The Military and Naval History of the Rebellion*. New York, 1866.

Terrell, W. H. H. Report of the Adjutant General of the State of Indiana. Indianapolis, 1865-69. 8 vols.

Terrell, W. H. H. *Indiana in the War of the Rebellion; Official Report of the Adjutant General*. Indianapolis, 1869. 2 vols.

United States, War Department. *The War of the Rebellion: Official Records of the Union and Confederate Armies*. Four series. Washington, D. C. v.d. 70 vols.

Warden, W. W. The Private Life and Public Services of Salmon P. Chase. Cincinnati, O., 1874.

Warren, Charles. *The Supreme Court in United States History*. Boston, 1922. 3 vols.

Weed, Thurlow. *Autobiography*. (Harriet E. Weed, ed.) Boston, 1883.

Welles, Gideon. *Diary*. (E. T. Welles, ed.) Boston, 1911. 3 vols.

White, Horace, *Life of Lyman Trumbull*. Boston, 1913.

Williams, T. Harry. *Lincoln and the Radicals*. Madison, Wis., 1941.

Willoughby, Westel W. *Constitutional Law of the United States*. New York, 1910. 2 vols.

Wilson, Woodrow. *Constitutional Government in the United States*. New York, 1921.

Weeden, William B. *War Government, Federal and State, 1861-1865*. Boston, 1906.

Bibliography

Woodburn, James A. "Party Politics in Indiana During the Civil War." *American Historical Association Report,* Washington, D. C., 1903.

Wall, Alexander J. *A Sketch of the Life of Horatio Seymour, 1810-1866.* New York, 1929.

INDEX

Abolitionists, grudging praise of emancipation, 94; disrespect toward Lincoln, 98; 99, 105, 107, 109, 110, 213

Acton, John Emerich Edward Dalberg, Lord, quoted on power, 141

Albany Evening Journal, attitude on emancipation, 108, 109; comment on Seymour's inauguration as Governor, 110

Albany mass meeting, adopts resolutions on Vallandigham's conviction, sends copy to Lincoln, 168

American Daily Line, lake carrier, 281

Ammen, Gen. Jacob, enforces order suppressing *Chicago Times*, 197

Anderson, Col. Benjamin, Confederate officer, in plan to capture Union prisons, 299, 325

Anderson, Major Robert, surrenders Fort Sumter, 20

Andrew, John Albion, Governor of Massachusetts, 104; negotiates with Gov. Seymour of New York on presidential candidate, 215

Antietam Creek, Battle of, an influence in Indiana election, 81; 103, 128

Army enrollment, direct in Federal service, plan attacked by Democrats and conservatives, 129, 130

Arms and ammunition sent in boxes as Sunday school books, 300, 313

Army of the Cumberland, 309

Army of the Ohio, removal of Gen. Buell from command, 131; hemmed in by Bragg, 189

Army of the Potomac, 94; McClellan withdrawn, but restored after Second Bull Run, 102, 103

Army of Tennessee, 178; Hood's scheme to turn it northward, 323

Arnold, Benedict, cited, 333

Asbury, Francis, Methodist Bishop, 191

Ashley, James Mitchell, introduces joint resolution for Constitutional Amendment on emancipation, 110; results in Thirteenth Amendment, 111

Ashmun, George, message to Stephen A. Douglas, 20, 21; 22; appointed special agent to Canada, 49

Associated Press, carries Douglas's endorsement of Lincoln's call for men, 22

Atlanta, captured by Sherman, 230, 231, 323

"Aunt Lucy" as name for the Confederacy, 266

"Australian ballots," 217

Ayer, I. Winslow, patent-medicine vendor, becomes spy, 299, 329; efforts to obtain money from the Government, 330

Baker, Gen. Edward Dickenson, killed at Battle of Ball's Bluff, 42

Baker, Lafayette Charles, employed by Secretary Seward as counterspy, wrote *The History of the United States Secret Service*, 51; story of his career, 52; 53; made Chief of U. S. Secret Service, 55; reports on Washington evils, 56; 57, 72, 74-76; arrests organizer of Knights of the Golden Square, 141; 205; his importance shrinks, 251; gives pass to Mme. Velasquez, 294; 296

Ball, Flamen, U. S. Attorney at Cincinnati, 50

Index

Index

Conkling, Roscoe, defeated for Congress in New York, 125

Conscription, not resorted to since War of Independence, 128, 129; act signed, 130, 141

Constitutional Conventions: North Carolina, 24, 25; Missouri, deposes Gov. Jackson, 26; of 1787, 41; in Georgia, 82

Constitutional Union Convention in New York, 119

"Contraband of war," applied to slaves by Gen. Butler, 97

Cook, Gen. John, commander of District of Illinois, 331

Copperheads, origin of the term, 192; swift spread of followers, 46; Gov. Morton's fight against them, 73, 74, 75, 77, 79, 87, 90, 104; compose the disloyal opposition, 117; fifth column affiliation, 136, 147, 206, 226; 137, 144, 157, 160, 170, 189, 191, 203, 209, 216, 237, 251, 254, 268, 292, 294, 300, 302-4, 306, 307, 331

Corps de Belgique, 65, 72, 136

Couch, Maj. Gen. Darius Nash, commander of the Department of the Susquehanna, complains of inoperation of civil law in his district, 141, 142

Council of Five Hundred, scattered by Napoleon, referred to by Gov. Seymour, 116

Counterespionage, employment of Lafayette C. Baker, 51; spy services set up, 74; against the Knights of the Golden Circle, 79, 87

Courts in Washington abolished, 48

Covode, John, on Radical Joint Committee, exposed printing scandals in Buchanan's Administration, 44

Cox, Gen. Jacob Dolson, safeguarding Johnson's Island against Confederate plot, 283

Cox, Samuel Sullivan ("Sunset"), witness in defense of Vallandigham, 166; 189

Crittenden, John Jordan, succeeds Clay, drafts resolution on nation's policy in the war, 39, 40

Crittenden Compromise, 166

Cromwell, Oliver, his action in Parliament cited by Gov. Seymour, 116

Crowder, Gen. Enoch, Provost Marshal General under President Wilson, studies Col. Fry's report on his handling the draft, 156

Curran, a Confederate spy, 263, 269

Curtin, Andrew Gregg, Governor of Pennsylvania, calls conference of war governors, 103, 104

Cutts, Adèle, Douglas's second wife and sister of the following, 164

Cutts, Capt. James Madison, Judge Advocate of commission trying Vallandigham, 164, 166; 189, 311

Damocles' sword cited, 272

Davis, Judge David, middle of the road man, 117; appeals for commutation of sentences of Sons of Liberty conspirators, 319; 320

Davis, Jefferson, candidate for President of U.S. at Charleston Convention, 30; 49, 64; his responsibility for continuance of the war, 106, 107, 126; his hope of getting Confederates out of Union military prisons, 153; regards Vallandigham as a liability to Confederate cause, 178; advises burning of Charleston if in danger of capture, 210, 211; 238, 262, 264, 271, 276, 278, 284; his hope for success in Northwest, 323, 324

Death records of New York City examined for persons killed in draft riots, 151, 152

Declaration of Independence, its phrases as battle cry in 1864 campaign, 209

Democratic National Convention of 1852, nomination of Franklin Pierce, 32; 1864 Convention, 215, 224; nominates McClellan, 228, 229; its effect on Lincoln, 230; 261, 302, 303

Democratic State Conventions: New York ratifies Whig nominee Horatio Seymour, 119; Ohio nominates Vallandigham for Governor, sends let-

[349]

Index

icately.

d leaves nothing. It's a proxy

d none of the blessings. One

orced and never been kissed.

reeps up like old age. Ya get

ts harder, and then....nobody

Index

Know-Nothings, 65; wrath at Gov. Seymour over entertaining Papal nuncio at dinner, 113; opposed by Tammany Society in New York, 242
Knox, John, 158

Lady Davis, blockade runner, takes Vallandigham to Bermuda, 179
"Lame duck" Congress, 159
Latter-Day Saints of Cromwell's day, cited by Gov. Seymour, 116
"Leader of his Majesty's Loyal Opposition" in the British House of Commons, 112
Leavitt, Humphrey Howe, Judge of U.S. Circuit Court, 166; refuses writ of habeas corpus to Vallandigham, 167, 183
LeCompton controversy, 309
Lee, Gen. Robert Edward, 101; comment on Pope's headquarters, 102, 104, 173; his loss at Gettysburg, 210; Grant's pressure on his lines, 231; 284
Leinster, Duke of, his palace the model for the President's House, 62
Letcher, John, Governor of Virginia, his message to Lincoln, 25
Lincoln, Abraham (16th President of the U.S.), his "repel force by force," 17; fighting the fifth column, 18; calls 75,000 men to repress rebellion, is advised by Douglas to make it 200,000, 20; likened by Stanton to an ape, 32; issues second call, for 42,000 volunteers, 36; his belief in his powers, 42; "master politician of the age," 94; plan for freeing slaves in Border States, 95; his powers as Commander in Chief, 98; replies to "Prayer of Twenty Millions," 99; goes to McClellan's headquarters, 101; issues preliminary Emancipation Proclamation, 120; signs Conscription Act, 130; surprised over Vallandigham case, 169, 170; his reply to the Albany resolutions, 173; to the letter of the Ohio Democratic Convention, 181, 182; fondness for quoting Jefferson, 209, 210; renom-

inated at Baltimore, 214; indifferent to Vallandigham's violation of his sentence, 224, 226; how he would have met McClellan's election, 231; reply to Chief Justice Taney in Merrimam case, 234, 235; re-elected, 238, 239; carries all but two States, 334; assassinated, 319.
Library of Congress, in the Capitol, buys Jefferson's private library, 59
Literature of the war, 18
"Local and distributed jurisdiction," enunciated by Gov. Seymour, 113
Locomotives, and their names, 58
Logan, John Alexander ("Black Jack"), denounces Douglas, 28; his sudden change of faith, 30; resigns from the Democratic party, 195
Longstreet, Gen. James, 252
"Lottery of life," applied to the draft, 145
Louisville Courier, accused of printing treasonable material, 50
Louisville Journal, 71, 91
Louisville & Nashville Railroad, as supply for the army, 222
Loyal opposition, 112, 117
Loyal States, determination to conquer the South, 96; their agitators and revolutionaries, 118; habeas corpus writ suspended, 120; 157, 168, 171, 190, 220, 225, 233, 240, 241, 244, 278, 285, 328, 334
Lyons, Richard Bickerton Pemell, Lord, British Minister to Washington, notifies Seward of Confederate plot, 282

Magoffin, Beriah, Governor of Kentucky, determines on keeping State neutral, 26; effort called "perfect humbug" by fifth columnist, 35
Maine, its prohibition law sweeping the country, 113; chooses a Democratic Congressman, 123
Majors, Capt., Confederate paymaster, 291, 293, 317
Malvern Hill, defeat of Lee, 101
"Manifest Destiny" doctrine, 67
Marcy, William Learned, Governor of

[355]

then arrests him, 85; 94; at Nashville, 129; ordered to send Vallandigham beyond Union lines, 171; hemmed in by Bragg, 189
Rules, Regulations and Principles of K. G. C., found in Dr. Bickley's trunk, 85
Russell, William Howard, correspondent of the London *Times,* 70

St. Nicholas Hotel, in New York City, 229
Saloon closing in Washington, 55
Sanders, George Nicholas, reported carrying dispatches from Davis to England, 49, 50; secret agent for Confederacy in Canada, 153
Sanderson, Col. John Philip, made Provost Marshal General of Missouri, investigates the secret societies, 255, 290, 305
Saratoga, armed lake vessel, 296
Scott, Gen. Winfield, seeks advice of Douglas, 23; candidate for President against Pierce, 32; orders advance that leads to First Bull Run, 38
Second Bull Run, a disaster, 102
Secret Service, U.S., its beginning, 51; War Department establishes its own, 55; Baker's organization, 74-76; his importance shrinking, 251
Secret society to aid Confederate cause, 36
Seven Days' Battle, 101
Seward, William Henry, asks Pierce to explain connection with Knights of the Golden Circle, 33; conditions release from prison of Mayor Berret, 47, 48; appoints Ashmun special agent to Canada, 49; seeks information about Knights of the Golden Circle, 50; his "Secret Service Letter Book" for 1861, 50; employs Lafayette Baker as chief counterspy, 51, 52, 75; arresting suspects, 53; cancels exequatur of Belgian consul in St. Louis, 72; told of Emancipation Proclamation by Lincoln, 102, 103; Radicals seek to force him out of

Cabinet, 108; middle of the road man, 117; ignores Vallandigham's appeal to re-enter U.S., 184; comment on Sherman's message from Atlanta, 230; retort to Lincoln's pre-election paper, 231
Seymour, Horatio, Governor of New York, declines invitation to Copperhead mass meeting in Indiana, 89; opinion of emancipation, 94; seeks to uphold McClellan for control of the army, 100; 105; elected Governor, 108, 125, 126; his place in opposition to the Administration, 112; vetoes prohibition law, 113; defeated for re-election, 114, 115; indulges in prophecy, 116; 118; his nomination by Whigs ratified by Democrats, 119; denounces conduct of the war, 121, 122; opposed to quota system in the draft, 135, 136; addresses crowd at City Hall in New York, 147; 153, 155; conference with Vallandigham, 159, 160; concern over latter's conviction, 168; praised by Indiana Legislature, 200; confers with Gov. Andrew on presidential candidate, 215; 219; importuned to become candidate, 220; address as permanent chairman of Democratic National Convention, 223, 224; 227; favors McClellan for nomination, 228; beaten by Dix for Governor, 238; 303
Shanks, J. T., a turncoat Confederate, 330; his pretended arrest, 332
Shannon, Frederick Albert, his *Organization and Administration of the Union Army—1861-65,* 137, 140
Sheahan, James Washington, editor of the *Chicago Times,* 197
Sherman, John, note from Murat Halstead on Lincoln, 207
Sherman, Gen. William Tecumseh, as choice for commander of Army of the Potomac, 46; his thinking sense, 77; 94; middle of the road in poli-

Index

for head of the Army of the Potomac, 40; middle of the road in politics, 117

Thompkins & Co., its business of furnishing substitutes, 138

Thompson, Jacob, Confederate Commissioner sent to Canada for plotting, 285, 286; initiated into the Sons of Liberty, 287; 289, 292, 298, 301; belief in Northwest, 324

Thurston, D., a detective, 281; gets information of plot to capture Johnson's Island, 282; refuses to reveal his informant, 284

Thornton band of guerrillas broken up, 294

Thrailkill band of guerrillas broken up, 294

Tilden, Samuel Jones, his influence on Seymour, 115; delegate at large to Democratic National Convention in Chicago, 220; prevents election of Vallandigham as head of Resolutions Committee, 226; 227, 228

Times (London), 70

Titles in the Order of American Knights, 193

Tod, David, Governor of Ohio, letter from Dr. Bickley protesting his innocence, 67, 86

Travel to Washington, 57, 58

Tribune (N.Y.), 36, 99, 122, 137; attacked in draft riots, 146; 147; prints list of persons killed, 151

Trollope, Mrs. Frances, her *Domestic Manners of the Americans*, 65

Troy Times, its printing plant destroyed by a mob, 150

Trumbull, David, an informer, 252

Trumbull, Lyman, bill defining escaping slaves as captives of war and thus free, 97

Tyler, John (10th President of the U.S.), in favor of the Union, 31

"Union as it was, Constitution as it is," simplification of resolutions, 40, 84, 94, 95, 120, 123

Union League, a countervailing secret organization, 81

Union Relief Society, 65

"Unseen Hand" in Lincoln's Cabinet, 108

Valentine's Manual of New York, statistics of New York deaths, 152

Vallandigham, Clement Laird, for peace at any price, 84; in prison when expected at a mass meeting, 89; among disloyal opposition, 117; defeated for Governor, 124; his background, 157; sent to Congress, 158; confers with Seymour, 159, 160; order for his arrest sought, 162; arrested and imprisoned, 164, 165; specifications of charges against him, 165; refuses to plead, 166; sentenced for the duration of the war, 167, 168; to be sent beyond the Union lines, 171; begins exile, 176; nominated for Governor in his absence, 180; appeals for permission to re-enter U.S., 183; issues from Canada an "Address to the People," 184; continues his exile, 185-88; defeated by Brough for governorship, 189, 215; made head of Sons of Liberty, 216, 217; his influence in the Democratic National Convention, 224; casts Ohio's vote for McClellan, 228; agrees to become Supreme Grand Commander of the Order of American Knights, name changed to Sons of Liberty, 245; adds Kentucky-Virginia Resolves of 1798 to new ritual, 247; determines to return to U.S., 264; loses control of Democratic Convention, 305; his trial before Military Commission in Cincinnati cited, 311

Valley Forge mentioned, 17

Van Buren, Col. James Lyman, on commission to try Vallandigham, 164

Van Buren, Martin (8th President of the U.S.), in favor of the Union, 31; his contempt for Buchanan, 32

Vanderbilt, Cornelius, the "Commodore," 115

Velasquez, Mme. Loreta Janeta, Con-

Index

federate suspect, 53, 76; gets pass from Baker, 294

Vice in Washington, 56, 57

Virginia, Constitutional Convention sends committee to Lincoln to discuss peace, 17

Voorhees, Daniel Wolsey, mentioned in letter of solicitation from Herschel Johnson, 83; for peace at any price, 84; at Democratic mass meeting, 89; pays tribute to Vallandigham, 90

Wade, Benjamin Franklin, his response to a challenge to a duel, 43; states objects of Joint Committee, 45; 100; among the Radicals, 118; 215; his faith in Andrew Johnson, 320

Wadsworth, Gen. James Samuel, nominated for Governor of New York, and defeated, 105, 122, 123

Walker, Dr. John L., 291, 293

Walker, Gen. William, filibuster, 67

Wall, James Walter, arrested by Baker's men, but elected to the Senate, 125

Walsh, Charles, head of Military Department of the Sons of Liberty, 291, 294, 302, 325, 330-32

War of Independence cited, 128

Washington, George, his view of the powers of the President, 41; mentioned, 129

Washington in wartime, 57-63

Washington Monument, 61

Webb, Col. William J., Confederate commander, 177

Webster, Daniel, 21

Wendell, Cornelius, Public Printer in Buchanan Administration, involved in scandals, 44

Weed, Thurlow, his attitude on emancipation, and that of his paper, the *Albany Evening Journal*, 108

Weller, John B., at the Democratic National Convention, 226

Welles, Gideon, told of the Emancipation Proclamation by Lincoln, 102,

103; 104; his Diary on Vallandigham, 169, 171; 172; Diary on Chase, 232, 233

Western Reserve of Ohio, 34

Wheeler, Gen. Joseph ("Fighting Joe"), 186

White, W. W., mentioned in letter of solicitation from Herschel Johnson, 83

White House, 60; formerly called the President's House, 62; its various rooms, 62, 63

Wilder, Gen. John Thomas, on Military Commission trying Harrison H. Dodd, 310

Wiles, Maj. William M., Provost Marshal General of Rosecrans's army, receives Vallandigham on his way to exile, 176

Willard, Caleb, hotel man, 61

Willard's Hotel, in Washington, 22, 59, 61, 62

Williams, of the Sons of Liberty, 291

Wilson, Henry, proclaims purpose of Radicals, 43; declares Chief Judge of Washington disloyal, 48; his bill for freeing slaves in the District of Columbia, 97; defends conscription, 130

Wilson, Dr. James B., 291; turns State's evidence in Sons of Liberty trial, 316, 317

Wilson, Thomas Woodrow (28th President of the U.S.), opposed formation of Joint Committee on Expenditures in the Conduct of the War, 46; orders study of Fry's report on draft law, 156

Winter & Co., 265

Wood, Benjamin, brother of the following, 154; one of the owners of the *New York Daily News*, 242, 243

Wood, Fernando, co-owner of the *New York Daily News*, fills paper with subversive propaganda, 33; his loyalty suspect, 100; advocates peace at any price, 148; 153; his responsibility in the riots, 154; calls on Lincoln